For Ashlynn
Confirmation Day!
May the Lord bless
and keep you
always.
Love, Dad & Mom
6-2-19

365 DEVOTIONAL READINGS WITH

MARTIN LUTHER

PSALM BY PSALM

CONCORDIA PUBLISHING HOUSE · SAINT LOUIS

1 2 3 4 5 6 7 8 9 10   26 25 24 23 22 21 20 19 18 17

INTRODUCTION

s a man who had spent seven years as a member of a monastic order, praying, singing, and reciting, out loud, all 150 Psalms, every single week, Martin Luther had the Psalms deeply committed to memory and would throughout the rest of his life draw on them constantly in every situation and circumstance. The words were always present with him and had taken deep and permanent root in his heart, mind and soul, as they should in ours as well. It is not surprising then that Dr. Luther, as a professor of Bible, would undertake first to provide a commentary on the Psalms. And so it is that with these daily devotional thoughts from Martin Luther, masterfully selected from Luther's Works by my colleague Dawn Weinstock, following on the previous resource she prepared, *Day by Day with Luther*, you will gain a fresh insight into what Luther regarded as worthy of being called a "little Bible"—the Psalms. Thus Luther:

> The Psalter ought to be a precious and beloved book, if for no other reason than this: it promises Christ's death and resurrection so clearly— and pictures his kingdom and the condition and nature of all Christendom—that it might well be called a little Bible. In it is comprehended most beautifully and briefly everything that is in the entire Bible. It is really a fine enchiridion or handbook. In fact, I have a notion that the Holy Spirit

wanted to take the trouble himself to compile a short Bible and book of examples of all Christendom or all saints, so that anyone who could not read the whole Bible would here have anyway almost an entire summary of it, comprised in one little book. (Luther's Works 35:254)

—Paul T. McCain

Blessed is the man.

PSALM 1:1

The Only Blessed One

he first psalm speaks literally concerning Christ thus: *"Blessed is the man."* He is the only blessed One and the only Man from whose fullness they have all received (John 1:16) that they might be blessed and men and everything that follows in this psalm. He is "the first-born among many brethren" (Romans 8:29), "the firstfruits of those who have fallen asleep" (1 Corinthians 15:20), so that He might also be the firstfruits of those who are awake, namely, in the Spirit. For it is also written in the roll of this book concerning Him, to do the will of God. . . . Thus He Himself says in Psalm 40:8: "I delight to do Thy will, O My God; Thy Law is within My heart." "I delight," He says, that is, "it is My desire, and not the compulsion of fear or the hope of gain. And therefore Thy Law is not in the outer edges and skin of My heart, but in the inside, in innermost and complete dedication."

From *First Lectures on the Psalms*, on Psalm 1
(Luther's Works 10:11, 13–14)

Blessed is the man
who walks not in the counsel of the wicked.

PSALM 1:1

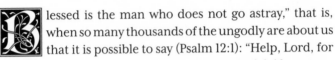

An Even Greater Victory

lessed is the man who does not go astray," that is, when so many thousands of the ungodly are about us that it is possible to say (Psalm 12:1): "Help, Lord, for there is no longer any that is godly; for the faithful have vanished from among the sons of men." And also with Micah 7:2: "The godly man has perished from the earth, and there is none upright among men." Is not he blessed and truly a man strong in faith who does not walk with the great throng on the broad way, who suffers much abuse and evil and still does not consent to walk with them, and who is not deceived by the attractive counsel of the ungodly which would lead even the elect astray (Matthew 24:24)? It is a great thing when a man is not overcome by riches, pleasures, and honors; but it is an even greater victory when a man overcomes the reasoning and the glittering righteousness of the ungodly, by which pure faith is attacked most of all.

From *Labors on the Psalms*, on Psalm 1 (Luther's Works 14:291)

But his delight is in the Law of the LORD.

PSALM 1:2

Christes Desire

he first root of all good is to have delight in the Law of the Lord. For nothing forced is permanent, and what is held without love and delight is not held for long, because the grain that fell on rocky ground does not have root (Matthew 13:20–21). . . . Therefore Christ does not want His rule to rest on force and violence, because then it would not stand firm, but He wants to be served willingly and with the heart and the affections. In this way His kingdom is eternal and will not be destroyed, since it does not rest on force. "God loves a cheerful giver" (2 Corinthians 9:7). It is for this that He gave His Spirit. Therefore, "anyone who does not have the Spirit of Christ does not belong to Him" (Romans 8:9). But "all who are led by the Spirit of God are sons of God" (Romans 8:14). These are the ones whose delight is in the Law of the Lord, since this is not something that comes out of us apart from the Spirit of God.

From *First Lectures on the Psalms*, on Psalm 1
(Luther's Works 10:14–15)

On His Law he meditates day and night.

PSALM 1:2

Rooted in the Law of the Lord

 editating is an exclusive trait of human beings, for even beasts appear to fancy and to think. Therefore the ability to meditate belongs to reason. There is a difference between meditating and thinking. To meditate is to think carefully, deeply, and diligently, and properly it means to muse in the heart. Hence to meditate is, as it were, to stir up in the inside, or to be moved in the innermost self. Therefore one who thinks inwardly and diligently asks, discusses, etc. Such a person meditates. But one does not meditate on the Law of the Lord unless his delight was first fixed in it. For what we want and love, on that we reflect inwardly and diligently. But what we hate or despise we pass over lightly and do not desire deeply, diligently, or for long. Therefore let delight be first sent into the heart as the root, and then meditation will come of its own accord. . . .

But what is the meaning of *day and night*? Here is a large sea. First, literally, it means at all times, or incessantly, since day and night comprise all of time. However, time is divided not only into day and night but, second, also into good times and bad times. Thus the day is the time of prosperity, while night is the time of adversity. Third, it is divided into a time of grace and a time of sin. Fourth, into a time of life and of death. . . . Fifth, into a time of quiet and of activity, or rest and work. Hence quiet (according to the spirit) is the day, but activity is the night. According to these distinctions there is a variety of uses of these words in the Scriptures. Therefore he who is rooted willingly and spontaneously in the Law of the Lord, no matter what time it is, does not go back, does not forget, does not put off meditation on the Law of the Lord. The fool, however, and he whose delight is not in His Law, changes at every difference in time.

From *First Lectures on the Psalms*, on Psalm 1 (Luther's Works 10:17–18)

He is like a tree planted by streams of water
that yields its fruit in its season,
and its leaf does not wither.

PSALM 1:3

The Tree of Life

eaves are words. It is clear, however, in which way these words of Christ have not withered, since they are written most splendidly in the Gospels and in the hearts of the faithful. The words which He speaks are life and spirit (John 6:63). Therefore they are worthy to be written not on stones and in dead books but in living hearts. Therefore *does not [wither]* says less and means more: Heaven and earth will pass away, but His words will not pass away (Matthew 24:35). He is therefore the "tree of life" (Revelation 22:2), firmly "planted in the house of the Lord" (cf. Psalm 92:13), producing His fruit in its season, the first-fruits of all the trees that imitate Him in these. . . . Perfect as the man is who makes no mistakes in a single leaf (cf. James 3:2), more perfect is certainly he whose leaves are blooming and plentiful, but most perfect is he whose leaf does not fall off, who is worthy to have his thoughts and sayings deserve eternal remembrance and authority.

From *First Lectures on the Psalms*, on Psalm 1 (Luther's Works 10:22)

Why do the nations rage and the peoples plot in vain?

PSALM 2:1

A Condition of His Kingdom

he prophet is filled with amazement and asks: "What is this, anyway? The nations conspire, and the peoples plot and take counsel not against the king of the Persians, not against the Turk, but against the Lord. Will these efforts not prove to be ridiculous, stupid, and foolish? Let no one therefore fear, let no one allow himself to be terrified by these counsels, whose net result will show that they have been in vain. For they are undertaken not against man, as it seems, but against the Lord." Thus right in the beginning he leads us from fear to hope and offers the comfort that the peoples and the nations will perish unless they abandon these counsels, because they plot against God and not against men. . . .

The Holy Spirit . . . teaches and consoles us in this psalm so that we cling bravely to this King [Christ] and think of Him much more than the tumults and other offenses. For it is a condition of His kingdom that it cannot exist without tumults. . . . Learn this and when the tumults swell, when the nations rage, the people plot, the kings rise up, and the rulers counsel together to suppress this King, then be in good spirits, and do not let yourself be moved by this peril. For the Second Psalm foretold that thus it would be, that the whole world would be moved when this King opens His mouth.

From *Commentary on Psalm 2* (Luther's Works 12:7, 10)

The kings of the earth set themselves,
and the rulers take counsel together,
against the LORD and against His Anointed.

PSALM 2:2

Rather, Have Compassion

he psalmist first says [the kings and rulers are] "against God" and then "against His Christ," because all sin first of all offends God. . . . It would not be sin if it did not offend God. But he also arranges the words in this manner that we may learn for our consolation and exhortation that we never suffer injustice without God suffering it first and more than we and that God the Father's solicitude for us is so great that He feels our suffering before we do and bears it with greater resentment than we ourselves. Therefore we should refrain from a feeling of revenge but should rather have compassion on those whom we see dashing themselves to their destruction against a majesty so great; for not only are they unable to do any harm, but they destroy themselves horribly. So it is written (Zechariah 2:8): "Whoever touches you, touches the pupil of My eye."

From *Labors on the Psalms*, on Psalm 2 (Luther's Works 14:316)

Sit in the Beauty of Peace

he world does not stop raging against and persecuting the members of Christ, and "the rulers take counsel together against the Lord," as we read also in Psalm 2:2. Yet in all this Christians do not succumb. So great is the peace of Christ, "which passes all understanding," as Paul says (Philippians 4:7); that is, so great is the peace in our hearts that in every tribulation we are so far from being overcome by fear that we even rejoice, as Paul says in Romans 5:3. Thus by not turning away evils or enemies but by turning them loose, the Lord causes us to feel safe, to rejoice always, not to be overcome by any evil, even though the whole world may bare its fangs against us. Let the pope rage. Let the emperor and his princes threaten us with evil. We shall sit in the beauty of peace, even though they throw us into prison. If they are allowed to give themselves over to their wrath, if finally they even slay us, we will rejoice no less than if we had been invited to a wedding.

From *Lectures on Zechariah (Latin)* (Luther's Works 20:25)

The Lord holds them in derision.
Then He will speak to them in His wrath,
and terrify them in His fury.

PSALM 2:4–5

Do Not Become Discouraged

Even if the time is not revealed to us in which the Lord will liberate the pious and will destroy the reprobate, nevertheless it will happen at some time, if only we do not become discouraged and if, strong in faith, we press on in constant prayer. . . . God wishes to be reminded and stirred up by our prayers. For this reason He wishes us to feel affliction and to bear it, but to believe in deliverance. But we shall not keep silence about our own experience, to make known not so much that this verse is true as that we are grateful to God, who is understanding, retaining with a sure memory, and proclaiming His marvelous kindnesses and wonderful way of saving and keeping us. . . . Let us, therefore, persevere in the faith and in the confession of the Word and let us not be found among the number of those who, as Ecclesiasticus says, "have lost their endurance" (Ecclesiasticus 2:16). They may suppress us, drive us, afflict us, even kill us; yet, if we do not become discouraged, if we suffer these evils in the hope of deliverance, our Lord will not desert us. For He here promises that He will speak in His wrath and that they will fall into confusion.

From *Commentary on Psalm 2* (Luther's Works 12:30–31)

Then He will speak to them in His wrath.

PSALM 2:5

More Than Words

n what manner will [God] speak? Here we must observe the Hebrew way of expression. For when Scripture says that God speaks, it understands a word related to a real thing or action, not just a sound, as ours is. For God does not have a mouth or a tongue, since He is a Spirit, though Scripture speaks of the mouth and tongue of God: "He spoke, and it came to be" (Psalm 33:9). And when He speaks, the mountains tremble, kingdoms are scattered, then indeed the whole earth is moved. That is a language different from ours. When the sun rises, when the sun sets, God speaks. When the fruits grow in size, when human beings are born, God speaks. Accordingly the words of God are not empty air, but things very great and wonderful, which we see with our eyes and feel with our hands. For when, according to Moses (Genesis 1), the Lord said: "Let there be a sun, let there be a moon, let the earth bring forth trees," etc., as soon as He said it, it was done. No one heard this voice, but we see the works and the things themselves before our eyes, and we touch them with our hands. Thus in this passage the Holy Spirit comforts the pious who sigh and breathe heavily under the cross, and at the same time terrifies the impious so that they are not smug but decide for certain that God will speak.

From *Commentary on Psalm 2* (Luther's Works 12:32)

As for Me, I have set My King on Zion, My holy hill.

PSALM 2:6

Christ Alone

he Gospel only holds up Christ to the souls and eyes of all and commands all to behold Him alone, to depend on Him alone, to trust and believe only in Him. Having assumed our flesh, in our flesh He conquered Satan, killed death, laid waste and destroyed hell. [The Gospel] proclaims that He alone is wise, because He alone knows and does the will of God the Father. Him alone it calls righteous, because He alone has done no sin, but is able and willing to communicate His righteousness to all who believe in Him. [The Gospel] speaks of Him alone as a power, because He alone conquered and despoiled the mighty one guarding his own house (Luke 11:21–22). Therefore [the Gospel] wishes us to trust in His wisdom, righteousness, and power; and then indeed it promises that we also will be wise, righteous, and powerful.

From *Commentary on Psalm 2* (Luther's Works 12:20)

The LORD said to Me, "You are My Son;
today I have begotten You."

PSALM 2:7

Sent to Preach

he doctrine of this King does not teach about works, but about the person to whom the Lord has said: "You are My Son." . . . This is a more majestic and excellent teaching than is the Law, whose purpose is only to tell us what we are to do. The Gospel does not, however, dispose of the Law. For the Law is also the voice of God, and it is fitting for all to be subject to it. Yet even though the Law remains, the Gospel teaches something higher. For because no one is able to obey the Law, [the Gospel] preaches about the Son of God, whom the Father has begotten today, that is, from eternity, and appointed King of Zion, that is, willed that He should be born a man and teach. Hereupon the hearts must be stirred up of their own free will to listen to this great King and observe His works. This is consequently the highest article of our faith, to know that the Son of Mary is the eternal Son of God, sent by the Father to preach, not to fight. For He has His strength in His mouth, not a sword in His hand. And this is the sum total of His teaching, that He says, "The eternal Father has begotten Me in eternity." This is the most import-ant part of our faith and the highest article of the Gospel.

From *Commentary on Psalm 2* (Luther's Works 12:45–46)

Ask of Me, and I will make the nations Your heritage,
and the ends of the earth Your possession.

PSALM 2:8

Victory Will Be Ours

hrist's kingdom is and will remain, and He shall rule in the midst of His enemies. In this way we should encourage ourselves also in our private struggle, when our hearts are terrified by the Law, sin, death. Then we should seize on this verse: "I will make the nations Your possession and the ends of the earth Your inheritance." That is, we should believe that by the authority of the Father, Christ was appointed Lord over all things so that salvation depends on Him alone. We have been baptized into His death (Romans 6:3); therefore when we call on His name, when we trust in His Word, we should believe that victory will be ours and that through Him we shall conquer death and hell. For God the Father is not preaching here about garlic and onions. He delivers all things into the hands of the Son so that those who believe in Him might be saved, but those who do not believe will be lost and condemned. Therefore the world, Satan, and our heart should not alarm us. We are indeed afflicted and oppressed in various ways, but the Son of God has preceded us in this very course. He also experienced the raging of the heathen and the threats and attacks of the kings, but at last He was declared to be the king over all the nations of the earth.

From *Commentary on Psalm 2* (Luther's Works 12:59)

You shall break them with a rod of iron.

PSALM 2:9

A Most Trustworthy Gospel

he] *rod of iron* is the holy Gospel, which is Christ's royal scepter in His church and kingdom. . . . It is called a "rod" because it directs, convicts, reproves, and upholds, etc. . . . [It is called a rod "of iron" because] it is inflexible and of an invincible straightness. For the Gospel could not be twisted into evil by any heretics or corrupters, though many have tried in vain to do so. But its straightness remains, iron, true, and unconquered. It is not a reedy rod or stick . . . something that could be swayed by the wind of any opinion whatever (cf. Ephesians 4:14) or that could be shattered when pressing down on something (cf. Isaiah 36:6). Rather, it is trustworthy and made of iron, so that whoever relies on it will be guided to salvation without fail. Therefore it is itself not moved by any violent twists. On the contrary all of us, who are frail and swayed by inconstant errors, will pour ourselves into it as into steadfast iron. Thus the most excellent praise of the Gospel is gathered up in this short word, and its power is strong and unconquered against all its corrupters.

From *First Lectures on the Psalms*, on Psalm 2
(Luther's Works 10:35–36)

You shall break them with a rod of iron
and dash them in pieces like a potter's vessel.

PSALM 2:9

The Word and the World

his verse is, therefore, threatening and terrifies the godless who oppose this King. On the other hand, it is comforting for us who ally ourselves with this King. We know that as far as the world is concerned He is a weak king, laboring in many infirmities and opposed by the tyrants and powers in the world, by false brothers and the founders of sects and heresies, and by our own conscience. Nevertheless neither the weakness of our being nor the power of His adversaries is so great as to prevent the eventual collapse and destruction of all who oppose Him. We should, therefore, cling to this consolation when the world rages and proceeds against this King with force and arms. For even if the world has great power and this King by contrast is completely weak, since He has nothing with which to fight except the Word of the Gospel, which we see thoroughly despised by the world; nevertheless this very Word, so despised and neglected by the world, will at last destroy all His enemies. It is truly, as the prophet says here, a rod of iron, whereas the world is a potter's vessel.

From *Commentary on Psalm 2* (Luther's Works 12:62–63)

Serve the LORD with fear.

Psalm 2:11

True Service of God

he Holy Spirit does not wish us to fear in such a way that we are overwhelmed by fear and despair. But just as He wishes presumption abolished and for that reason commands that we should fear, so He also wishes despair abolished, and commands that we should travel on the royal road, fearing and hoping at the same time. It is as though He wished to say: "Just as this King does not wish to tolerate the pride of kings and the righteousness of saints, so also He does not wish to tolerate the despondency of the poor and foolish who cannot counsel themselves. But He wills that you should fear and so escape pride or presumption, and that you should rejoice and so escape despair. Those who do not wish to fear Him, He threatens with blows, for He has a rod of iron. Those, however, who fear Him in such a way that they rejoice at the same time, that is, who believe they are justified by the mercy of God alone and by the favor of Christ, they are truly the children of God. They fear God not as a tyrant, but as children fear their parents, with respect. For they temper the fear of God with joy and hope. And yet they remain in humble reverence, lest their spirit grow too big and pass over into presumption." This is the true service of God, which, we acknowledge, can never be learned thoroughly.

From *Commentary on Psalm 2* (Luther's Works 12:75)

And rejoice with trembling.

PSALM 2:11

Pure Worship

here is an important reason why He unites joy with trembling. For if one feels pure joy, smugness follows; presumption follows smugness, but damnation follows presumption. For God cannot tolerate presumption. We shall, however, mix these in such a way if we rejoice in God but are disturbed within ourselves. For we are not only foolish but also miserable sinners. There is cause enough, then, for us to tremble and fear. But you must not stop here. For if you see nothing else than that you are a sinner, despair will follow. You must lift up your eyes, then, and behold Christ. Then joy will follow upon fear. Thus truly we shall speak: "I am surely a sinner, but I shall not despair for that reason. For Christ is righteous. Yes, Christ took my sins upon Himself and suffered and rose again in order that I might be clothed in His righteousness. If, therefore, I am without counsel, He has been appointed for me by God to be my Wisdom. I am poor and helpless, He is powerful and rich." This, at last, is the pure worship with which Christ wants us to worship Him.

From *Commentary on Psalm 2* (Luther's Works 12:79)

Kiss the Son, lest He be angry,
and you perish in the way,
for His wrath is quickly kindled.

PSALM 2:12

An Important Distinction

his is, therefore, a most serious threat, full of terror, the very thought of which would slay us if the Holy Spirit had not added the necessary consolation. For He distinguishes between those who kiss this Son and those who do not kiss Him. Accordingly He is angry and threatens ruin to those who do not wish to kiss this Son but are proud of their own righteousness. But He declares those blessed who kiss the Son, who are in fear because of their sins and yet have hope on account of God's Son. Thus the angels made a distinction at the Lord's tomb, when they said to the women (Matthew 28:5), "Do not be afraid." Certainly they had not come to frighten those who loved and sought Christ. But they had come to terrify the guards to whom the Pharisees and priests had given the job of suppressing Christ's glory. And so as the persons differ, the messages also differ. The sermon of wrath and punishments, however, is suitable for the hardened and secure. They must be broken with the hammer of the Law.

From *Commentary on Psalm 2* (Luther's Works 12:92)

Kiss the Son, lest He be angry. . . .
Blessed are all who take refuge in Him.

PSALM 2:12

Hope and Believe

here are two worlds, as it were. The one is the devil's, in which men are secure, proud, neglecting God and the Gospel. . . . The other is Christ's. In it are the afflicted and miserable men who are disturbed by the sense of their sins and fear punishment for their sins, eternal death, and the wrath of God. And yet, because they see that the Son of God was made a sacrifice for their sins, they have hope for mercy. The Holy Spirit comforts them with the marvelous word: "Blessed are all who take refuge in Him," or hope. At the same time, however, He teaches about the true worship of God. To worship God means nothing else than to put one's whole trust in this King and to depend upon His aid and support against death, sin, and Satan. The word "hoping," then, explains the kiss about which He spoke above; as if He wished to say: "Behold this King, be joyful and happy, and fill your heart with good thoughts about God through this Son, whom the Father proposes you should kiss. For everything else in the world, even the most holy life, good works, or your righteousness, will make you sad, will not offer consolation or aid against death and sin. In this Son, however, you will find the fountain of salvation and comfort. Do not only hope in Him, then, but firmly believe that you are blessed when you believe in Him."

From *Commentary on Psalm 2* (Luther's Works 12:92–93)

January 19

O Lᴏʀᴅ, how many are my foes!
Many are rising against me. . . .
But You, O Lᴏʀᴅ, are a shield about me,
my glory, and the lifter of my head.

Pꜱᴀʟᴍ 3:1, 3

What It Means to Hope

W ithout a testing . . . hope would founder, indeed, it would no longer be hope, but presumptuousness; in fact, it would be worse, for it would be the enjoyment of the creature instead of the Creator. And if a person remained in this state, he would be confounded for all eternity. Therefore suffering comes, through which a man is made patient and tested; it comes and takes away everything he has and leaves him naked and alone, allowing him no help or safety in either his physical or spiritual merits, for it makes a man despair of all created things, to turn away from them and from himself, to seek help outside of himself and all other things, in God alone, and thus to sing in the words of Psalm 3:3: "But Thou, O Lord, art my Protector and my Glory." This is what it means to hope and that hope is created in times of testing.

From *Lectures on the Romans* (Luther's Works 25:292)

Answer me when I call, O God of my righteousness! . . .
Be gracious to me and hear my prayer!

PSALM 4:1

The Gifts of God

By the very fact that [God] has mercy on me He justifies me. His mercy is my righteousness. For unless He Himself has mercy, I am not righteous. What is mercy if I do not receive it? But if I receive it, then I have been made righteous. Therefore, since this psalm, as I said, is an "invitation," it ought to teach one how to confess and praise. As I said, he is best who sets before him for contemplation the gifts he has received. We are excited by the gifts we have received. But now the noun "mercy" denotes what is given by the one who has mercy, whereas my righteousness denotes what has been received from the one who has mercy. . . . You see, then, that the prophet in a most excellent way acknowledges the gifts of God which he has received, and all of them, as I have said, at least the spiritual ones, are subsumed under righteousness and mercy. It is with these that a man is something in the presence of God.

From *First Lectures on the Psalms*, on Psalm 4 (Luther's Works 10:47)

You have given me relief when I was in distress.

PSALM 4:1

Prepare Your Soul for Trial

ruly He is a faithful and kind God, who for His own name's sake alone deems us, who are unworthy and evil, worthy of such great blessings. And who can be worthy in the presence of such great majesty except one whom He Himself has made worthy? This indeed is what reason affirms. For He is the highest and has no need of anyone's blessings. Hence these brief words comprise all of the blessings of God that He offers in adversity. However, [the psalmist] correctly made mention of his prosperity first. For God first adorns and equips, He first justifies and makes alive, and then He quickly subjects to battle, so that strength may increase, which otherwise would quickly be consumed by rust and inactivity. No matter what, it is because of His work as the end. But that work meets with the opposition of tribulation and trial. Therefore this verse agrees with Ecclesiasticus 2:1: "My child, if you come forward to serve the Lord," namely, through justification, "prepare your soul for trials." "Note then the kindness of God" (Romans 11:22). What great things He offers in adversity, and with what faithful love He sends tribulation!

From *First Lectures on the Psalms,* on Psalm 4 (Luther's Works 10:48)

But know that the Lord has set apart
the godly for Himself.

<small>PSALM 4:3</small>

A Most Pleasant and Beautiful Game

ust as in the discipline of a household the correction of children is by no means pleasing, so the chastening of the Lord seems exceedingly hard and bitter. Yet "blessed is the man," says James, "who endures trial; for when he has stood the test, he will receive the crown of life which God has promised to those who love Him" (1:12). Therefore let us conclude for certain that disasters, sobs, sighs, and our death are nothing else than a most pleasant and beautiful game of God's goodness. . . . The psalm tells you to learn, to listen, and to let it be told to you whenever you are disturbed by various difficulties and by troubles of every kind [cf. Psalm 4:4]. Consider that God is playing with you, and that this game is wonderful for you and gives pleasure to God. For if He did not embrace you with His fatherly heart, He would not play with you this way. Therefore this is proof of His ineffable mercy toward you, that you are numbered among those with whom God is pleased, and that He takes delight in you. Accordingly He gives you His promise, Word, and Sacrament as most certain symbols and testimonies of grace, that He has adopted you as His son, and that He requires nothing else than that you bear His games, which are pleasing to Him and salutary to you.

From *Lectures on Genesis* (Luther's Works 7:226)

But know that the Lord has set apart the godly for Himself;
the Lord hears when I call to Him.

Psalm 4:3

PSALM 4:3

Held Fast

hen you think that our Lord God has rejected a person, you should think that our Lord God has him in His arms and is pressing him to His heart. When we suppose that someone has been deserted and rejected by God, then we should conclude that he is in the embrace and the lap of God. So Jacob feels and thinks nothing else but that he will be destroyed. But when he takes stock of matters, he is held fast in the embrace of the Son of God [cf. Genesis 32:22–32]. The example of Job in his humiliation and affliction teaches the same. For in this wonderful manner the Lord treats His saint (Psalm 4:3), namely, when we think that it is all over with us, He embraces and kisses us as His dearest sons. This is what Paul means when he says: "When I am weak, I am strong; when I die, I live" (cf. 2 Timothy 2:11; 2 Corinthians 12:10). But we do not understand, and the reason is that the flesh stands in the way. It cannot endure the mortification of itself and hinders the spirit so that it cannot perceive the boundless love and goodwill of God toward us until it comes forth from this struggle and repels the hindrances of the flesh.

From *Lectures on Genesis* (Luther's Works 6:149–50)

January 24

But know that the L<small>ORD</small> has set apart the godly for Himself;
the L<small>ORD</small> hears when I call to Him.

P<small>SALM</small> 4:3

Resolved Contradictions

 od made His Christ wonderful in a number of ways. First, He made Him do miracles and thus repudiated the Jews who denied that this man was from the Lord. Second, His manner of life was opposed to the whole world, namely, that He would flee what the whole world sought above all and would seek what the world fled above all. Thus in the first place "He made foolish the wisdom of the world" (1 Corinthians 1:20) by being Himself made foolish to the world; then "He chose what is weak" (that is, sufferings and punishments) "to shame the strong" (that is, agreeable and peaceful things); hence "what is despised and things that are not" (1 Corinthians 1:27f.), such as poverty, contempt, the cross, death, and in general every opinion and "wisdom of the flesh" (Romans 8:6) and of the world. . . . Third, He made Him wonderful in a superexcellent way in that He who alone is wonderful and the author of wonders made Him to be God. This is a great miracle, that the same person is God and man, dead and alive, mortal and immortal, and almost every contradiction is here resolved in Christ.

From *First Lectures on the Psalms*, on Psalm 4, where the comments follow the Latin translation, which reads: "The Lord hath made His holy one wonderful." (Luther's Works 10:61)

Offer right sacrifices,
and put your trust in the LORD.

PSALM 4:5

Good Advice

hat else does "sacrifice" mean but to make sacred, and a sacrifice something made holy and offered and set apart for sacred purposes? But all of us ought to be such a sacrifice. . . . But note that he adds, "trust in the Lord." There is a difference between "trusting in the Lord" and relying "on the Lord." For to "trust in the Lord" is to be in Christ, our God, and to share in Him and thus by being in Him to rely on the Lord. In Him and with Him and through Him we dare to hope and present every work. For "without Him we can do nothing" (cf. John 15:5). Therefore, no matter how holy and righteous you may be, beware of ever relying on the Lord by means of yourself or on the basis of your own righteousness. But you can have hope in Christ, as the apostle argues, "through Him we have access and confidence" (cf. Romans 5:2). . . . Therefore "trust in the Lord." "Trust in Him at all times, O people" (Psalm 62:8).

From *First Lectures on the Psalms*, on Psalm 4
(Luther's Works 10:67–68)

O L<small>ORD</small>, rebuke me not in Your anger,
nor discipline me in Your wrath.

P<small>SALM</small> 6:1

Kind Father, Stern Judge

od chastens in two ways. At times He does so in grace as a kind Father, temporally; at times He does so in wrath as a stern Judge, eternally. Now when God seizes man, man is by nature weak and disheartened, because he does not know whether God is taking him in hand out of anger or in grace. In fear of His anger he begins to cry out: "O Lord, rebuke me not in Thy anger; let it be in grace and temporally; be a Father, not a Judge." . . . Thus he implores here, not that he wants to go unpunished altogether, for this would not be a good sign, but that he be punished as a child by his father. However, that these words are spoken by a sinner or in the person of a sinner follows from the fact that he mentions punishment. For God's punishment is not sent for the sake of righteousness. Therefore all saints and Christians must recognize themselves as sinners and fear God's wrath, for this psalm is general and excludes no one. Therefore woe to all those who do not fear, do not feel their own sins, and walk about smugly in the face of the awful judgment of God, before whom no good work can avail!

From *Seven Penitential Psalms*, on Psalm 6 (Luther's Works 14:140–41)

Be gracious to me, O Lord, for I am languishing;
heal me, O Lord, for my bones are troubled.

PSALM 6:2

A Prayer for Body and Soul

Be gracious to me, O Lord. That is, show me grace, so that I do not dissolve and despair in fear and terror. *O Lord, heal me.* That is, strengthen me; help me in this wretchedness. *For my bones are troubled.* That is: "All my strength and power passes away at the terror of Thy punishment. Since, therefore, my strength leaves me, give me Thy strength." And here it must be noted that this psalm and others like it will never be thoroughly understood or prayed unless disaster stares man in the face as it does in death and at the final departure. Blessed are they who experience this in life, for every man must finally meet his end. When man thus declines and becomes as nothing in all his power, works, and being, until there is nothing but a lost, condemned, and forsaken sinner, then divine help and strength appear, as in Job 11:11–17: "When you think you are devoured, then you shall shine forth as the morning star."

From *Seven Penitential Psalms*, on Psalm 6 (Luther's Works 14:141)

My soul also is greatly troubled.
But You, O LORD—how long?

Psalm 6:3

Goodness and Mercy Disguised

od's strength and consolation are given to no one unless he asks for it from the bottom of his heart. But no one who has not been profoundly terrified and forsaken prays profoundly. He does not know what ails him, and he remains secure in the strength and consolation of another, his own or that of creatures. In order, therefore, that God might dispense His strength and consolation and communicate it to us, He withdraws all other consolation and makes the soul deeply sorrowful, crying and longing for His comfort. Thus all God's chastisements are graciously designed to be a blessed comfort, although through weak and despairing hearts the foolish hinder and distort the design aimed at them, because they do not know that God hides and imparts His goodness and mercy under wrath and chastisement.

From *Seven Penitential Psalms*, on Psalm 6 (Luther's Works 14:141–42)

The Lord has heard the sound of my weeping.

PSALM 6:8

The Good Life

od is so disposed that He gladly hears those who cry and lament, but not those who feel smug and independent. Therefore the good life does not consist in outward works and appearances but in a lamenting and sorrowful spirit, as we read in the fourth of these psalms (51:17): "The sacrifice acceptable to God is a broken spirit; a broken and contrite heart, O God, Thou wilt not despise." And again (Psalm 34:18): "The Lord is near to the brokenhearted." Therefore weeping is preferred to working, and suffering exceeds all doing.

From *Seven Penitential Psalms*, on Psalm 6 (Luther's Works 14:145)

The LORD has heard my plea;
the LORD accepts my prayer.

PSALM 6:9

Cry, Implore, Pray

hese words refer to a soul that is poor in spirit and has nothing left but crying, imploring, and praying in firm faith, strong hope, and steadfast love. The life and behavior of every Christian should be so constituted that he does not know or have anything but God, and in no other way than in faith. Therefore those who are not like this are not heard by God, for they do not call with the heart. They are not poor, nor are they in need of calling and praying; for they are sated and filled.

From *Seven Penitential Psalms*, on Psalm 6 (Luther's Works 14:145–46)

All my enemies shall be ashamed and greatly troubled;
they shall turn back and be put to shame in a moment.

PSALM 6:10

The Greatest Blindness on Earth

y enemies] stand there in their sense of well-being as a threat and a menace, and they glory in themselves as if all were well with them. O God, they do not know how devoid of all blessing they are! It would be good for them if they came to their senses and realized how very shameful and poor they are in the sight of God. For the proud in spirit and the worldly-wise cannot but be satisfied with themselves, feel secure, esteem themselves highly, never feel foolish, always say the right thing, do the right thing, have holy intentions, stand out among others, and acknowledge few as their equals. This is the greatest blindness on earth; for to the extent that they think, esteem, and consider themselves great in these things, to that extent they are despised and dishonored before God. It is the psalmist's wish that they realize this, for they would be different if they came to their senses and were terrified at themselves.

From *Seven Penitential Psalms*, on Psalm 6 (Luther's Works 14:146)

O LORD my God, if I have done this . . .
if I have repaid my friend with evil
or plundered my enemy without cause . . .
lay my glory in the dust.

PSALM 7:3–5

The Christian Religion

[I]t] is not enough before God, that someone does good only to the good and to friends, unless he is roundly and completely the same person to all the good and evil, to friends and enemies. For this is the Christian religion, to be just to all without a selection according to the person and physical partiality. Just as the fig tree produces figs, whether it stands among thorns or among roses, so it is with the vine (cf. James 3:12). "A sound tree cannot bear evil fruit" (Matthew 7:18). But those who are friends only to their friends are confused. Concerning them the Lord says (Matthew 7:16): "Are figs gathered from thistles?" Thus they do not gather thorns from fig trees, because they are thorny to enemies, but gentle to friends. Hence they are not whole and rounded and the same for all. Then [the psalmist] adds: *If I have paid back those who have done evil to me.* The Lord teaches abundantly in Matthew 5:48: "You must be perfect," that is, rounded and whole like a circle. . . . And this is what the word "justice" (*aequitas*) means, namely, that one who is just (*aequus*) is the same toward all without regard for or discrimination of persons.

From *First Lectures on the Psalms,* on Psalm 7 (Luther's Works 10:83)

The wicked man . . . makes a pit, digging it out,
and falls into the hole that he has made.
His mischief returns upon his own head.

PSALM 7:14–16

No Fairer Law

his is the wonderful wisdom of God, that He does not punish the ungodly except with their own stratagems, He mocks them with their own mockeries, He pierces them with their own javelins, as David did with Goliath and Christ did with the devil. . . . And always God observes the rule: "No law is fairer than that the schemers of destruction perish by their own device" [Ovid]. And blessed Augustine says, "You have commanded, O Lord, and so it is done, that every disordered spirit be its self-punishment." And in this passage (v. 16) we read: *His mischief shall be turned on his own head.* This is what happened to Saul, Absalom, and many others who harmed themselves when they wanted to harm others.

From *First Lectures on the Psalms,* on Psalm 7 (Luther's Works 10:86)

O Lord, our Ruler,
how glorious is Thy name in all the lands!
PSALM 8:1 (according to Luther's translation)

His Divine and Human Names

he name "Lord" is ascribed to no creature on earth, no, not even to an angel in heaven, but only to God. Therefore it is a special and proper name of God and means "the right, true, and eternal God." But the word "lord" or "ruler" is a common name, which Holy Scripture uses even for princes and heads of the household. . . . [David] gives Christ the King two names—a great divine name, Lord; and a small human name, Ruler. Thus he indicates the two natures in Christ, the divine and human nature; yet he speaks not of two, but of one single Lord and Ruler, to show the unity of the person, that Christ the Lord, our Ruler, is one single person. He distinguishes the natures and gives each nature a special name. Yet he does not divide the person, but keeps the person undivided. Let us follow this prophet, as by the Holy Spirit he prophesies that Christ is the Lord and the Ruler of us all and yet is not two Lords nor two Rulers nor two Messiahs nor two Kings, but one single Lord, our Ruler, one single Messiah and King.

From *Commentary on Psalm 8* (Luther's Works 12:99–100)

O Lord, our Ruler,
how glorious is Thy name in all the lands!
PSALM 8:1 (according to Luther's translation)

Who Can Compare?

he greatness and glory of this name call for such amazement. If a physician were to be found on earth who could cure one or two incurable sicknesses or diseases, or could even rescue a man from death, what praise and fame do you think such a physician would have throughout the world? If a prince or king had the might and power to make a blind man see, to cast out a devil, or to raise a dead man, everyone would sing and say about him, "This is a lord." If the Roman emperor could cleanse a leper of his leprosy—if he were not emperor already, they would soon crown him. Yet what would all this be in comparison with what this King and Ruler has done for the children of men, and still does daily and will do throughout the world until the Last Day? He has forgiven many sinners their sins and still forgives them daily. He has made many blind to see and has cleansed many lepers. He has raised many from the dead and made them alive, and on the Last Day He will raise all men and make them alive. Therefore this is an excellent and glorious name, at which everyone might well be amazed.

From *Commentary on Psalm 8* (Luther's Works 12:102–3)

You have set Your glory above the heavens.

PSALM 8:1

Already Home

The Lord, our Ruler, has established and prepared a dominion and kingdom in which we are already in heaven according to the spirit, heart, and soul, even though according to the body we are scattered hither and yon among the lands. Paul speaks the same in Philippians 3:20–21: "Our commonwealth is in heaven, and from it we await a Savior, the Lord Jesus Christ, who will change our lowly body to be like His glorious body, by the power which enables Him even to subject all things to Himself." Our citizenship or homeland, he says, is not here on earth, but in heaven; there we have our real existence and life. . . . There we are citizens and heirs of God, brothers and fellow heirs with Christ. Yes, we are already there with our hearts according to the spirit and faith; for we believe, as the children's Creed teaches us, "a holy Christian Church, resurrection of the body, and life everlasting." Therefore we have this firm hope and confidently expect that on the Last Day we shall arise and possess eternal life.

From *Commentary on Psalm 8* (Luther's Works 12:105)

Out of the mouth of babies and infants . . .

Psalm 8:2

Established with the Word

ow does [Christ] found such a power and kingdom, and what sort of people does He use? "Out of the mouths of infants and sucklings," [the psalmist] says, "hast Thou ordained strength. Thou hast ordained a strength or established a kingdom full of might and power against sin, death, devil, and world, not with physical weapons, armor or sword or gun, but with the mouth of men, and of infants and sucklings at that." This is the way Christ's kingdom is established, namely, not with human force, wisdom, counsel, or power, but with the Word and the Gospel preached by infants and sucklings. The Turkish emperor strengthens and fortifies his kingdom with the sword. So does the pope. But Christ founds, strengthens, and fortifies His kingdom only through the oral Word.

From *Commentary on Psalm 8* (Luther's Works 12:108)

Out of the mouth of babies and infants,
You have established strength because of Your foes,
to still the enemy and the avenger.

PSALM 8:2

The Weak Confound the Strong

hrist] did not bring about this destruction [of our foes] by the sword or by force, but entirely by the opposite. For it is not a matter of force against force, but He chose the "infants and sucklings" against the great and wordy legal experts and scribes. And through humility He fought and brought low whatever was high. "He chose the weak things to confound the strong" (1 Corinthians 1:27). And throughout, whatever is worthless in the world He chose and by it destroyed whatever amounts to anything in the world. Hence He has done these things "out of the mouth of infants," but not by their strength. . . . In vain, therefore, do the Jews look for their Messiah to destroy their enemies by physical strength and power. For the warfare of Christ was not of this kind, nor by equal strength with equal, nor by greater strength against lesser, but altogether by the opposite. Whoever heard of strength being destroyed by weakness? Who has seen glory crushed by shame and not rather by greater glory? But this is what Christ did. In lowliness, weakness, and shame He stripped the whole world of its strength, honor, and glory, and altogether annihilated it and transferred it to Himself.

From *First Lectures on the Psalms*, on Psalm 8 (Luther's Works 10:89)

When I look at Your heavens, the work of Your fingers,

the moon and the stars, which You have set in place,

what is man that You are mindful of him?

PSALM 8:3–4

The New World

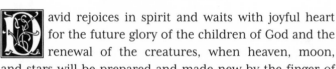avid rejoices in spirit and waits with joyful heart for the future glory of the children of God and the renewal of the creatures, when heaven, moon, and stars will be prepared and made new by the finger of the Lord, our Ruler, that is, by the Holy Spirit. As though he were to say: "I hope for this and am sure that one day I shall come out of this vale of tears into another world, out of this night into brightness, out of this darkness into light, when the Lord, our Ruler, will reveal and manifest Himself with the works of His fingers, that is, the Holy Spirit. Then I shall see a new heaven, new moon, and new stars, and I myself shall be clothed in a new and beautiful body and adorned with new and sharp eyes." By this he teaches that in the world to come the life of the elect and saved will be in heaven and will be a heavenly being and life, where we shall no longer have to work, have toil or trouble, eat, drink, mourn, or be sorrowful, as we must in this world. We shall have an eternal Sabbath and holy day, be eternally satisfied in God, eternally joyful, safe, and free of all sorrow.

From *Commentary on Psalm 8* (Luther's Works 12:119–20)

What is . . . the Son of Man that You care for Him?

PSALM 8:4

Did God Forget?

avid] pictures Christ in distinction from all men on earth and says, "What is Man that Thou art mindful of Him, and the Son of Man that Thou dost care for Him?" He says this about the height and depth of Christ's humiliation. . . . In such humiliation no one regarded Him as a man, but all those who passed by (Lamentations 1:12) shook their heads and said: "Ugh! How God has cursed this man that He should hang on the cross!" . . . [David] is amazed at this and says: "Is it really possible or ought one believe that God would be mindful of such a wretched and miserable man and care for a son of man who dies so miserably, executed on a cross? Is He supposed to be the dearest child and the chosen one of God, He whom everyone spits upon, mocks, and blasphemes? How foolishly God acts! Is He supposed to be God's Son, the Lord, our Ruler, whose name is glorious in all the lands and to whom thanks are given in heaven—He who hangs on the cross and is regarded as a mockery and curse of the people?" David says this in great amazement, as though he were to say: "The whole world thinks that God has forgotten this Man and does not care for this Son of Man. But 'the stone which the builders rejected has become the chief cornerstone. This is the Lord's doing; it is marvelous in our eyes' (Psalm 118:22–23)."

From *Commentary on Psalm 8* (Luther's Works 12:123–24)

Thou wilt let Him be forsaken of God for a little while.

PSALM 8:5 (according to Luther's translation)

In Our Place

t. Paul speaks of it in this way in Philippians 2:6–7: Jesus Christ, "though He was in the form of God, did not count equality with God a thing to be grasped, but emptied Himself, taking the form of a servant." He says that Christ emptied Himself of the divine form; that is, He did not use His divine might nor let His almighty power be seen, but withdrew it when He suffered. In this emptying and humiliation the devil tried all his hellish might. The Man and Son of Man stands there and bears the sins of the world (John 1:29), and because He does not give the appearance of having divine consolation and power, the devil set his teeth over the innocent Lamb and wanted to devour It. Thus the righteous and innocent Man must shiver and shake like a poor condemned sinner and feel God's wrath and judgment against sin in His tender, innocent heart, taste eternal death and damnation for us—in short, He must suffer everything that a condemned sinner has deserved and must suffer eternally.

This is what David talks about here, as though he wanted to say: "Sin and death are conquered, the enemy is destroyed, the kingdom of heaven is won. It happened in this way, that the Lord, our Ruler, true Man and Son of Man, travailed with body and soul in His tender humanity. He underwent such need and anguish that He sweat blood and felt nothing so much as that He was forsaken of God. In His soul He had to quench and extinguish the temptation of being forsaken by God, the devil's flaming darts (Ephesians 6:16), hellish fire, anguish, and everything that we had deserved by our sins." By this the kingdom of heaven, eternal life, and salvation were secured for us, as Isaiah also says (53:11): "He shall see the fruit of the travail of His soul and be satisfied." His body and soul, he says, travail in deep and difficult suffering. But He does this for our great benefit and for His own great joy. For He conquers His enemies and triumphs, and by His knowledge He makes many righteous.

But the best part is that the prophet adds to this: "Thou hast let Him be forsaken of God for a little while." The forsaking is not to be for long, much less forever, but only a little time, namely, only for several hours and not always or over and over.

From *Commentary on Psalm 8* (Luther's Works 12:127)

Thou wilt let Him be forsaken of God for a little while,
but Thou wilt crown Him with honor and adornment.

PSALM 8:5 (according to Luther's translation)

Dressed, Adorned, and Crowned

 hus the prophet preaches preciously and powerfully about the suffering of Christ. It is a brief and clear sermon. . . . He indicates His physical suffering [and] His sublime spiritual suffering when he says that for a little time He will be forsaken by God. . . . Now there follows His joyful resurrection from the dead. *But Thou wilt crown Him with honor and adornment.* Him whom no one will support, who is forsaken by God and the whole world, Him Thou wilt snatch from suffering to peace, from anguish to consolation and joy. Because of the contempt, mockery, and shame He has endured Thou wilt adorn Him with honor. Because of the ugly form He had on earth Thou wilt dress Him preciously, so that He will be dressed, adorned, and crowned on all sides. Not only will He be beautiful in body and soul for His own person, full of eternal life, full of joy, salvation, wisdom, power and might, full of heavenly majesty and deity, so that all creatures will regard and adore Him; He will also be gloriously adorned and decorated with His Christians and believers on earth and with the elect angels in heaven, in this world and in the world to come.

From *Commentary on Psalm 8* (Luther's Works 12:128)

Thou wilt crown Him with honor and adornment.

PSALM 8:5 (according to Luther's translation)

The Coronation of Christ

ings are usually adorned when they are to put on a spectacle. . . . On that day [Christ] will be decked out in the right dress and adornment, when He comes in glory with His elect and holy angels. As St. Paul says (2 Thessalonians 1:10), Christ will come "to be glorified in His saints and to be marveled at in all who have believed." And Christ Himself says (Matthew 25:31–32): "When the Son of Man comes in His glory, and all the angels with Him, then He will sit on His glorious throne. Before Him will be gathered all the nations." Then He will have around Him all the works of His fingers, a new heaven, moon, stars, and all creation. David means to express all this by the "honor and adornment" with which Christ is to be crowned. Therefore these words are a glorious prophecy of the resurrection of Christ and of His coronation, and this honor and adornment will have no end.

From *Commentary on Psalm 8* (Luther's Works 12:129–30)

You have given Him dominion
over the works of Your hands;
You have put all things under His feet.

PSALM 8:6

True Man and True God

n this verse David describes Christ as true man and yet at the same time true God and Lord over all creatures. For the [Hebrew] word [translated as "Thou wilt make Him Lord"] . . . really means to make lord the way a man is made a lord. . . . [David] says, "Thou wilt make Him Lord over the works of Thy hands" and "Thou hast put all things under His feet." Thereby he testifies that Christ, true man, is also at the same time true God. For God does not make anyone Lord over the works of His hands nor put all things under anyone's feet unless He is His equal, that is, unless He is God. God alone is Lord over the works of His hands and has all things under His feet. Since this Man Christ, who was forsaken of God for a little time, is to be made Lord over God's works—heaven, angels, sun, moon, earth, men, air, water, and everything that is in heaven, on earth, and in the water—it follows that He is true God.

From *Commentary on Psalm 8* (Luther's Works 12:130–31)

You have put all things under His feet,
all sheep and oxen, and also the beasts of the field,
the birds of the heavens, and the fish of the sea.

PSALM 8:6–8

Everything Belongs to Christ

 his is the last part of Christ's dominion, a dominion that Adam also received in Paradise, as is written in Genesis 1:26. . . . What Adam received in Paradise, David subjects here to Christ. Hence we should not get some such idea as this: "If Christ has a special, peculiar dominion and kingdom, He has nothing in common with Adam's dominion and kingdom." The Christians must still live in the world. Where are they to stay and find something to eat and drink, if Christ has nothing to do with Adam's kingdom and the world is their enemy and will not grant them even a crust of bread? To avoid such ideas, David also subjects to Christ the dominion that Adam has on earth over fish, birds, cattle, etc., and says that under Christ's feet are put all sheep, all oxen, all wild beasts, all birds of the air, all fish in the sea. Therefore, everything in the wide world belongs to Christ, the Ruler. . . . Because He does have everything in His power, His Christians are richly provided for and will get along well, so that they may remain in the world; they will also have enough to eat and drink on earth.

From *Commentary on Psalm 8* (Luther's Works 12:134–35)

O LORD, our Lord,
how majestic is Your name in all the earth!

PSALM 8:9

A Verse Worth Repeating

his verse is the end of the song. David concludes this psalm just the way he began it. He thanks the Lord, our Ruler, for His great and inestimable blessing, for establishing such a kingdom and calling and gathering His Church, which gloriously praises His name throughout the world and thanks Him in heaven. Let us follow the example of this singer of praises as he prophesies to us. The Lord is our Ruler, too, and His kingdom is established and founded from the mouths of babes and sucklings. We entered it by Baptism, and we are called to it daily through Word and Gospel. With David we also hope to come to where we shall see the heavens, the work of His fingers, the moon and the stars which He will prepare. He won the kingdom with great trouble and anguish. Now He is crowned with honor and adornment and has everything under His feet. For this we give God our praise and thanks, but especially for the fact that He has brought us to a light and knowledge that does not spring up out of human reason but out of Christ. He is our Sun, who died for us and was raised from the dead, lives and reigns, so that through Him we might be saved.

From *Commentary on Psalm 8* (Luther's Works 12:135–36)

February 16

I will give thanks to the Lord with my whole heart;
I will recount all of Your wonderful deeds.

PSALM 9:1

Sluggish Confessions

 onfess is a single word in Hebrew that among Hebrews means as much as all these among us: praise, give thanks, recompense, and acknowledge a benefit received. . . . Some people confess with their lips only. They are the ones who say one thing in the heart and another with the mouth, like the sinner who has evil intentions and sings to God nevertheless. Concerning them Psalm 78:36–37 says: "They lied to Him with their tongue, but their heart was not right before Him." Others confess with their heart, but not with the whole heart. These are the ones who confess with half a heart and do not do, or do sluggishly, what they say and understand. But those *confess with the whole heart* who are ready to do and suffer with all their powers, just as it is in their hearts.

From *First Lectures on the Psalms*, on Psalm 9
(Luther's Works 10:91–92)

He judges the world with righteousness,
He judges the peoples with equity.

PSALM 9:8 (RSV)

The Fair Judge

quity and *justice* are generally distinguished in the Scriptures in this way, that equity looks to persons while justice deals with causes. He is fair (*equus*) who is the same toward all and conducts himself fairly, and neither by hatred nor by love, neither by riches nor by poverty is he influenced in favor of one more than of another. Thus God is called fair, because He sets forth His grace not only to the Jews but without discrimination to all men . . . for He is the same for all, of the same severity and leniency, and for no one more or less [for the rich man as for the poor man, for the Jew as for the Gentiles]. Human laws, however, are often like "webs of a spider" (Isaiah 59:5f.) and unfair. . . . "Justice," however, is said to be the restoration to each one of what belongs to him. Hence equity comes before justice and is, as it were, the prerequisite. And equity distinguishes merits, while justice returns reward. Thus the Lord "judges the world in equity" (for He is the same for all, He desires all to be saved), and He "judges in justice" (Psalm 98:9), because He gives to each one his own reward. An example of both is in the Gospel parable, where after the individuals had received the day's wage, some complained about unfairness (Matthew 20:10–12).

From *First Lectures on the Psalms*, on Psalm 9, commenting on the Latin translation of this verse (Luther's Works 10:94–95)

The LORD is a stronghold for the oppressed,
a stronghold in times of trouble.

PSALM 9:9

In Due Time

hen the Lord appeared to Abram, and said: *To your descendants I will give this land* [Genesis 12:7]. After Abram, the exile, has been annoyed and troubled among the Canaanites long enough and in various ways, he finds great comfort in his trials, to keep him from being overcome by impatience. For it is true that no flesh would be saved (Matthew 24:22) unless at that time the days were shortened and comfort followed. He who perseveres in faith will surely experience in the end that God does not forsake His own. He indeed defers His comfort and strains the sinew to such an extent that you think it is about to tear. But in due time He is at hand; and when we seem to be on the verge of collapse, He supports us with His help. For this reason Psalm 9:9 bestows this title on God, calling Him "a Helper at the appropriate time."

From *Lectures on Genesis* (Luther's Works 2:283)

Those who know Your name put their trust in You,
for You, O Lord, have not forsaken those who seek You.

PSALM 9:10

It's Not Always What It Seems

 od] is really a helper in need. For He does not forsake His saints who hope in Him, although they seem to be forsaken and cast off. For this is what it means not to forsake those who are nearly forsaken. But God makes an affirmative out of a negative. When the godly say: "There is no help in God: I am lost," God replies: "You are not lost, and you will not be lost as you conclude, but I shall give you a mouth and wisdom even in the extremity of the greatest dangers so that you are not forsaken." It certainly appears to be forsaking, but in reality it is not. Therefore God again sends forth His Word and comforts the troubled old man [Jacob]. . . . "Your prayer and tears," He wants to say, "compel Me to come to your aid. The things which seemed to threaten you with destruction will not harm you at all. I am the Lord your God!"

From *Lectures on Genesis* (Luther's Works 6:221–22)

Why, O Lᴏʀᴅ, do You stand far away?
Why do You hide Yourself in times of trouble?
Psᴀʟᴍ 10:1

In the Meantime

 e find those mournful laments in the psalms, such as "Arise!" in Psalm 7:6 and "Why does Thou stand afar off?" in Psalm 10:1. Similar words are spoken by hearts that are in doubt as to whether we have a God and ask: "Where is your God?" (Psalm 42:10). "We do not have to believe in Him who conceals and withdraws Himself from us, do we?" . . . But we have nothing from God except the pure Word, namely, that the Lord Jesus sits at the right hand of the Father and is the Judge of the living and the dead, and that through Him we are kings and priests (Revelation 1:6). But where can this be discerned? Not in the indicative mood, but in the imperative and the optative. Why He hides Himself in this way we shall see on that Day, when all enemies will have been put under His feet (1 Corinthians 15:25). Meanwhile we should believe and hope. For if one could see it now before one's eyes, there would be no need of faith.

From *Lectures on Genesis* (Luther's Works 4:356–57)

[The Lord's] eyes see,
His eyelids test the children of man.

PSALM 11:4

~~~

A God Who Sleeps?

ccording to Cassiodorus . . . "eyes" denote God's clear knowledge concerning the righteous, while "eyelids" are, as it were, sleep and ignorance concerning the unrighteous. Not that God did not see both with equal clarity, but that He appears to the people themselves to be like this. For the righteous always act (in fear) as if the Lord saw them. But the ungodly walk along smugly, as if God has His eyelids closed and did not see them, even though He examines them, too, and knocks, warning their conscience, as Revelation 3:20 says: "I stand at the door and knock, etc." . . . Therefore if a person does not yet fear and see God everywhere and at all times, the eyes of the Lord do not yet look at him, for God is sleeping as far as he is concerned, even though God cannot sleep. . . . His "eyes" are open when He causes us to have open eyes and to be watchful. But they are "eyelids" for Him when He lets us sleep and snore or permits us not to think about Him at all, etc.

From *First Lectures on the Psalms*, on Psalm 11
(Luther's Works 10:99–100)

February 22

Save, O Lord, for the godly one is gone;
for the faithful have vanished
from among the children of man.

PSALM 12:1

You Are Not Alone

Since the ingratitude and the wickedness of the burghers, the peasants, and the classes of every kind are so great, we, too, are often driven to conclude that the entire world is possessed by Satan. Moreover, the very sad spectacle troubles the hearts of the godly. But one must hold fast to the hope which is here before Abraham: that nevertheless there are some pious and saintly people still living. For God is not without a people. He is a God of mercy and of judgment. Therefore He preserves and guides those who are not impenitent but humble themselves and seek forgiveness. Thus Psalm 12:1 states: "The faithful have vanished from among the sons of men"; that is, the world casts aside and hates the truth and the Word. Yet at the end the Lord says (Psalm 12:5): "I will arise because of the poor." Therefore there always remain some who keep and receive the Word.

From *Lectures on Genesis* (Luther's Works 3:345)

May the LORD cut off all flattering lips,
the tongue that makes great boasts,
those who say, "With our tongue we will prevail,
our lips are with us; who is master over us?"

PSALM 12:3–4

Be Not Wise in Your Own Conceits

ote this word ["with our tongue we will prevail"], for it is a word of stubbornness, a word of pride and heresy. You must never be so learned that you should not always be ready to hear also the opinion of others, even if you have spoken the truth, but especially when you have spoken doubtful things. From this arise heresies and strife, and in their midst even the truth itself is lost, since truth is not contentious. Romans 12:15: "Be not wise in your own conceits." As a result of this people become incorrigible. Note the example of Jeremiah 28:1ff., and of Moses, Exodus 18:13ff. And the apostle says, 1 Corinthians 14:30: "If a revelation is made to another sitting by, let the first be silent." For "God is wonderful in His saints" (Psalm 68:35), and in a remarkable way He has the proud and the contentious in derision (Psalm 2:4).

From *First Lectures on the Psalms,* on Psalm 12 (Luther's Works 10:102)

The words of the LORD are pure words,
like silver refined in a furnace on the ground,
purified seven times.

PSALM 12:6

A Most Beautiful Analogy

he Gospel is called "silver," first, because it is precious, not according to the flesh, but because it makes the soul precious in the sight of God; second, because it is solid, that is, because it makes people solid and full, not like an empty reed and a carnal letter [nor wormeaten like a twig or a rush]; third, because it is heard far and wide. Thus the sound of the Gospel has gone out through all the world (Psalm 19:4), and it makes the disciples sonorous and eloquent. Fourth, it is weighty, because it does not contain fables or superficial things, and it makes men serious and mature, as stated below, "I will praise Thee in a strong people" (Psalm 35:18). Fifth, it is white and shining, because it is modest and chaste and teaches modesty, it speaks modestly. Therefore because of this characteristic, when he had said, "the promises of the Lord are pure," he immediately called it "silver" altogether. . . . The preacher of the Word of God should also be like this, namely, first, valuable and genuine; second, solid and full of knowledge, not of the emptiness of opinions; third, eloquent; fourth, sober and steadfast; fifth, shining, reproving without malice and rage.

From *First Lectures on the Psalms,* on Psalm 12 (Luther's Works 10:103)

The fool says in his heart, "There is no God."

PSALM 14:1

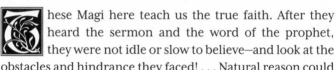

Go Farther Than You Feel

hese Magi here teach us the true faith. After they heard the sermon and the word of the prophet, they were not idle or slow to believe—and look at the obstacles and hindrance they faced! . . . Natural reason could in no way have held its own here. If they had not found the king as they had expected, they would have at once pouted and become arrogant and said: "The devil led me here. A king cannot have been born here since everything is so quiet and wretched. There is more shouting when a child is born to our shepherd, and a calving cow is more talked about than this king." See, reason and nature always do this; they go no farther than they can feel. If they no longer feel, they at once dare to deny God and say as the psalmist says of them: Here "there is no God" (Psalm 14 [:1]). . . . The light of nature and the light of grace cannot be friends. Nature wants to perceive and be certain before it believes. Grace believes before it perceives. For this reason, nature does not go farther than her own light. Grace joyfully steps out into the darkness, follows the mere word of Scripture, no matter how it appears; whether nature holds it true or false, [grace] clings to the Word.

From the *Church Postil*, sermon for Epiphany on Matthew 2:1–12 (Luther's Works 76:102–3)

The LORD looks down from heaven on the children of man,
to see if there are any who understand,
who seek after God.
They have all turned aside.

PSALM 14:2–3

The Office of the Holy Spirit

e draw the universal conclusion that without the Holy Spirit and without grace man can do nothing but sin and so goes on endlessly from sin to sin. . . . Statements of Holy Scripture prove the same thing. Or is not Psalm 14:2–3 general enough? . . . Paul repeats this in Romans 3:10. Likewise Psalm 116:11 states in general: "Every human being is a liar"; and Paul (Romans 11:32): "God has shut up all under sin." All these passages are very general and most emphatically conclude in our favor that without the Holy Spirit, whom Christ alone bestows, man can do nothing else than err and sin. For this reason Christ also declares in the Gospel (John 15:5): "I am the vine, you are the branches; apart from Me you can do nothing. Without Me you are like branches that are cut off, dry, dead, and ready for the fire." This is also the reason why it is the office of the Holy Spirit to reprove the world (John 16:8), namely, that He might recall the world to repentance and to a recognition of this fault.

From *Lectures on Genesis* (Luther's Works 2:40)

There is none who does good, not even one.

Psalm 14:3

Righteousness Looks Down

aul uses Psalm 14:3 to prove that "a person is not justified by works of the Law," Galatians 2:16. Thus Luther writes:] Therefore the works of the Law must be sins; otherwise they would certainly justify. Thus it is clear that Christian righteousness and human righteousness are not only altogether different but are even opposed to each other, because the latter comes from works, while works come from the former. No wonder, therefore, that Paul's theology vanished entirely and could not be understood after Christians began to be instructed by men who declared falsely that Aristotle's ethics are entirely in accord with the doctrine of Christ and of Paul, by men who failed completely to understand either Aristotle or Christ. For our righteousness looks down from heaven and descends to us. But those godless men have presumed to ascend into heaven by means of their righteousness and from there to bring the truth which has arisen among us from the earth. Therefore Paul stands resolute: "No flesh is justified on the basis of works of the Law," as Psalm 143:2 also says: "No man living will be justified before Thee."

From *[First] Lectures on Galatians* (Luther's Works 27:224–25)

The LORD is my chosen portion and my cup;
You hold my lot. . . .
Indeed, I have a beautiful inheritance.

PSALM 16:5–6

Our Lord's Double Claim

n this life God is the "portion" of the saints or a partial reward, as the apostle says in 1 Corinthians 13:12: "We know in part." But in the future "God will be all in all" (1 Corinthians 15:28), since what is now in part will have been done away (cf. 1 Corinthians 15:24). Therefore Christ here calls the Lord the portion of His lot and of His cup. . . . And if the text were carefully considered, our Lord is here claiming a double right that He has in relation to God. First, there is the inheritance; because He is innocent and the Son of God, He rightfully has everything as an inheritance; and in line with this He says, "the Lord is the portion of My inheritance," because, as above, in this life even Christ did not have everything that by right of inheritance belonged to Him. The second is the right of merit, and thus He says, "the Lord is the portion of My cup." But all this is ours, because we, too, have a share in the Lord in this life, in the cup and suffering of Christ. For that reason there follows, *Thou art the One who will restore My inheritance to Me*, that is, "My faithful people, My Church," as above in Psalm 2:8: "I will give Thee the Gentiles for Thy inheritance."

From *First Lectures on the Psalms*, on Psalm 16
(Luther's Works 10:106–7)

I have set the LORD always before me;
because He is at my right hand, I shall not be shaken.

PSALM 16:8

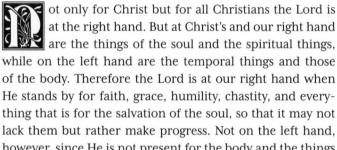

At Your Right Hand

Not only for Christ but for all Christians the Lord is at the right hand. But at Christ's and our right hand are the things of the soul and the spiritual things, while on the left hand are the temporal things and those of the body. Therefore the Lord is at our right hand when He stands by for faith, grace, humility, chastity, and everything that is for the salvation of the soul, so that it may not lack them but rather make progress. Not on the left hand, however, since He is not present for the body and the things of the body, yes, He lets it be scourged, humbled, suffer want, and be afflicted. And therefore it is rather the devil who is at our left hand. 1 Peter 5:8 reads: "Your adversary, the devil, prowls around like a lion, seeking, etc." However, the Lord is in our midst (Psalm 46:7). But the devil is outside, going around, and therefore at our left hand.

From *First Lectures on the Psalms,* on Psalm 110
(Luther's Works 11:369)

Wondrously show Your steadfast love,
O Savior of those who seek refuge
from their adversaries at Your right hand.

PSALM 17:7

The Gracious Strength of God

he right hand is Christ, the Son of God, as Psalm 118:16 says: "The right hand of the Lord has made strength," for the Son of God is the strength, power, and wisdom of God, 1 Corinthians 1:24, 30. Second, the right hand of God is the grace or faithfulness or work of God. Thus blessed Augustine correctly says by way of explanation that the right hand means God's propitiation and favor, according to Psalm 45:4: "The right hand shall conduct Thee wonderfully." The left hand, however, is God's rule or freely given grace, which is common to all. Third, the right hand is the awarding of glory in the future, as Matthew 25:33–34 says, "He will place these on His right hand and those on His left, and then He will say, etc." Therefore the right hand is, first, Christ; second, it is the merit of Christians; and third, it is their reward. . . . Therefore the right hand of God is the gracious strength of God with which He helps the elect.

From *First Lectures on the Psalms*, on Psalm 17 (Luther's Works 10:111)

March 2

Keep me as the apple of Your eye;
hide me in the shadow of Your wings.

PSALM 17:8

A Shadow of Protection

 he shadow of Thy wings in a mystical sense is faith in Christ, which in this life is mysterious and shadowy. But the wings of Christ are His hands stretched out on the cross. For just as the body of Christ on the cross produces a shadow, so it casts a spiritual shadow on the soul, namely, faith in His cross, under which every saint is protected. Second, the shadow of the wings is the protection and watch of the holy angels or of contemplative men, who are the wings of God, for in them He soars and dwells in affectionate and encaptured minds. Third, the shadow of the wings is the learning of Scriptures, in which there is rest for those who devote themselves to this learning.

From *First Lectures on the Psalms*, on Psalm 17 (Luther's Works 10:111)

The Lord is . . . the horn of my salvation.

PSALM 18:2

Victorious Salvation

 n Scripture the horn often denotes royal power as the chief power, or the king himself as the chief, especially the victorious and warlike power. Therefore also the Church is called the horn of Christ, Psalm 112:9: "His horn will be exalted in glory"; and Psalm 75:10: "The horns of the righteous shall be exalted," that is, the kingdoms and churches of Christ. . . . Thus Luke 1:69 reads: "He has raised up a horn of salvation," that is, Christ as victorious salvation, "for us in the house of His servant David." . . . But the kingdom of Christ is called His horn. Accordingly, He Himself has one horn, or one realm, as it were, because He is the Lord of only one Church. For just as a horned beast . . . fights and wages war with the horns as weapons, so Christ fights and vanquishes the world and its prince through the Church, which is His exceedingly strong and invincible horn. The Church, on the contrary, calls Christ her horn, because it also denotes the King Himself, as I have said, because Christ is the strength of His Church through whom it triumphs over the world. He Himself is strength and wisdom for all who believe in Him. Thus the avenging God is the strength and invincible might of Christ, in which He has overcome all things. Accordingly, He says here, "the horn of My salvation," for God is the victorious might of Christ for salvation.

From *First Lectures on the Psalms*, on Psalm 18
(Luther's Works 10:113)

March 4

The cords of death encompassed Me;
the torrents of destruction assailed Me;
the cords of Sheol entangled Me;
the snares of death confronted Me.

PSALM 18:4–5

Not without Grief

 ome take this in the literal sense of the words: "the ropes of death," that is, the bonds that held Christ three days in death, and "the ropes of hell," that is, the bonds that held His soul in hell for three days. This seems to be the sense of Psalm 16:10, which says that His soul was in hell. But here He says that He endured even the sorrows of death. . . . Peter, too, bears witness to this in Acts when he says (Acts 2:24): "God raised Him up, having loosed the pangs of death," or hell. Therefore [Christ] even sorrowed in death, and God loosed these sorrows by raising Him. . . . I firmly believe that Christ did not feel the punishments and griefs of the damned, who are the children of despair, but that Christ always hoped. Nevertheless, these words testify that He was not altogether without grief. And if there had been no other griefs, yet because He was held by the ropes and in the power of death and hell, this in itself was without doubt loathsome and irksome to His most noble soul, for without putting off the substance He desired freedom and His own brilliant glorification.

From *First Lectures on the Psalms*, on Psalm 18
(Luther's Works 10:115–16)

March 5

He bowed the heavens and came down;
thick darkness was under His feet.
He rode on a cherub and flew;
He came swiftly on the wings of the wind.

PSALM 18:9–10

Going Up and Going Down

 od's] feet stand in the soul, but in the fog and darkness of faith; then, however, we shall rise up to Him in the future by sight. But now He comes down to us by faith. And this is the first meaning. Second . . . the darkness covers the ungodly, who are the earth and His footstool when He lights up the low-hanging heavens. Third, the darkness covers and blinds the flesh of sin so that it may not see desirable things, and lies beneath the feet, that is, the desires of God. . . . There follows, *and He ascended upon the cherubim* (v. 10). God does not ascend physically but in our understanding and love, when He is acknowledged to be the most high and incomprehensible and supremely lovable. And thus, the more we advance in our understanding of Him, the more He ascends, because His exalted state is recognized ever more clearly. But this going up does not take place except where there is a previous going down, just as Christ first descended and then ascended.

From *First Lectures on the Psalms*, on Psalm 18
(Luther's Works 10:118–19)

March 6

He made darkness His covering,

His canopy around Him,

thick clouds dark with water.

PSALM 18:11

Concealed in Humanity

he hiding place of God is darkness. In the first place, because [God] dwells in the riddle and darkness of faith. Second, because He dwells in an unapproachable light (1 Timothy 6:16), so that no mind can penetrate to Him. . . . For thus God is hidden and beyond understanding. Third, this can be understood as referring to the mystery of the incarnation. For He is concealed in humanity, which is His darkness. Here He could not be seen but only heard. Fourth, this refers to the Church or the blessed Virgin, for He was concealed in both and continues to be hidden in the Church to the present. The Church is dim to the world but clear to God. Fifth, it refers to the sacrament of the Eucharist, where He is most completely concealed.

From *First Lectures on the Psalms*, on Psalm 18
(Luther's Works 10:119–20)

With the merciful You show Yourself merciful;
with the blameless man You show Yourself blameless.

PSALM 18:25

An Occasion for Something Good

ot only the passive evils that are inflicted on us result in good, but also the active ones, that is, the evils which we ourselves do. "How can this be?" you say. Because when a godly person is aware of his fall, he becomes ashamed and is perturbed. Thus his fall leads first to humility and then also to fervent prayer. It is for this reason that Solomon says (Proverbs 24:16): "A righteous man falls seven times in a day and rises again." For they do not persist in their sins; they groan and grieve. . . . Therefore God leads His saints in a wonderful manner, as the psalm (4:3) states. "With the pure Thou dost show Thyself pure; and with the crooked Thou dost show Thyself perverse" (Psalm 18:26). But these statements should not be understood as though we maintained that a failing is something good. For a failing remains something intrinsically evil; but in the case of the saints it becomes the occasion for something good, according to the statement (Psalm 18:25): "With the blameless man Thou dost show Thyself blameless." Whatever the saints do is sanctified; that is, even if those fall who are saintly or justified or believe and fear God, their faith is nevertheless disciplined and increased. To this extent God is wonderful in His saints.

From *Lectures on Genesis* (Luther's Works 3:334)

With the pure Thou dost show Thyself pure;
and with the crooked Thou dost show Thyself perverse.

PSALM 18:26 (RSV)

All Are Not Treated Alike

he persons of the saints need to be distinguished from those of the perverse. For since the saints live uprightly in faith toward God and in love toward their neighbor, all that they do therefore is pleasing as well, whether sacrifices or the work of their hands, etc. Indeed, God is so well-pleased with His people that even their sins and errors do them no harm, and God is holy together with His saints even amid their sins. On the other hand, since the godless live perversely, caring nothing about faith toward God and mercy toward their neighbor, but boasting about their sacrifices and works and reveling in them, God also along with them makes Himself perverse and becomes perverse also to them. It is as if He were saying: "Since you reject My commandment about faith and mercy and do not deign to give it any place, I, in turn, will have no regard for your most sublime work of sacrifice—or, rather, to put it plainly, I do not want it! So far are your sins from being harmless to you that even your greatest merits are, for you, the greatest sins."

From *Annotations on Matthew 1–18* (Luther's Works 67:70)

With the pure Thou dost show Thyself pure;
and with the crooked Thou dost show Thyself perverse.
PSALM 18:26 (RSV)

The Saints and the Perverse

aith can use all things for its purpose, whether good or bad, except unbelief and its fruits. . . . To a Christian, therefore, the entire world is holiness, purity, utility, and piety. Contrariwise, to a non-Christian the whole world is unholiness, impurity, uselessness, and destruction—even God with all His goodness, as Psalm 18:26–27 says to God: "With the pure Thou dost show Thyself pure; and with the crooked Thou dost show Thyself perverse." Why is this? Because the pure, that is, the believers, can use all things in a holy and blessed way to sanctify and purify themselves. But the unholy and the unbelievers sin, profane, and pollute themselves incessantly in all things. For they cannot use anything in a right, godly, and blessed way, so that it might serve their own salvation.

From *Commentary on 1 Corinthians 7* (Luther's Works 28:35)

He made my feet like the feet of a deer
and set me secure on the heights.

PSALM 18:33

Soaring and Flying

 his verse appears also in the prophet Habakkuk (3:19), where Luther comments:] That is equivalent to saying: "The Lord is still my God and my whole strength, We shall rejoice over that, skipping about and leaping like hinds [deer]. That is how our feet will be, no longer wading and crawling in the mire but soaring and flying joyfully on the heights. We shall do nothing but sing happily, play, and express our joy in every way. That will happen when the Babylonian scepter is cursed and destroyed and we are delivered and the Christ has appeared with His kingdom. Amen."

From *Lectures on Habakkuk (German)* (Luther's Works 19:237)

The heavens declare the glory of God,
and the sky above proclaims His handiwork.

PSALM 19:1

Beautiful Daybreak

 he psalmist describes both the sun and the day, Christ and the Gospel, in a most delightful way when he says, "The heavens proclaim the glory of God" (Psalm 19 [:1]); that is, just as the natural heavens bring the sun and the day, and the sun is in the heavens, so the apostles in their preaching bring and have in themselves the true sun, Christ. The psalmist continues: "In them He has set a tent for the sun, which comes out like a bridegroom from his wedding chamber. It rejoices like a strong man to run its course. It rises from one end of the heavens, and runs back again to the same end, and there is nothing hidden from its heat" (Psalm 19 [:4–6]). All of this is said about the beautiful daybreak, that is, about the Gospel, which Scripture praises highly, for it makes alive, happy, joyous, active, and brings all goodness with it. Therefore, it is called "Gospel," that is, joyous news.

From the *Church Postil*, sermon for Advent 1 on Romans 13:11–14
(Luther's Works 75:18–19)

Who can discern his errors?

PSALM 19:12

Faced with Reality

hoever wants to drown out sin and death with works will, of necessity, fail; for it is impossible to recognize all sins (Psalm 19:12). Only the lesser part of sin is recognizable, and the devil or God's judgment will reveal those sins that man cannot recognize or know. Then the conscience will be terrified and say: "O Lord God, I have done nothing to atone for this sin!" For it thought that sins could be paid for with works, and now it is suddenly faced with many and great sins which it knew nothing of, much less paid for. Then this conscience is cast down into despair, and the devil lends a hand and turns all the good works into sins. What can be done then? This soul knows nothing of the kingdom of grace, or that God's steadfast love prevails over us; nor is it in the habit of trusting in His grace.

From *Commentary on Psalm 117* (Luther's Works 14:28)

Who can discern his errors?
Declare me innocent from hidden faults.

PSALM 19:12

A Most Ardent Plea for Grace

nly before God should one acknowledge guilt which does not exist, not before men. I can truthfully say that I have not committed adultery and have not stolen, but I cannot say in general that I have committed no sin against the Sixth and Seventh Commandments. For in these circumstances I must be afraid of God's judgment, even though I am not conscious of anything. Sin has not yet been done away with, nor has it been completely buried; and to have restrained one's hands is not enough for God. He condemns even the lust of the heart. Therefore we are right in acknowledging before Him guilt where there is no guilt, that is, where we are not conscious of anything. We are right in saying with David (Psalm 19:12): "Who can discern his errors? Cleanse me of my hidden faults." For God holds even our original sin against us. . . . God always regards us as responsible and answerable to Him.

From *Lectures on Genesis* (Luther's Works 3:349–50)

O Lord, in Your strength the king rejoices,
and in Your salvation how greatly he exults!
You have given him his heart's desire
and have not withheld the request of his lips.

Psalm 21:1–2

God Hears You

In the presence of God our prayers are regarded in such a way that they are answered before we call. I wish that this promise were made use of to its utmost extent by all in all kinds of dangers, because we are subject to the world, the papacy, the Turk, and the tyrants. . . . In this state of despair we must cry to God, if not with our voice, then at least with our mouth. The prayer of the righteous man is answered before it is finished. Before they begin to formulate, when they are still speaking in general, as elsewhere, "Thou hast given him his heart's desire" (Psalm 21:2). So God heard Moses, groaning and laboring in the anguish of his heart; He heard the groan and sob of his heart. Then He struck the sea. So Bernard says to his brothers, "Do not despise prayers, and know that as soon as you will have raised your voices, they are written in heaven, and it will come to pass and it will be given you. If it is not given, then it is not good for you, and God will give you something in its place that is better and more useful."

From *Lectures on Isaiah* (Luther's Works 17:392–93)

I am a worm and not a man.

PSALM 22:6

Despised by All

ince the enemy's iniquity is great and his anger violent, this Ruler [Christ] takes pleasure and joy in making a fool of such a wicked, fierce, and proud spirit, and mocking him. In order to ordain this strength, He degrades Himself so profoundly and becomes a man, yes, even degrades Himself below all men, as it is written in Psalm 22:6: "I am a worm and no man; scorned by men, and despised by the people." Therefore He goes about in poverty, as He Himself says, Matthew 8:20: "Foxes have holes, and birds of the air have nests; but the Son of Man has nowhere to lay His head." In such physical weakness and poverty He attacks the enemy, lets Himself be put on the cross and killed, and by His cross and death He destroys the enemy and the avenger, as St. Paul says, Colossians 2:15: "He disarmed the principalities and powers and made a public example of them, triumphing over them in Him."

From *Commentary on Psalm 8* (Luther's Works 12:110)

But I am a worm and not a man,
scorned by mankind and despised by the people.

PSALM 22:6

His Richest Consolation

ince it thus seems good to God and it cannot be otherwise but that there should be a flock which for God's sake is . . . a reproach of men and rejected by the people (cf. Psalm 22:6), we are certainly not reluctant to be regarded as such in the world. For we have His richest consolation, which has said (cf. Matthew 5:11–12): "Blessed will you be when men hate you and when they cast you out, insult you, and utter your name like an evil omen on account of the Son of Man. Be glad on that day and rejoice, for behold, your reward is great in heaven." It is a matter of a short time. Life is brief and wretched, but the joy and glory we await is eternal. Since, therefore, it pleases God that we should be a little flock, insignificant and despised, let us bear the troubles of this life with a calm and joyful heart.

From *Lectures on Genesis* (Luther's Works 6:52)

The LORD is my shepherd.

PSALM 23:1

A Sweet and Comforting Name

ome of the other names which Scripture gives God sound almost too splendid and majestic and at once arouse awe and fear when we hear them mentioned; for example, when Scripture calls God our Lord, King, Creator, etc. The little word "shepherd," however, is not of that kind but has a very friendly sound. When the devout read or hear it, it immediately grants them a confidence, a comfort, and a sense of security that the word "father" and others grant when they are attributed to God. Therefore this metaphor is one of the most beautiful and comforting and yet most common of all in Scripture, when it compares His Divine Majesty to a pious, faithful, or as Christ says, "good shepherd" (John 10:14), and compares us poor, weak, miserable sinners to sheep. One can, however, understand this comforting and beautiful picture best when one goes to nature, from which the Prophets have taken this picture and similar ones, and carefully learns from it the traits and characteristics of a natural sheep and the office, the work, and the care of a pious shepherd. Whoever does this carefully, will not only readily understand this comparison and others in Scripture concerning the shepherd and the sheep, but will also find the comparisons exceedingly sweet and comforting.

From *Commentary on Psalm 23* (Luther's Works 12:152–53)

The Lord is my shepherd.

PSALM 23:1

The Voice of the Gospel

he voice of this Shepherd, however, with which He speaks to His sheep and calls them, is the Holy Gospel. It teaches us how we may win grace, forgiveness of sins, and eternal salvation: not by the Law of Moses, which makes us even more shy, unstable, and discouraged, though even in times past we were excessively timid, shy, and frightened; but by Christ, who is "the Shepherd and Bishop of our souls" (1 Peter 2:25). For Christ has sought us miserable, lost sheep and has brought us back from the wilderness. That is, He has redeemed us from the Law, sin, death, the power of the devil, and eternal damnation. By giving His life for us He has obtained for us grace, forgiveness of sin, comfort, help, strength, and eternal life against the devil and all misfortune. To the sheep of Christ this is a dear, sweet voice. They are sincerely glad to hear it, for they know it well and let themselves be guided by it.

From *Commentary on Psalm 23* (Luther's Works 12:155)

The LORD is my shepherd;
I shall not want.

PSALM 23:1

An Ever Happy Life

Whenever God's Word is preached properly and purely, it creates as many good things and results as the prophet here gives it names. To those that hear it diligently and seriously—and they are the only ones whom our Lord acknowledges as His sheep—it is pleasant green grass, a cool draught, by which the sheep of the Lord are satisfied and refreshed. It keeps them in the paths of righteousness and preserves them from suffering misfortune and harm. And it is to them an ever happy life, in which food and drink and all kinds of joy and pleasure abound. In other words: these sheep of the Lord are not only instructed and guided, refreshed, strengthened, and comforted by God's Word, but they are also continuously kept on the right path, protected in body and soul in all kinds of distress, and finally they conquer and overcome all tribulation and sorrow, of which they must endure only as much as verse four mentions. In short, they live in complete safety as men whom no sorrow can befall, because their Shepherd tends and protects them.

From *Commentary on Psalm 23* (Luther's Works 12:148–49)

I shall not want.

PSALM 23:1

A Thousand Times More

s little as a natural sheep can feed, direct, guide itself, or guard and protect itself against danger and misfortune—for it is a weak and quite defenseless little animal—just so little can we poor, weak, miserable people feed and guide ourselves spiritually, walk and remain on the right path, or by our own power protect ourselves against all evil and gain help and comfort for ourselves in anxiety and distress. . . . As little as a natural sheep can help itself in even the slightest degree but must simply depend on its shepherd for all benefits, just so little—and much less—can a man govern himself and find comfort, help, and counsel in himself in the things that pertain to his salvation. He must depend on God, his Shepherd, for all of that. And God is a thousand times more willing and ready to do everything that is to be done for His sheep than is any faithful human shepherd.

From *Commentary on Psalm 23* (Luther's Works 12:154)

March 21

He makes me lie down in green pastures.
He leads me beside still waters.

PSALM 23:2

Richly Provided For

he prophet . . . calls God's people and the Holy Christian Church a "green pasture," for it is God's pleasure ground, decorated and adorned with all kinds of spiritual gifts. The pasture, however, or the grass in it, is God's Word, with which our consciences are strengthened and restored. Into this green pasture our Lord God gathers His sheep, feeds them in it with precious grass, and restores them with fresh water. That is, He commits to the Holy Christian Church the office of a shepherd, entrusts and gives to it the holy Gospel and the Sacraments, so that by means of these it may care for and watch over His sheep and so that these sheep may be richly provided with instruction, comfort, strength, and protection against all evil. . . . This, then, is the first fruit of the dear Word: that the Christians are instructed through it in such a way that they grow in faith and hope, learn to commit all their doings and ways unto God, and hope in Him for everything they need in soul and body. [The second fruit is:] It is not only the believers' pasture and grass, with which they are satisfied and grow strong in the faith; to them it is also pleasantly cool, fresh water, through which they gain refreshment and comfort. . . . That is, in all kinds of afflictions, anxieties, and distresses—spiritual and physical—when I cannot find help and comfort anywhere, I cling to the Word of grace.

From *Commentary on Psalm 23* (Luther's Works 12:162–63)

March 22

He restores my soul.
He leads me in paths of righteousness
for His name's sake.

PSALM 23:3

His Name

he name of God is the preaching of God, by which He is glorified and made known as the gracious, merciful, patient, truthful, and faithful one; although we are the children of wrath (Ephesians 2:3) and are guilty of eternal death, He forgives us all our sins and receives us as His children and heirs. That is His name, and that name He causes to be proclaimed through the Word. . . . Thus, without ceasing, He strengthens and restores our souls spiritually and keeps us from falling into error, and also feeds us bodily and wards off all misfortune. But only those who cling to His Word, and who believe and confess boldly that all the gifts and possessions of body and soul that they own, they have received from God purely out of grace and kindness, that is solely for His name's sake and not because of their own deeds and merits—only they give Him the honor of being exactly as we have just been told. They thank Him for His blessings and also proclaim these blessings to others.

From *Commentary on Psalm 23* (Luther's Works 12:166)

Even though I walk through the valley
of the shadow of death,
I will fear no evil, for You are with me.

PSALM 23:4

Alive with God

ust as in . . . Christ, our Head, death and all the works of the devil have been destroyed, so it will have to happen in each of His members. For just as Christ was at once a mortal and an immortal Person, He was indeed subject to death by reason of His humanity; but because His whole Person could not be slain, it happened that death failed, and the devil succumbed in slaying Him; and thus death was swallowed up and devoured in life. In this way the curse was swallowed up and conquered in the blessing, sorrow in joy, and the other evils in the highest good. Thus now, too, it pleases our most gracious God to destroy death and the works of the devil in us through Christ. We Christians should learn, in order that we may die joyfully. For just as it is impossible for Christ, the Victor over death, to die again (cf. Romans 6:9), so it is impossible for one who believes in Him to die; as Christ says in John 11:26, 25: "He who believes in Me shall never die. And though he dies, he shall live." Whatever becomes alive with God is immortal.

From *Lectures on Hebrews* (Luther's Works 29:136)

Your rod and Your staff, they comfort me.

PSALM 23:4

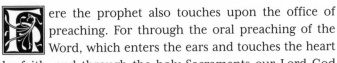

Word and Sacrament

ere the prophet also touches upon the office of preaching. For through the oral preaching of the Word, which enters the ears and touches the heart by faith, and through the holy Sacraments our Lord God accomplishes all these things in His Christendom, namely, that men are brought to faith, are strengthened in faith, are kept in pure doctrine, and in the end are enabled to withstand all the assaults of the devil and the world. Without these means, Word and Sacrament, we obtain none of these things. For since the beginning of the world God has dealt with all the saints through His Word and, in addition, has given them external signs of grace. This I say so that no one may venture to deal with God without these means or build for himself a special way to heaven, lest he fall and break his neck. . . . Therefore he is speaking here about the office of preaching in the New Testament, which proclaims to the world that "Christ came into the world to save sinners" (1 Timothy 1:15) and that He has gained this salvation for sinners by giving His life for them. Whoever believes this should not perish but have eternal life (John 3:16). That is the rod and the staff by which the souls obtain rest, comfort, and joy.

From *Commentary on Psalm 23* (Luther's Works 12:170–71)

You prepare a table before me
in the presence of my enemies.

PSALM 23:5

Retaining Victory

ow, then, does it happen that Christendom, which is so weak, can withstand the craft and the tyranny of the devil and the world? The Lord is its Shepherd; therefore it does not want. He feeds and restores it spiritually and physically; He keeps it in the right path; He also gives it His rod and His staff as a sword. . . . Moreover, the Lord has prepared a table or paschal lamb before it, in order to destroy its enemies completely when they rage greatly, gnash their teeth against it, become mad, insane, raging, and raving, and call to their aid all their craft, strength, and power. Thus the dear Bride of Christ can sit down at the Table of her Lord, eat of the paschal lamb, drink of the fresh water, be happy and sing: "The Lord is my Shepherd, I shall not want." These are her weapons and guns, with which she has defeated and conquered all her foes until now. With these she will also retain the victory until Judgment Day. The more the devil and the world plague and torture her, the better she fares. For her betterment and growth come in persecution, suffering, and dying.

From *Commentary on Psalm 23* (Luther's Works 12:174)

Surely goodness and mercy
shall follow me all the days of my life,
and I shall dwell in the house of the LORD forever.

PSALM 23:6

To the Very End

Because the devil never stops tormenting the believers—inwardly with terror, outwardly with the wiles of false teachers and the power of the tyrants—the prophet here at the end earnestly asks that God, who has given him this treasure, would also keep him in it to the end. . . . Blessed David, a prophet enlightened with all kinds of divine wisdom and knowledge and endowed with so many kinds of great and splendid gifts of God, prayed often and earnestly that he might remain in possession of the blessings of God. We, then, who surely must be considered as nothing at all in comparison with David and who, besides, live at the end of the world—and that, as Christ and the apostles tell us, is a horrible and dangerous time—ought much more to awake and to pray with all earnestness and diligence that we may remain in the house of the Lord all the days of our life, that is, that we may hear God's Word, through it receive the many kinds of blessings and fruit that were shown us above, and endure therein unto the end. May Christ, our only Shepherd and Savior, grant us this! Amen.

From *Commentary on Psalm 23* (Luther's Works 12:178–79)

For Your name's sake, O Lᴏʀᴅ,
pardon my guilt, for it is great.
Psᴀʟᴍ 25:11

Call Upon the Name of the Lord

Sins are not forgiven because of application to works; they are forgiven when I call upon the name of the Lord Jesus Christ because I believe that He is the expiation for our sins. This is the truth. But the devil does not let us remain on this road. He immediately brings up our works. Therefore let no one cleave to his own works. It is our nature to say: "I have sinned with a deed. Therefore I shall make expiation with a deed." The devil, who strengthens our error, is present. One must attack this sin with the promise that sins are remitted for His name's sake, as Psalm 25:11 says.

From *Lectures on 1 John* (Luther's Works 30:245)

Vindicate me, O Lord, for I enter in my innocence.

PSALM 26:1 (according to Luther's translation)

Confidence to Continue On

"To enter" means to have a station in the congregation, for instance, to preach or to govern. One does not conduct his life and work as a private affair; but since he deals with God's Word, he speaks as a minister of the Word. A preacher knows this. He is sure that the doctrine is correct and that he has a divine office, that in the congregation he enters the office of God. Thus I know for sure that my ministry is pleasing to the Divine Majesty, though other people slander me and claim that I am a scoundrel. Still I can say, "I know that on the Last Day God will attest that I have preached rightly." If I were not sure of this so that in my heart I could build upon it and depend upon it, it would be much better for me to keep my mouth shut. But a preacher must have this confidence. Thus St. Paul is confident (2 Corinthians 13:3) that he is speaking not his own word, but the Word of the Lord Christ. Thus we, too, can say that He has put it into our mouth. We have not invented it ourselves, but He has given it to us. If we have Christ's Word and speak it, then we also have this confidence. We know we shall abide and continue even though the world should perish with all schismatics and heretics.

From *Commentary on Psalm 26* (Luther's Works 12:186)

March 29

Vindicate me, O LORD,
for I have walked in my integrity,
and I have trusted in the LORD without wavering.

PSALM 26:1

What Eventually Comes

here is no other counsel or help in this matter than to look to heaven, sigh, and pray God to be the Judge in the matter. One should say: "Dear God, Thou knowest that we are right and they are wrong. But we cannot tell this to anyone. They will not let us tell them, but with their false doctrine they keep gaining ground. Therefore, dear God, take Thou the sword in Thy hand and intervene. Put a stop to the game." This often happens when the schismatics perish and come to naught in their lies, while the divine Word, so long neglected and despised, is restored to honor. Our Lord God works this way. His own, who have God's Word, must first be overcome, oppressed, and vexed; but defeat must eventually come to those who have been on top for so long. . . . Because God hears this crying, the fanatics and schismatics must eventually come to naught and perish.

From *Commentary on Psalm 26* (Luther's Works 12:185)

March 30

Thy loving kindness is before mine eyes:
and I have walked in Thy truth.

PSALM 26:3 (KJV)

The Right Way

 n this David's heart relies and says: "I am on the right way. The divine Word has brought me onto the right path. I have nothing before my eyes except Thy kindness." . . . But we cannot do this unless we pray daily and say: "O God, help arrange my life properly. I am not pure or without sin. But I have begun to go the right way, even though I am still mangy and sordid and many sins and infirmities are still upon me." "In Thy truth," in God's truth. Truth is what is right, what is not false, what does not have a glitter or shine, but is right before God. Thus a man in faith walks before God and therefore goes on the way of love in serving his neighbor. That is the right way: inwardly, before God, one has the right faith in His Word; outwardly, one is on the path and walks on it and lives according to faith.

From *Commentary on Psalm 26* (Luther's Works 12:191)

The Lord is my light and my salvation;
whom shall I fear?
The Lord is the stronghold of my life;
of whom shall I be afraid?

Psalm 27:1

Mutual Conversation

know for a certainty that I have a kind and loving God. Therefore, from whom should I flee? of whom shall I be afraid [Psalm 27:1]? For I know that He is a God who is kind and loving toward humanity. If you can be convinced of this on the basis of this word ["kind," Titus 3:4], [then] there is no doubt. Then follows praise and thanksgiving, and you do not remain joyless but say: "Now this is a God who does not send lightning and thunder down on me, but who wills to deal with me in a kind and loving way." He is always with you; whether you are awake or asleep, you have faith in your heart; wherever you go, He is present; He speaks with you and you with Him, and there is mutual conversation between Him and you. He speaks with you like a good friend [Exodus 33:11], and you in turn praise, proclaim, and call upon Him.

From *Afternoon Sermon for the First Sunday after Epiphany,*
on Titus 3:4–8 (Luther's Works 58:392–93)

One thing have I asked of the Lord,
that will I seek after:
that I may dwell in the house of the Lord
all the days of my life.

Psalm 27:4

The Temporal and the Spiritual

ere we are taught not to seek many things, but rather "one thing is needful." Martha was concerned about many things; she believed that temporal, not spiritual things should be sought (Luke 10:41–42). For temporal things divide a man into many things, while spiritual things draw the divided man together into one, as the apostle says, 1 Corinthians 6:17: "He who is united with the Lord is one spirit," that is, he is spiritual, he is one and not temporal.

From *First Lectures on the Psalms*, on Psalm 27
(Luther's Works 10:127)

In the time of trouble He shall hide me in His pavilion:
in the secret of His tabernacle shall He hide me.

PSALM 27:5 (KJV)

Invincible Benefits of Faith

abernacle is the Church or the Body of Christ, which, however, in a mystical sense is also the Church. And in it is hidden every believer. This hiding must not be understood in a physical sense, because the saints are certainly placed on the candlestick (cf. Mark 4:21). This does not mean, however, that all his glory is in his soul alone, but rather because man is called inward and hidden in that he does not live in a worldly and carnal fashion, that is to say, he withdraws himself from the life, the customs, and the activity of the world. Indeed, as the apostle says (2 Corinthians 10:3), that even though they live in the flesh, they do not wage war according to the flesh. And 1 Peter 4:4 says: "They are surprised that you do not join them, etc." Therefore *to be hidden* is nothing else than not running with those who live carnally, something the carnal people certainly see plainly. . . . *The cover* [cf. Psalm 27:5 in the ESV] therefore is the Church's faith, or spirit, which is the same. For they live by faith and in spirit, that is, by the recognition and love of what is invisible. . . . And note that the Church is protected, not in the open and in visible things; no, in these the Church is abandoned to the will of tyrants and wicked men. . . . But the Church is defended in spiritual things, so that they cannot be taken away from her or she be harmed in them, for they are the invincible and eternal spiritual benefits of faith.

From *First Lectures on the Psalms*, on Psalm 27 (Luther's Works 10:125)

April 3

Cling to the Word

hose who are afflicted feel and complain that they are perishing and dying. Nor can nature think anything else when it is being mortified. It can say nothing else than "I am lost." But oh, how happy and blessed the voice of Christians is if they can cling to the Word and say: "I have been baptized. I believe in God the Father. I believe in Jesus Christ"! Let only this remain firmly fixed in the heart. Then all will be well. To be sure, the flesh is distressed and tortured. It hurts. Reason despairs. The will murmurs. Finally all the senses are completely downcast. Thus David says of himself: "I had said in my alarm: 'I am driven far from Thy sight'" (Psalm 31:22). But these words and thoughts must be censured, and one must fight against a corrupt nature and reason which can feel and say nothing else. "What, then, shall I do," you will say, "when I have been placed at the very door of hell and in despair? Shall I say with the psalmist: 'I am lost, I am cast off, etc.?'" By no means! But you must determine as follows: "I have been baptized; I have been called through the Word; I believe in the Son of God, who suffered for me. 'Father and mother have forsaken me, but the Lord has taken me up'" (Psalm 27:10).

From *Lectures on Genesis* (Luther's Works 8:8–9)

Wait for the LORD;
be strong, and let your heart take courage;
wait for the LORD!

PSALM 27:14

Hold On!

od knows the end and outcome of trial, which you do not know. "Hold on! I want to mix in the sugar in such a way that, even though you die, you are overwhelmed with perpetual joy in the resurrection of the dead." For these exercises are useful to this end, that we learn to understand the mercy of God and the mystery of faith and hope and in some manner comprehend the inscrutable plans of God concerning us, as is stated in Psalm 4:3: "Know that the Lord has set apart the godly for Himself," and likewise in Psalm 16:3: "As for the saints, they are the noble, in whom is all My delight," and in Psalm 17:7: "Wondrously show Thy steadfast love, O Savior of those who seek refuge from their adversaries at Thy right hand." Mercy, grace, and the promise are certainly present, but it is wonderfully fulfilled beyond all our thoughts, desires, and wishes.

From *Lectures on Genesis* (Luther's Works 6:354)

Wait for the LORD;
be strong, and let your heart take courage.

PSALM 27:14

What Faith Is

aith is an all-powerful battle which, in opposition to the battle of the flesh, clings to the Word and the promise with one and the same prospect. . . . [David] felt much more unbelief than faith, for faith seems and is weak, because the flesh not only wages war but even takes captive, as Paul says in Romans 7:14. Formerly I had no other conviction than that Paul gave no thought at all to exerting himself and battling against the flesh. But he says (2 Corinthians 12:7): "A thorn was given me in the flesh, a messenger of Satan, to harass me." He teaches me what faith is. I see the glorious victories of the saints and the martyrs. But my faith cannot accomplish this. And they also exerted themselves and overcame death. They did not do this without a great conflict. Thus we, too, have the same Baptism, the same God to give consolation, and the Holy Spirit, the Comforter who offers us rich comfort in the Word. And although I gladly hear the account of the conflicts and the victories of the saints, I cannot do the same things. Therefore one must take hold of the Word (Psalm 27:14): "Wait for the Lord; be strong, and let your heart take courage." God does not abandon even him who is weak in faith.

From *Lectures on Genesis* (Luther's Works 5:131)

Wait for the LORD!

PSALM 27:14

What Else Should You Do?

 oday we are tormented and afflicted by Satan and the world in various ways. . . . But what else should you do than wait for the Lord? You have the promise that God is your Father. Add faith and love to this, have no doubt about the promise, and wait, since what is promised is not shown immediately. For although "hope deferred makes the heart sick" (Proverbs 13:12), nevertheless what the author of the Epistle to the Hebrews points out should be kept in mind: "God is treating you as sons" (12:7). Thereupon we should encourage and arouse ourselves by such examples to bear any difficulties, dangers, and griefs. But if we are killed, it is certain that by this means we are truly liberated and rescued from all evils. . . . But if we are preserved, we should persevere and wait in hope and faith; for God does not hate us or turn us away in hostile fashion, no matter how He may conduct Himself toward us otherwise. Let us rather conclude: "I know that I have been baptized, that I have eaten the body and drunk the blood of the Son of God, that I have been absolved by divine authority, that all my sins have certainly been forgiven me, and that victory over the devil, death, and hell has been promised me. What more should I ask for?"

From *Lectures on Genesis* (Luther's Works 7:131–32)

April 7

The voice of the LORD is over the waters;
the God of glory thunders,
the LORD, over many waters.

PSALM 29:3

Just like Water

aters is a designation for us, the people (Revelation 17:15: "the waters that you saw are peoples") principally because of our fleeting and transitory life, 2 Samuel 14:14: "We all die, and like water we dissolve into the ground"; second, because we are inconstant and unstable like water, not like a rock or anything solid; third, because of the tumults of disturbances, that is, the inner drives of our desires and cravings, of which also the poets are aware. But to those who do not resist, the voice of the Lord and the Gospel remain forever upon the waters as the rays of the sun shine steadily upon the turbulent water.

From *First Lectures on the Psalms*, on Psalm 29
(Luther's Works 10:133)

April 8

The voice of the Lord breaks the cedars;
the Lord breaks the cedars of Lebanon.
He makes Lebanon to skip like a calf,
and Sirion like a young wild ox.

PSALM 29:5–6

To Become like Calves

e must overcome *the cedars*, that is, manifestations of pride, not by might but by humility and patience. So Christ conquered the wisdom of the world not by wisdom but by foolishness, and the power of the world by weakness. He did not conquer evil by evil, not life by life, not bitter by bitter, but by their opposites, life by death, and evil by good. For He was like a *calf of Lebanon*, not like a king and tyrant, but rather like a weakling in the offering of His flesh, and by the example of His humility even unto death. In this way He conquered the life of the flesh by death, so that henceforth no one might live for himself in the flesh but for Him. In this way He wrested the cudgel away from Hercules, that is, He deprived the devil of power and life and wisdom. This is what we, too, must do when we want to overcome malice, and we must become calves, that is, patient and humble.

From *First Lectures on the Psalms*, on Psalm 29
(Luther's Works 10:135–36)

The voice of the Lᴏʀᴅ shakes the wilderness.

Pꜱᴀʟᴍ 29:8

Thunder and Lightning

 hat is how God's Word proceeds. It challenges the whole world. It reaches into the mouth of the lords and the princes and of everyone else, denouncing and cursing their whole way of life, something that is not proper for you or me to do as individual Christians except in our office and our teaching position. In Psalm 2:10–11, David dares to do this. He tells all the kings and lords to think, to humble themselves, to fall at the feet of the teaching about Christ, and to let themselves be rebuked and instructed. Otherwise they will be damned instantly and turned over to the devil. I would not dare to do that. But that is the way God's Word proceeds. It hammers the great and mighty mountains with its thunder and lightning and storms, so that they smoke. It shatters everything that is great and proud and disobedient, as Psalm 29 says. But on the other hand, it is also like a fruitful rain, sprinkling and moistening, planting and strengthening whatever is like the poor, parched plants that are weak and sickly.

From *Sermon on the Mount* (Luther's Works 21:120)

His anger is but for a moment.

PSALM 30:5

A Reason to Give Thanks

et us be warned . . . and learn this: the longer God puts up with idolatry and other sins, and the longer He pays no attention to them, the more intolerable will His wrath reveal itself to be later on. Therefore we ought to consider it a great kindness if He does not permit our sins to go unpunished for a long time. Psalm 30:5 exhorts the church to give thanks because the wrath of the Lord is "for a moment" and because He loves life. It says: "Weeping may tarry for the night, but joy comes with the morning" [v. 5]; and Psalm 89:30, 32: "If his children forsake My Law and do not walk according to My ordinances, I will punish their transgression with the rod and their iniquity with scourges." This is a wrath of grace, when the punishment comes quickly and calls us back from sin.

From *Lectures on Genesis* (Luther's Works 2:223)

His anger is but for a moment,
and His favor is for a lifetime.

PSALM 30:5

The Art of Joy

It is, therefore, easy to say that the true fear of God is a filial fear, that is, a fear mixed with joy or hope. But if you follow your feeling, you will perceive that joy is all but overwhelmed and extinguished by fear. But you must not on that account let your heart sink or despair, but trust in the Lord and lay hold on His Word, which declares that God's anger is but for a moment (Psalm 30:5) and His favor is for a lifetime. That is, God wants us to live. He does not want us to perish. And for this very reason He sends us blows. And so it happens that you feel at least some small drop of joy. It will grow little by little until it finally overcomes fear. The practice is difficult, but is nevertheless of the kind which the saints of God learned to do, as their examples show. We, too, must follow in their footsteps and learn this art also. Moreover, the Holy Spirit will come to our aid, especially when we pray.

From *Commentary on Psalm 2* (Luther's Works 12:78)

Weeping may tarry for the night,
but joy comes with the morning.

PSALM 30:5

Founded on the Rock

his means that that disaster will be of short duration. One bad night before the morning breaks. . . . But every trial seems permanent to our mind, and our reason does not see the end of the trial. Therefore divine mercy appoints an end for it which we cannot grasp. With God our trial is but of an evening's duration. The flesh, however, does not know how to reckon this but judges according to the senses. Therefore we must rather cling by faith to the Word of God. But these promises apply to us by way of example. For although we have the Word, we must expect all the trouble that others have sustained. Therefore, for the same affliction we make use of the same promise and comfort. Trials seem long lasting, but they are short before God, who provides the outcome and will indeed permit us to be afflicted but not overcome. For we are founded on the solid Rock, which is Christ.

From *Lectures on Isaiah* (Luther's Works 16:156–57)

April 13

By Your favor, O Lord,
You made my mountain stand strong;
You hid Your face; I was dismayed.

PSALM 30:7

God's Training Method

his is the usual way of training saintly and godly men. . . . Why or how does God rule in this manner? Why does He not make this joy complete and lasting for His saints? I do not know, except for the fact that I observe this pattern and common example in all the saints, even in Christ Himself, their Head, who sometimes rejoices in spirit and joyfully gives thanks to God in the Holy Spirit. Afterward He is again troubled in spirit, prays for protection, and laments that He has been forsaken in the hour of death, as one can see in Psalm 8:5 and in Psalm 22:1. Therefore one should learn this example and this pattern of the saints, yes, this method by which God governs His saints.

From *Lectures on Genesis* (Luther's Works 3:4)

To you, O Lord, I cry,
and to the Lord I plead for mercy:
"What profit is there in my death, if I go down
to the pit? . . . Hear, O Lord, and be merciful to me!"

Psalm 30:8–10

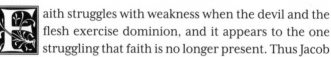

From the Abyss

aith struggles with weakness when the devil and the flesh exercise dominion, and it appears to the one struggling that faith is no longer present. Thus Jacob complains [Genesis 34:30]: "I have become abominable to all my neighbors, I have been thrown into extreme danger, and I think of nothing but destruction." Where is faith here and the remembrance of the promises? Why does he not induce his heart to say: "You have prevailed against God. How much more, then, will you prevail against neighboring nations?" All this has slipped away from him. Trial devours the splendid promises and most glorious victories of faith. But he does not yet despair, although he is very similar to one in despair. He does not fall into misbelief and is not an unbeliever, although it appears so. This is trial, just as Paul says of himself: "So that we might not rely on ourselves, we had the sentence of death in ourselves" (cf. 2 Corinthians 1:8–9). It is necessary for the saints to be disciplined in this way, to descend into hell and the abyss, and to be recalled from there into heaven.

From *Lectures on Genesis* (Luther's Works 6:219)

Be gracious to me, O Lord, for I am in distress;
my eye is wasted from grief;
my soul and my body also.

Psalm 31:9

A Prayer of a Penitent Heart

his is] a beautiful prayer of a conscience that is fearful and that acknowledges it has sinned. . . . Indeed, this is the rule for tropological language: Wherever in the Psalms Christ complains and prays in bodily affliction according to the letter, there, in the same words, every faithful soul, born and trained in Christ, complains and prays, confessing that it has been tempted to sin or has fallen into sin. For to the present day Christ is spitted on, killed, scourged, crucified in us ourselves. Even now there lie in ambush for Him without ceasing the flesh with its feelings, the world with its pleasures, and the devil with his offers and temptations.

From *First Lectures on the Psalms*, on Psalm 31
(Luther's Works 10:139)

My times are in Your hand;
rescue me from the hand of my enemies
and from my persecutors!

PSALM 31:15

The Whole World in His Hands

he Holy Spirit reminds us . . . that we should learn the doctrine of creation correctly, namely, that all things are in God's hand, and that we should accustom and encourage ourselves to confident trust in our Creator, which, to be sure, is still very small and weak in us. For if we firmly concluded that God is our Creator, we would certainly believe that He has heaven and earth in His hands and all things which are contained by these. To be sure, if we saw the world shattered and falling into ruin with all the elements and hanging over our necks, we would nevertheless say: "Even in falling you will not fall unless God wills it." Even if it were hanging over our head, we would say: "You will do no harm and not overwhelm me. And even if it seems good to God that I should be overwhelmed by your huge mass, let what is good in the Lord's eyes be done. My times are in His hands (cf. Psalm 31:15). But if it seems otherwise, I shall scoff at you, O heaven and earth, together with the Turks and Papists and all other ragings of the whole world."

From *Lectures on Genesis* (Luther's Works 6:242–43)

Let the lying lips be mute,
which speak insolently against the righteous
in pride and contempt.

PSALM 31:18

Deadly Words

eceitful lips become dumb . . . when they are removed by death and borne away in the wrath of punishment, so that they can no longer rage against God's righteousness. Thus we read in Psalm 63:11: "The mouth of those who speak evil is stopped"; and in Psalm 107:42: "All iniquity shall stop its mouth"; and in Psalm 75:5: "Do not speak iniquity against God." But this is the iniquity which they speak against God, because they oppose the righteous Christ and His righteousness, as if it were neither necessary nor useful, as if their own were enough. This is evil and against God. He wants this righteousness of Christ and indeed demands it. Therefore John says, "If we say that we have no sin, we make God a liar" (1 John 1:10). This is so because He Himself has asserted that we have sin, and He sent His Son into death for our sins [since Scripture everywhere promises righteousness and truth on His account, it follows that there was none on earth], as all the prophets testify, Isaiah 53:8: "For the wickedness of My people have I struck Him."

From *First Lectures on the Psalms*, on Psalm 31
(Luther's Works 10:143–44)

*Love the L*ORD*, all you His saints!*
*The L*ORD *preserves the faithful*
but abundantly repays the one who acts in pride.
Be strong, and let your heart take courage,
*all you who wait for the L*ORD*!*

PSALM 31:23–24

A Droplet of Spiritual Trust

ow often it is repeated in the Psalms: "Wait for the Lord; be strong, and let your heart take courage; wait for the Lord!" (Psalm 27:14). "Love the Lord, all you His saints! The Lord preserves the faithful but abundantly requites him who acts haughtily. Be strong, and let your heart take courage, all you who wait for the Lord!" (Psalm 31:23–24). We know all this, and it is pointed out to us daily, yet we neither believe nor follow God, who calls us to confess the Word and promises help and deliverance. There certainly is no reason for us to think that God is pleased with that doubt and mistrust in us. Indeed, this one sin is by far the gravest of all the sins which will condemn the world and the unbelievers. For the magnitude of the sin can be gauged from the magnitude of God's promise, oath, pledge, and imprecation. Therefore whoever has either a droplet or a spark of that spiritual trust should know that it is a blessing of God and an extraordinary gift. If we firmly and unquestioningly held promises of this kind as true, there would be given to our hearts strength far greater than our fear of the world or the devil or all the gates of hell.

From *Lectures on Genesis* (Luther's Works 4:147)

April 19

Be strong, and let your heart take courage,
all you who wait for the Lord!

PSALM 31:24

His Promises Are True

ince we have the promise, let us hold out in trials and conclude: "The Lord, who said to me: 'Believe,' will surely keep His promise. Meanwhile I shall wait in accordance with the words 'Wait for the Lord, be strong, etc.' (Psalm 27:14), 'Be strong, and let your heart take courage, all you who wait for the Lord'" (Psalm 31:24). The godly should wait and persevere even in greatest dangers and adversities; for He has promised that He wants to take care of us. 1 Peter 5:7 states: "Cast all your anxieties on Him, for He cares about you." The exercises of faith are necessary for the godly; for without them their faith would grow weak and lukewarm, yes, would eventually be extinguished. But from this source they assuredly learn what faith is; and when they have been tried, they grow in the knowledge of the Son of God and become so strong and firm that they can rejoice and glory in misfortunes no less than in days of prosperity and can regard any trial at all as nothing more than a little cloud or a fog which vanishes forthwith.

From *Lectures on Genesis* (Luther's Works 5:56)

Blessed is the one whose transgression is forgiven,
whose sin is covered.

<small>PSALM 32:1</small>

Free in Christ

his is at once in opposition to the hypocrites, who do not need forgiveness and, like healthy people, have no use for a doctor. For they do not think they have iniquities but rely on themselves as righteous and do not eat with the tax collectors and sinners, because they are not like other people (cf. Luke 15:2; 18:9ff.). . . . Let us hear, then, what the line of argument is here. No one is blessed except the one whose iniquities are forgiven. Therefore the corollary is: No one is without iniquity, no one is not a child of wrath, and so he needs to have his sins forgiven. But this happens only through Christ. Therefore no one will be saved on his own, but through Christ alone. And this is also the argument of blessed Paul's entire Epistle to the Romans, to which almost all the words of the Epistle speak, as is clear to anyone who looks into it. For he says (Romans 1:18, 17): "The wrath of God is revealed from heaven"; again: "The righteousness of God is revealed, etc." The meaning is this: No human being knew that the wrath of God is upon all men and that all are in sin before God, but through His Gospel He has revealed from heaven both how we may be saved from that wrath and by what righteousness we may be set free, namely, through Christ.

From *First Lectures on the Psalms*, on Psalm 32
(Luther's Works 10:145)

Blessed is the man against whom the LORD counts no
iniquity, and in whose spirit there is no deceit.
For when I kept silent, my bones wasted away
through my groaning all day long.

PSALM 32:2–3

Separated by Grace

he first [type of confession] is before God, of which
the prophet David says: "I confess my sin, and I do
not cover my iniquity. I said, 'I will confess my transgressions to the Lord,' and You forgave the iniquity of my sin"
(Psalm 32 [:5]). . . . No one can stand before God unless he
brings this confession with him. Psalm 130 [:4] says, "With You
there is grace, that You may be feared"; that is, whoever deals
with You must deal in such a way that he confesses from his
heart: "Lord, if You are not compassionate, it does not matter
how godly I can be." . . . Thus this confession teaches us that we
are all equally evildoers and sinners. . . . If anyone has special
grace, then he should thank God for it, and not boast about
himself. If anyone has fallen into sin, then it is [because of]
his blood and flesh; no one has fallen so deeply that another
who now stands cannot fall deeper still. Therefore, there is
no distinction among us who are so many; rather, God's grace
alone separates us. This kind of confession is so highly necessary that it should not be omitted for a moment, but should
be the whole life of a Christian, so that he does not stop prais-
ing God's grace and reviling his life before God's eyes."

From *Sermon on Confession and the Sacrament* (Luther's Works 76:434)

I acknowledged my sin to You,
and I did not cover my iniquity.

PSALM 32:5

No Need to Hide

his is in contrast to those in whom deceit of the spirit produces such false confidence that they can unabashedly justify and excuse themselves. Because of this they get into quarrels with other people and lapse into pride, anger, hatred, impatience, condemning, and slander. Their innocence makes them really guilty, and yet they claim to have done justly and rightly and to have acted fairly. They conceal deeply their own iniquity, for they look at their own righteousness and do not confess their sins to God sincerely and without deceit of the inner spirit. Righteous people, however, do not hide their iniquity, do not become angry, do not grow impatient even when they are wronged; for they do not feel that they can be wronged, since they find no righteousness in themselves. These are the blessed to whom God remits iniquity and cancels it because they confess it. Since they do not hide and cover their sin, God covers and hides it.

From *Seven Penitential Psalms*, on Psalm 32 (Luther's Works 14:150)

I said, "I will confess my transgressions to the Lord,"
and You forgave the iniquity of my sin.
Therefore let everyone who is godly
offer prayer to You at a time when You may be found.

PSALM 32:5–6

(Un)Knowingly Righteous

nasmuch as the saints are always aware of their sin and seek righteousness from God in accord with His mercy, for this very reason they are always also regarded as righteous by God. Thus in their own sight and in truth they are unrighteous, but before God they are righteous because He reckons them so because of their confession of sin. They are actually sinners, but they are righteous by the imputation of a merciful God. They are unknowingly righteous and knowingly unrighteous; they are sinners in fact but righteous in hope. And this is what he is saying here: "Blessed are they whose iniquities are forgiven, and whose sins are covered" (Psalm 32:1). Hence, these words follow (v. 5), "I said, I will confess my transgressions to the Lord" (that is, I am always conscious of my sin, because I confess it to Thee). Therefore, "Then Thou didst forgive the guilt of my sin," not to me only but to all. Hence these words follow (v. 6): "Therefore let everyone who is godly offer prayer to Thee."

From *Lectures on Romans* (Luther's Works 25:258)

I will instruct you and teach you
in the way you should go.

PSALM 32:8

Let Him Lead You

od is saying:] This is where I want you to be. You ask that I deliver you. Then do not be uneasy about it; do not teach Me, and do not teach yourself; surrender yourself to Me. I am competent to be your Master. I will lead you in a way that is pleasing to Me. You think it wrong if things do not go as you feel they should. But your thinking harms you and hinders Me. Things must go, not according to your understanding but above your understanding. . . . Thus Abraham went out from his homeland and did not know where he was going (Genesis 12:1ff.). He yielded to My knowledge and abandoned his own knowledge; and by the right way he reached the right goal. Behold, that is the way of the cross. You cannot find it, but I must lead you like a blind man. Therefore not you, not a man, not a creature, but I, through My Spirit and the Word, will teach you the way you must go.

From *Seven Penitential Psalms*, on Psalm 32 (Luther's Works 14:152)

I will counsel you
with My eye upon you.
PSALM 32:8

True, Simple Faith

od is saying:] "I will not leave you; you shall not go down and perish; I will not forget you. Your eyes shall be closed because My eyes are open over you. Have you not read (Psalm 34:15) that 'the eyes of God are toward the righteous,' and that Mount Moriah is called 'the Lord shall behold' (Genesis 22:14)? Surely I alone shall see, just as I did when Abraham failed to see; and yet he did not fail to see." In brief, God wants us to have a true, simple faith and firm trust, confidence, and hope. While faith, hope, humility, and patience are not mentioned by name in these words, yet the mode and the true nature of such virtue are expressed. There are many who write about virtues, but they praise their names rather than teach their nature.

From *Seven Penitential Psalms*, on Psalm 32
(Luther's Works 14:152–53)

I will instruct you and teach you
in the way you should go;
I will counsel you with My eye upon you.
Be not like a horse or a mule, without understanding.

PSALM 32:8–9

Knowledge of the Mind of Christ

In the Holy Scriptures *understanding* takes its name from the object rather than from any capacity, the opposite of what it is in philosophy. Understanding is the recognition or knowledge of the mind of Christ, about which the apostle teaches excellently in 1 Corinthians 1 and 2, for he says (1 Corinthians 2:7–8): "We speak a wisdom hidden in a mystery . . . which none of the princes of this world understood." In brief, this is nothing else than the wisdom of the cross of Christ, which is folly to the Gentiles and a stumbling block to the Jews, namely, to understand that the Son of God was incarnate and crucified and put to death and raised for our salvation. It is to the understanding of this wisdom that the title of the psalm refers.

From *First Lectures on the Psalms*, on Psalm 32
(Luther's Works 10:147–48)

Be glad in the LORD,
and rejoice, O righteous,
and shout for joy,
all you upright in heart!

PSALM 32:11

Bold and Courageous

You may rejoice in the Lord, you who trust in the Lord, who do not trust or rejoice in yourselves but rather despair of yourselves and are sorrowful, who are your own enemies and find no satisfaction in your own opinion. . . . Be bold and courageous; rise up and sing praises; be of good cheer, like a man who shouts for joy. For the heart that is right with God and is not wrapped up in itself or in something other than God is founded on the eternal good and stands firm. Therefore it has an abundance out of which it can praise, glory, strut, and boast, as the apostle says (1 Corinthians 1:31): "Let him who boasts, boast of the Lord."

From *Seven Penitential Psalms*, on Psalm 32 (Luther's Works 14:154)

*Rejoice in the L*ORD*, O ye righteous:*
for praise is comely for the upright.

PSALM 33:1 (KJV)

Blessed Are Those Who Mourn

 ome *rejoice* in the Lord by taking pleasure in the blessings of spiritual salvation. It is these the apostle encourages with the words (Philippians 4:4): "Brethren, rejoice in the Lord, and again I say, rejoice." At the same time these people have sadness in the world, for "blessed are those who mourn" (Matthew 5:4). Thus they have affliction in the world and peace in the Lord Christ at the same time. Therefore we read in 2 Corinthians 1:4: "Who comforts us in all our affliction."

From *First Lectures on the Psalms*, on Psalm 33
(Luther's Works 10:152)

Sing to Him a new song;
play skillfully on the strings,
with loud shouts.

<small>Psalm 33:3</small>

The Old and the New

Only a new man can sing *a new song*. But the new man is a man of grace, a spiritual and inner man before God. The old man, however, is the man of sin, the carnal and outer man before the world. The newness is grace, the oldness, sin. Therefore the devil is called the "old serpent" (Revelation 12:9), and Christ "a new thing which the Lord created on the earth" (Jeremiah 31:22), through whom God the Father made all things new, according to Revelation 21:5. It is clear, then, that this "new song" is so called not because of time, but because of the new holy thing, for Scripture is holy, and it speaks of the holy.

From *First Lectures on the Psalms*, on Psalm 33
(Luther's Works 10:154)

For the word of the LORD is upright,
and all His work is done in faithfulness.

PSALM 33:4

As Promised

he Word of the Lord is upright. First of all, in itself, and then because it makes upright, it straightens out the man who is bent in on himself and turns him upward so that he acknowledges and loves God by faith. *All His works are done in faithfulness.* First . . . they are faithful, or done in faithfulness, as He promised. And thus it corresponds to the upright Word . . . because He does not promise something fictitiously or deviously, but with a straightforward and clear meaning. And thus the works promised in the Word are in faithfulness, so that they might demonstrate that the Word was upright, in that what it promised straightforwardly, it faithfully observed and accomplished. Second, the works of the Lord, those which the Lord wants to be done and which are done according to Him, with Him, and in Him through us, are done in faithfulness, that is, by faith. For we live and act by faith, or, in faith, that is, faithfulness, which is one of the twelve fruits of the Spirit (Galatians 5:22–23). . . . Third, in faith, that is, His works are true or firm, works that must be believed, contrary to the works of hypocrisy, which are reedy, faked, and upright only in appearance, untrue and fictitious, like the wolf in sheep's clothing.

From *First Lectures on the Psalms*, on Psalm 33
(Luther's Works 10:154–55)

May 1

By the word of the Lᴏʀᴅ the heavens were made,
and by the breath of His mouth all their host.

PSALM 33:6

By One Indivisible Essence

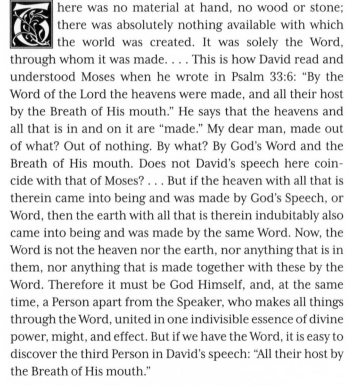

here was no material at hand, no wood or stone; there was absolutely nothing available with which the world was created. It was solely the Word, through whom it was made. . . . This is how David read and understood Moses when he wrote in Psalm 33:6: "By the Word of the Lord the heavens were made, and all their host by the Breath of His mouth." He says that the heavens and all that is in and on it are "made." My dear man, made out of what? Out of nothing. By what? By God's Word and the Breath of His mouth. Does not David's speech here coincide with that of Moses? . . . But if the heaven with all that is therein came into being and was made by God's Speech, or Word, then the earth with all that is therein indubitably also came into being and was made by the same Word. Now, the Word is not the heaven nor the earth, nor anything that is in them, nor anything that is made together with these by the Word. Therefore it must be God Himself, and, at the same time, a Person apart from the Speaker, who makes all things through the Word, united in one indivisible essence of divine power, might, and effect. But if we have the Word, it is easy to discover the third Person in David's speech: "All their host by the Breath of His mouth."

From *On the Last Words of David* (Luther's Works 15:301)

He spoke, and it came to be;
He commanded, and it stood firm.

PSALM 33:9

Outside the Scope of Time

 f you look at my person, I am something new, because sixty years ago I was nothing. Such is the judgment of the world. But God's judgment is different; for in God's sight I was begotten and multiplied immediately when the world began, because this Word, "and God said: 'Let Us make man,'" created me too. Whatever God wanted to create, that He created then when He spoke. Not everything has come into view at once. Similarly, an arrow or a ball which is shot from a cannon (for it has greater speed) is sent to its target in a single moment, as it were, and nevertheless it is shot through a definite space; so God, through His Word, extends His activity from the beginning of the world to its end. For with God there is nothing that is earlier or later, swifter or slower; but in His eyes all things are present things. For He is simply outside the scope of time. Therefore these words, "God said: 'Let there be, grow, multiply,'" established the creatures as they are now and as they will be to the end of the world. . . . It is as Christ says (John 5:17): "My Father is working still, and I work." The Word which He spoke in the beginning is still in existence.

From *Lectures on Genesis* (Luther's Works 1:76)

The Lᴏʀᴅ brings the counsel of the nations to nothing;

He frustrates the plans of the peoples.

The counsel of the Lᴏʀᴅ stands forever,

the plans of His heart to all generations.

Psᴀʟᴍ 33:10–11

Futile Things

What makes Christ bold and fills His enemies with dismay is not the work of man but of God, to whom Christ is obedient; for it is futile to set yourself against God. It is the experience of Christians that if they put their reliance in God, their enemies, with all their wrath, will not be able to harm them; for He holds their hearts in His hand and controls all their thoughts. Psalm 33:10 confirms this: "The Lord brings the counsel of the nations to naught; He frustrates the plans of the people." Despite emperor and pope the Lord our God can easily thwart the plans they have against us in their hearts. A roadblock has been placed in their path, and it bears the name: "I defy you to carry out your plans and plots." . . . It is bad to combat enemies who cause you to lose heart. If I have that power over an opponent, I have soon defeated him. His resistance will be short-lived. Thus God, too, makes His enemies lose courage and heart, and fills them with despair. At the same time He grants courage to those who rely on Him but are timid and dejected, and He enables them to carry out their plans.

From *Sermons on John 6–8* (Luther's Works 23:221)

*I will bless the L*ORD *at all times;*
His praise shall continually be in my mouth.

PSALM 34:1

At All Times and in All Things

ime is twofold. As Ecclesiastes 3:2–8 says four-teen times: "A time of peace, a time of war, a time of prosperity, a time of adversity." Therefore many bless the Lord at one time, namely, according to Psalm 49:18: "He will praise Thee when Thou dost well to him." At other times, however, when God has tried them as He did Job, when something has befallen them different from what they have in mind, they "thunder against the gods three hundred times with their mouth" [*Aeneid* v4.510]. But it is the part of Christians to say, "Praise the Lord, nights and days, light and darkness, and all beasts and cattle, praise the Lord" (cf. Psalm 148:3, 10). For all things work together for good to the saints (Romans 8:28), therefore God is to be blessed in all things. *His praise shall continually be in my mouth.* This happens whenever we say good and holy things. In them God is praised, as when we speak truth, wisdom, and good-ness, because God is all of these. Therefore He says to Moses (Exodus 4:12): "I will be with your mouth," for the mouth of the righteous will ponder wisdom, which is God Himself.

From *First Lectures on the Psalms*, on Psalm 34
(Luther's Works 10:159–60)

*My soul makes its boast in the L*ORD*;*
let the humble hear and be glad.
*Oh, magnify the L*ORD *with me,*
and let us exalt His name together!

PSALM 34:2–3

Disparaged and Praised

he beginning of the psalm is full of the example of humility, for no one blesses the Lord except the one who is displeased with himself and curses himself and to whom God alone is pleasing. . . . He who regards himself as anything but completely detestable clearly has praise of himself in his mouth, and the praise of God is not "continually in my mouth" (v. 1). Therefore the confession of sin glorifies and praises God, and we never praise God correctly unless we first disparage ourselves. For He does not permit something else to be praised alongside Himself, nor does He want anything loved beside Himself. . . . But if this is so, how then are we to understand what follows here, "In the Lord shall my soul be praised" (v. 2)? How can we be disparaged and praised before the Lord at the same time? But it must, of course, be understood that it is indeed permitted us in the Lord, yes, it behooves us to be praised, to rejoice, and to be pleasing in the Lord. For it is a sweet business to ponder and magnify your Creator and to say, "Behold, I am the creature of so great a Lord! How happy I am that my Creator is such a person, that such a person has given me such things and such great things!"

From *First Lectures on the Psalms*, on Psalm 34
(Luther's Works 10:162–63)

May 6

*The angel of the L*ORD *encamps*
around those who fear Him,
and delivers them.

PSALM 34:7

Guardian Angels

f we have a promise, then it follows without fail that angels are round about us. This is why Psalm 34:7 states: "The angel of the Lord encamps around those who fear Him." Likewise Psalm 91:11: "He will give His angels charge of you." This [Isaac and his family] believed firmly and without doubt. Therefore we, too, if we are godly, should believe in the promise of Him who cannot lie. Then we are surely under His protection, and it is also certain that angels are with us. But if any evil befalls us beyond, or contrary to, this trust and protection, this happens because of a special purpose that is hidden from us and especially from our adversaries. But the godly should comfort themselves in this manner: "I know that I have guardian angels; but that I have to bear some misfortune, this I leave to the will of God. For I am in the camp of the angels. God is not a liar. Therefore He will not forsake me."

From *Lectures on Genesis* (Luther's Works 5:62)

Oh, taste and see that the LORD is good!
Blessed is the man who takes refuge in Him!

PSALM 34:8

Patient Endurance

et us consider these matters carefully so that, after we have begun to believe and have hope in the future life that has been granted us through the Word and Baptism, we may learn to endure patiently whatever evils ensue and come to the conclusion that all things take place for our salvation not haphazardly but according to the Father's plan. This is the understanding which we eventually have when the trial is ended. When one is in the very throes of trial, this is not understood, for the feeling of the flesh tears us away from the promise. When a man is involved in tribulation and anxiety, it does not enter his mind to say: "I have been baptized; I have God's promise," but his heart is quite overwhelmed by complaints, grief, and tears according to the flesh. However, the flesh should be crucified and mortified, for it hinders the understanding of the promise and the truth of God's Word, which is perceived in temptation if one clings to it in firm faith. What is stated in the psalm (34:8) follows: "O taste and see that the Lord is good!" God allows us to be tempted that He may have an opportunity for satisfying, comforting, and filling those who have been emptied of all strength and stripped of all help.

From *Lectures on Genesis* (Luther's Works 6:356–57)

The LORD is near to the brokenhearted
and saves the crushed in spirit.

PSALM 34:18

Battle against the Feelings

he comfort is this, that in your deep anxieties—in which your consciousness of sin, sadness, and despair is so great and strong that it penetrates and occupies all the corners of your heart—you do not follow your consciousness. For if you did, you would say: "I feel the violent terrors of the Law and the tyranny of sin, not only waging war against me again but completely conquering me. I do not feel any comfort or righteousness. Therefore I am not righteous but a sinner. And if I am a sinner, then I am sentenced to eternal death." But battle against this feeling, and say: "Even though I feel myself completely crushed and swallowed by sin and see God as a hostile and wrathful judge, yet in fact this is not true; it is only my feeling that thinks so. The Word of God, which I ought to follow in these anxieties rather than my own consciousness, teaches much differently, namely, that 'God is near to the brokenhearted, and saves the crushed in spirit' (Psalm 34:18), and that 'He does not despise a broken and contrite heart' (Psalm 51:17)."

From *Lectures on Galatians* (Luther's Works 27:25–26)

Many are the afflictions of the righteous,
but the Lord delivers him out of them all.

PSALM 34:19

Be Strong and Take Courage

he Holy Spirit points out the hypothetical asser-
tion, as they call it in the schools, when He states in
Psalm 34:19: "Many are the afflictions of the righteous, but the Lord delivers him out of them all." Therefore when the saints see that they are afflicted, they still do
not for this reason depart from the commands of God; but
to this minor premise they add the conclusion of faith and
maintain that they, too, will be delivered from those adversities and dangers. These are revelations of the Holy Spirit;
philosophy is not aware of them. Therefore it is offended; it
denies providence and concludes that God does not concern
Himself with human affairs, but everything happens by acci-
dent and by chance. . . . What is the reason for this blindness?
No doubt it is this: reason looks only at the adversities of the
present and is impressed and overwhelmed by them, but of
the promise concerning the future it has no knowledge at
all. The Holy Spirit, however, commands us to disregard the
things of the present and to look at those of the future. He
says (Psalm 27:14): "Wait, be strong, and let your heart take
courage; yea, wait for the Lord." Thus these passages are
intended to teach and strengthen faith and hope.

From *Lectures on Genesis* (Luther's Works 2:307–8)

Transgression speaks to the wicked deep in his heart;
there is no fear of God before his eyes.
For he flatters himself in his own eyes
that his iniquity cannot be found out and hated.

PSALM 36:1–2

The Ungodly and the Godly

he godly make no claims for themselves, but rather whatever they have they acknowledge to be a gift of God's grace; they have nothing to offer God, but they only receive from Him. The ungodly in their desire to influence God by their works despise God and make gods of themselves. . . . Sham avails nothing but is an abomination to God. However, the people of Christ's kingdom are the poor, the mean, the insignificant, the fainthearted, the harassed, the lowly, the fearful. These He will judge; that is, He will make the just cause prevail. He will justify them, He will give them grace, He will forgive the sins of those who acknowledge and confess them and do not rely on themselves. He says in Matthew 5:3: "Blessed are the poor in spirit, etc." Therefore they will be judged with righteousness, that is, they will have righteousness and will increase in it, they will be reproved with equity, which is the righteousness of faith, whereby they are upright before God and men; they do for both God and men what pleases them: glory to God and kindness to men.

From *Lectures on Isaiah* (Luther's Works 16:121)

Fret not yourself because of evildoers;
be not envious of wrongdoers!
For they will soon fade like the grass
and wither like the green herb.

PSALM 37:1–2

Hay That Is Soon Harvested

his is a fine illustration; it is frightening to the hypocrites and comforting to the suffering. How wonderfully [the psalmist] takes us out of our own sight and puts us before the sight of God! Before our own sight the mob of hypocrites grows green, blooms, and increases until it covers the whole world; only they seem to amount to anything, as the green grass covers and adorns the earth. But in God's sight, what are they? Hay that is soon to be harvested. The higher the grass grows, the closer are the scythes and pitchforks. Thus the faster the wicked grow and the higher they soar, the closer is their downfall. Then why should you be angry, since their wickedness and their good fortune are such a brief thing? But you may say: "What am I to do meanwhile? What shall I hold on to until that happens?" Listen to the great promise: *Trust in the Lord, and do good; remain in the land, and make your living in faith* [Psalm 37:3].

From *Four Psalms of Comfort*, on Psalm 37 (Luther's Works 14:211–12)

Delight yourself in the LORD,
and He will give you the desires of your heart.
Commit your way to the LORD;
trust in Him, and He will act.

PSALM 37:4–5

Content with His Will

D o not permit yourself to be vexed that God lets [the wicked] prosper so; indeed, take pleasure in it as the very gracious will of God. Content yourself with His will. Then your dissatisfaction at the prosperity of the wicked will pass away. Look, here you have this comforting promise: "He will give you all that your heart desires." What more do you want? Only be sure that instead of this vexation you find joy and satisfaction in the will of God. Then your enemies will not only do you no harm, but your heart will also be full of peace and will joyfully await the fulfillment of this promise of God. . . . Committing our way to God does not mean that we do nothing. It means that though the hypocrites may denounce, ridicule, slander, or frustrate what we do, we must not give in to them or quit, but keep right on with it, letting them have their stubbornness and entrusting the whole cause to God, who will make it come out right on both sides.

From *Four Psalms of Comfort*, on Psalm 37
(Luther's Works 14:212–13)

Be still before the Lord and wait patiently for Him;
fret not yourself over the one who prospers in his way,
over the man who carries out evil devices!

PSALM 37:7

The Success of Scoundrels

 t is as if [the psalmist] were saying: "It will tend to vex you when you encounter misfortune in a righteous cause, while they get along very well in their wickedness and do not disappear, as you wish they would. You see the wicked man succeed so well in all his evil devices that a proverb has been coined about it: 'The greater the scoundrel, the greater his success.' But be wise, dear child, and do not let that get you down. Cling to God, and your heart's desire will come—in abundance! But it is not yet time; the scoundrel's success must pass by and have its appointed time before it is all over. Meanwhile you must commit it to God, take your pleasure in Him, and find satisfaction in His will, so that you do not hinder His will in you or in your enemy. For that is what happens when people will not stop raging; either they ram their cause through headfirst, or they smash it to bits."

From *Four Psalms of Comfort*, on Psalm 37
(Luther's Works 14:213–14)

The wicked plots against the righteous
and gnashes his teeth at him,
but the LORD laughs at the wicked,
for He sees that his day is coming.

PSALM 37:12–13

No Greater Comfort

This is said for the consolation of those who are weak in faith, who do not want to endure the attacks of the wicked and are vexed that God does not punish them right away but lets them get along so well. . . . How could we receive a greater comfort? The raging enemies of the righteous use all their power and wickedness and are bent on devouring the righteous (that is, the believer in God). And God has such contempt for them that He laughs at them, for He sees how brief their rage will be and how soon their day will come. This does not mean that God laughs as a man laughs, but that it is truly ridiculous to behold how, despite their rage and their ambitious plans, these madmen do not make one whit of progress. They are like the silly fool who would take a long spear and a short dagger and try to bring the sun down from the sky, and then would dance for joy, as though he had really accomplished something.

From *Four Psalms of Comfort*, on Psalm 37
(Luther's Works 14:215–16)

Better is the little that the righteous has
than the abundance of many wicked.
For the arms of the wicked shall be broken,
but the LORD upholds the righteous.

PSALM 37:16–17

Abstain from Unjust Gain

njustice does not bestow happiness or peace of conscience. He who accumulates gets no pleasure from it, and the heir is impoverished. For in the house of the godless man it is wiped out. Although riches are scraped together there, yet they are wiped out; for God blows, and he who accumulates does so into a pouch with a hole in it, as the poets relate about the sieve of the Danaides. Therefore he who is godly should be satisfied with a little, in accordance with the statement of Psalm 37:16. He should enjoy this, be glad with his wife and children, and abstain from unjust gain. The histories and books of all nations teach the same thing, namely, that it is far better for you to live on one or two guldens acquired in an honorable manner than on many thousands obtained in a shameful manner with harm to others.

From *Lectures on Genesis* (Luther's Works 5:66)

The Lord knows the days of the blameless,
and their heritage will remain forever.

Psalm 37:18

At the Appropriate Time

od recognizes their days, their appointed time; that is, because they trust Him fully and do not want to know when and how their help is to come, God takes their side. And though it seems to the wicked that God has forgotten the blameless, this is not true; God knows well when it is the appropriate time to help them. As Psalm 9:9 says: "God is a Helper at the appropriate time," and Psalm 31:15: "My times are in Thy hand." It is as if he were saying: "They are poor and few in number, while the others are rich and numerous. But never mind; they will still have enough and will not suffer want. God knows well when it is the appropriate time to help and counsel them, and they trust in Him without relying on their own help and counsel." In addition, their heritage will be eternal, not only in the world to come but also in this world. For they will and must always have enough, even though they may not have extra grain, as the wicked do. God is their grain and their granary, their wine cellar and their entire property.

From *Four Psalms of Comfort*, on Psalm 37 (Luther's Works 14:217–18)

They are not put to shame in evil times;
in the days of famine they have abundance. . . .
I have not seen the righteous forsaken
or his children begging for bread.

PSALM 37:19, 25

From the Midst of Heaven

[he righteous] may hunger indeed, but he will not die of hunger; for hunger exercises his faith in the Word, but then faith gains food also for the body. Therefore the splendid word of Moses stands: that God deals with His own by testing them with hunger and exercising them in His Word, and then feeds the believer from the midst of heaven if it cannot be done otherwise. Thus they are to learn by experience that they should not be concerned for their belly, and that life does not lie in the things we possess or in bread but in the Word by which we become rich toward God, as the Gospel says (Luke 12:15). For while we live by the Word in the heart, we force God, as it were, to feed the belly too. . . . To understand these and similar wonderful and faithful promises of God is truly to understand the promise of the First Commandment, in which He says: "I am the Lord your God." "Yours, yours," He says, "who will show and display Myself to you as God and will not forsake you, if only you believe this." All such promises depend on and flow from the First Commandment.

From *Lectures on Deuteronomy* (Luther's Works 9:94)

May 18

The wicked borrows but does not pay back,
but the righteous is generous and gives;
for those blessed by the LORD shall inherit the land.

PSALM 37:21–22

Genuine Possession

his is a comforting difference among possessions. Not only are the possessions of the wicked perishable and transitory, but they are evil and damnable possessions, because they have only been heaped up and have not been distributed to those in need. This violates the nature of possessions. The possessions of the righteous, on the other hand, not only have no end—because he trusts in God and waits for his possessions from Him—but they are truly useful possessions which are distributed to others and are not just heaped up. Thus he has enough, even without temporal grain, and gives enough to others too. This is a genuine possession. Even though you may not have much, it is God-pleasing and useful.

From *Four Psalms of Comfort*, on Psalm 37 (Luther's Works 14:219)

The steps of a man are established by the Lord,
when He delights in his way.

PSALM 37:23

Yield to the Lord

till more comfort! Not only are you to have plenty of temporal possessions, but everything you do, your whole life and conduct, will succeed and prosper, because you trust God, surrender yourself and your cause to Him, and remain yielded to Him throughout your life. Thus you cause Him to find pleasure, delight, and satisfaction in advancing your works and ways. But this is opposed by the fact that a God-pleasing way of life receives no support but only hindrance and rejection from the wicked. This is a vexation for human nature. Therefore one must find consolation in God's approval and support of our way of life, regardless of the hindrance and rejection of the wicked.

From *Four Psalms of Comfort*, on Psalm 37 (Luther's Works 14:220)

The steps of a man are established by the Lord,
when He delights in his way;
though he fall, he shall not be cast headlong,
for the Lord upholds his hand.

PSALM 37:23–24

A Promise to Believe

o far as the care and protection of God are concerned, we are loved no less than [the greatest saints]. As a sure pledge of this most tender and burning love we have God's Son, for whose sake the Father loves us and makes us sit in the heavenly places, as Paul says (Ephesians 2:6). We should know that what is stated very sweetly in Psalm 37:23–24 also applies to us. There we read: "The steps of a man are from the Lord, and He establishes him in whose way He delights; though he fall, he shall not be cast headlong, for the Lord is the stay of his hand." Let us only believe, and give assent to, this promise. For just as parents guard their little ones with all care, lest perchance they fall, lest they stumble somewhere or offend, and, if they see a spot or mucus smeared on their cheeks, dry it and wipe it off—which an enemy or a stranger does not do—and if a feather sticks to their hair, comb and adorn it, so great also is God's care, love, and true fatherly feeling toward all who believe in Him.

From *Lectures on Genesis* (Luther's Works 5:278)

I have been young, and now am old,
yet I have not seen the righteous forsaken
or his children begging for bread.

PSALM 37:25

The Purpose of Affliction

he godly, too, are afflicted, just as Isaac endured want and famine in his time. . . . The purpose of these afflictions should be carefully noted. Although public misfortunes affect the saints and the prophets, this does not happen as a punishment or because of anger, as in the case of the godless and the ungrateful; it happens for their salvation and to test and prove their faith, love, and patience, in order that the godly may learn to bear the hand of God in the management of their household. For God has promised that He wants to support them in the time of famine, as it is written (Psalm 37:25): "I have not seen the righteous forsaken." Likewise (Psalm 37:19): "In the days of famine they have abundance." God confirms these promises with such examples of the saints, and by means of this tribulation in the household He instructs the godly in the Word, in faith, in humility of spirit, in love, and in other virtues.

From *Lectures on Genesis* (Luther's Works 5:12)

The mouth of the righteous utters wisdom,
and his tongue speaks justice. . . .
Wait for the LORD and keep His way,
and He will exalt you to inherit the land;
you will look on when the wicked are cut off.

PSALM 37:30, 34

Clear as Noon

his is the basis of the conflict: the wicked refuse to listen to the wisdom and justice of God. They persecute it, condemn and denounce it as foolishness and injustice. Because these rascals are successful at this for a while, the righteous are irked and provoked, and it incites them to wickedness and vengeance or impatience. Therefore this psalm teaches them to be still and to go right on with their duties: teaching, writing, and speaking wisdom and justice; entrusting their cause to God; letting the wicked bite, rage, scowl, slander, strike, draw their swords, bend their bows, and build up their mobs and their power, as has already been said. For God will set it right, if only we wait for Him to do it, staying on our course, and not letting them make us quit or give up. Ultimately the judgment of this verse must prevail and become as clear as noon: that the righteous man has been speaking justly and wisely, and the wicked have been foolish and unjust.

From *Four Psalms of Comfort*, on Psalm 37 (Luther's Works 14:223)

The mouth of the righteous utters wisdom,
and his tongue speaks justice.
The Law of his God is in his heart; his steps do not slip.

PSALM 37:30–31

Where the Law of God Is

He speaks justice and utters wisdom because the Law of God is not in a book, not in his ears or on his tongue, but in his heart. No one can rightly understand the Law of God unless it is in his heart, and he loves it and lives according to it; this is done by faith in God. Therefore although the wicked make much talk about God and His Law, and boast that they are teachers and experts in the Scriptures, they never speak justice or wisdom. For they do not have it in their heart; therefore they do not understand it. . . . In addition the steps of the righteous do not slip but go straight ahead, safe and sure, in good conscience, because he is certain of his cause and will not let himself be seduced by the laws and doctrines of men. But the wicked always fall and slide around, and their step is uncertain, because they remove the Law of God from faith and thus misunderstand it. Thus they wander about as their own ideas lead them or the laws of men instruct them to do first this, then that work.

From *Four Psalms of Comfort,* on Psalm 37
(Luther's Works 14:223–24)

The salvation of the righteous is from the LORD;
He is their stronghold in the time of trouble.
The LORD helps them and delivers them;
He delivers them from the wicked and saves them,
because they take refuge in Him.

PSALM 37:39–40

A Threefold Delivery

hat a rich promise, what a great consolation, what an abundant admonition, if only we trust and believe! First, God helps them in the very midst of evil. He does not leave them lying there but stands by them, strengthens them, and preserves them. Secondly, He not only helps them but delivers them and enables them to escape. For the precise meaning of this Hebrew word is "to escape misfortune and to get away from it." And as a vexation to the wicked he mentions them by name and says: "He delivers them from the wicked." They may not like it; but their rage will not do them a bit of good, though they believe that the righteous man will not escape them and will surely be destroyed. Thirdly, He not only delivers them but goes right on helping them, so that they do not remain in any trouble, no matter when it comes. And He does all this because they have trusted in Him.

From *Four Psalms of Comfort*, on Psalm 37 (Luther's Works 14:228)

O LORD, rebuke me not in Your anger,
nor discipline me in Your wrath!
For Your arrows have sunk into me,
and Your hand has come down on me. . . .
There is no health in my bones because of my sin.

PSALM 38:1–3

A Shot to the Heart

his psalm portrays most clearly the manner, words, acts, thoughts, and gestures of a truly penitent heart. *O Lord, rebuke me not in Thy anger.* The chastisement is understood by means of words, as one rebukes an evildoer. . . . *For Thy arrows have sunk into me.* The words with which God rebukes and threatens in Scripture are arrows. Whoever feels them cries out: "O Lord, rebuke me not in Thy anger." However, only he feels them into whose heart they are thrust and whose conscience is terrified. It is the sensitive into whose heart God shoots the arrows. From the smug, who have become hardened, the arrows glance off as from a hard stone. . . . The arrows of God and His angry words make real the sin within the heart. This causes restlessness and terror in the conscience and in all the powers of the soul, and it makes the body sick throughout.

From *Seven Penitential Psalms*, on Psalm 38
(Luther's Works 14:156–57)

There is no soundness in my flesh
because of Your indignation;
there is no health in my bones because of my sin.

PSALM 38:3

The Weakness of Human Nature

 here is no soundness in My flesh. This is understood literally concerning the flesh of Christ bruised in suffering and His bones shaken and dispersed. And this was done in the face of God's wrath, that is, in the presence of, and before, God's wrath. This wrath comes *in the face of our sins*, before, or in the presence of. . . . Second, it is also understood of the weakness of the human nature, which is so weakened by sin that it is quick and inclined to evil all the time from youth onward and in all its own powers slow to the good. And for this, too, the Lord cries here in a most devout way for our sake, that He might take it away. Third, it refers to the bodily weaknesses and sufferings, sicknesses and ills without number, to which human nature is subject because of sin, as is clear from experience. And for these, too, Christ grieved [for He bore all our evils].

From *First Lectures on the Psalms*, on Psalm 38
(Luther's Works 10:177)

My iniquities have gone over my head;
like a heavy burden, they are too heavy for me.

PSALM 38:4

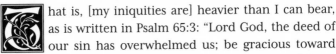

An Amazing Thing

hat is, [my iniquities are] heavier than I can bear, as is written in Psalm 65:3: "Lord God, the deed of our sin has overwhelmed us; be gracious toward our iniquity." Thus our sin treads us underfoot until grace comes, treads sin underfoot, and raises our head above it so that we become master and rule over sin, not sin over us. Those, however, who lie in sin, who are either dead or too holy, do not sense these things. Therefore it is an amazing thing: He who has no sin feels and has it, and he who has sin does not feel it and has none. For it would be impossible for him to complain about and against sin if he did not live in righteousness and grace. One devil does not drive out the other (Luke 11:18); sin does not accuse its kind; and one wolf does not cry out against the other. And yet it is impossible for him who cries out against sin to be without it, for he dare not speak to God in fiction. It must be true that he has sin, as he says, and yet also true that he is without sin. Just as Christ was at the same time truly alive and dead, so also those who are real Christians must be full of sin and without sin at the same time.

From *Seven Penitential Psalms*, on Psalm 38
(Luther's Works 14:157–58)

My wounds stink and fester because of my foolishness,
I am utterly bowed down and prostrate;
all the day I go about mourning.

PSALM 38:5–6

Heart Bowed Down

ust as wounds and swellings of the body decay, fester, and stink, so also the evil sores of human nature get worse and begin to stink if they are not treated and healed daily with the ointment of grace and the water of the Word of God. Now others go on smugly, not heeding these sores, just as though they were well. . . . But it is foolishness when a man does not know himself but imagines he is altogether well. The arrows, however, reveal this foolishness that man may realize how blind he has been in knowing himself. Hence this is the meaning: When I recognized my own foolishness and lack of self-understanding, I also recognized how very foul and stinking my wounds really are. Formerly, in my foolishness, I did not see this. Therefore *I am utterly bowed down and prostrate. . . . All the day I go about mourning.* These are true signs of real repentance for sin, just as the publican in the Gospel did not dare raise his eyes (Luke 18:13) but considered himself evil and bowed down to the ground, more with his heart than with his body.

From *Seven Penitential Psalms*, on Psalm 38 (Luther's Works 14:158)

But for You, O Lord, do I wait;
it is You, O Lord my God, who will answer.

Psalm 38:15

Words of Faith

hese are words of a true and strong faith, which in time of trouble lets everything else go and clings to the Word and grace of God, and does not doubt that God will hear and help him. Yet he does not prescribe to God the time or manner but simply says: "Thou wilt answer; I will hope and continue to hope."

From *Seven Penitential Psalms*, on Psalm 38 (Luther's Works 14:160)

Do not forsake me, O Lord!
O my God, be not far from me!
Make haste to help me, O Lord, my salvation!

PSALM 38:21–22

God's Material

 t is God's nature to make something out of nothing; hence one who is not yet nothing, out of him God cannot make anything. . . . Therefore God accepts only the forsaken, cures only the sick, gives sight only to the blind, restores life only to the dead, sanctifies only the sinners, gives wisdom only to the unwise. In short, He has mercy only on those who are wretched, and gives grace only to those who are not in grace. Therefore no proud saint, no wise or righteous person, can become God's material, and God's purpose cannot be fulfilled in him. He remains in his own work and makes a fictitious, pretended, false, painted saint of himself, that is, a hypocrite. . . . God is not a Father of the rich but of the poor, widows, and orphans. The rich He has left alone (Luke 1:53). "O God of my salvation," that is, that I seek no help or salvation either in myself or in anyone else, but only in Thee. Thus also Psalm 4:1: "The God of my righteousness has heard me," that is, He is the one who gives help.

From *Seven Penitential Psalms*, on Psalm 38 (Luther's Works 14:163)

Hear my prayer, O L<small>ORD</small>, and give ear to my cry. . . .
For I am a sojourner with You,
a guest, like all my fathers.

P<small>SALM</small> 39:12

Citizens in Hope

o those who believe and have God's promise, this life is a wandering in which they are sustained by the hope of a future and better life. And it seems that David took those words of the psalm, "like all my fathers," from the words of Jacob: "And they have not attained to the days of the years of the life of my fathers in the days of their sojourning" [Genesis 47:9]. Accordingly, before God we are all citizens in hope; but before the world we are sojourners in fact. The godly should carefully remember these things and order their life according to this method. For those who consider this are few; but most people pursue the advantages and pleasures of the world, which they regard as Paradise and their kingdom and heaven. They cast aside the expectation of the other life.

From *Lectures on Genesis* (Luther's Works 8:115)

Then I said, "Behold, I have come;
in the scroll of the book it is written of Me:
I delight to do Your will, O My God."

PSALM 40:7–8

One Will

he right basis for knowing Christ's suffering is to know and understand not only His suffering but also His heart and will for that suffering. Whoever looks at His suffering without seeing His will and heart in them must be terrified at it rather than rejoice in it. But if we see His heart and will in [His suffering], this produces true comfort, confidence, and joy in Christ. For this reason Psalm 40 [:7–8] praises this will of God and of Christ in suffering: "In the book it is written of Me that I should do Your will, O My God, and I do it gladly." The Epistle to the Hebrews says: "By that will we all have been sanctified" (Hebrews [10:10]). He does not say "through the suffering and blood of Christ" (which is certainly true), but "through the will of God and of Christ," because they both were of one will: to sanctify us through the blood of Christ.

From the *Church Postil*, sermon for Quinquagesima
on Luke 18:31–43 (Luther's Works 76:350–51)

My iniquities have overtaken me,
and I cannot see. . . .
Be pleased, O LORD, to deliver me!

PSALM 40:12–13

A Light to See

hen the conscience blames, then man is distressed and says with David in Psalm 40:12: "My iniquities have overtaken me till I cannot see"; see also Psalm 49:6. Then a sinner sobs and says: "I do not know what I ought to do." But in opposition to this darkness of the heart it is said: "God knows everything." One's conscience is always fearful and closes its eyes, but God is deeper and higher than your heart and examines it more intimately. He gives us a light, so that we see that our iniquity has been taken away from us. Satan often disturbs our conscience even when we do what is right. . . . But then one must close one's eyes and consider that God is wiser in His Word and that we are not saved by such vain works. . . . God, who strengthens you in the truth, is more powerful than the devil. . . . You must always consider that *God is greater than our heart* [1 John 3:20]. The heart knows nothing that is right. God knows everything and teaches me better things in the Word of the Gospel.

From *Lectures on 1 John* (Luther's Works 30:280–81)

Why are you cast down, O my soul,
and why are you in turmoil within me?
Hope in God; for I shall again praise Him,
my salvation and my God.

PSALM 42:5

Something Greater

he time of grace is when the heart is encouraged again by the promise of the free mercy of God and says (Psalm 42:5): "Why are you cast down, O my soul, and why are you disquieted within me? Do you not see anything except Law, sin, terror, sadness, despair, death, hell, and the devil? Are there not also grace, the forgiveness of sins, righteousness, comfort, joy, peace, life, heaven, God, and Christ? Stop troubling me, O my soul. What are Law, sin, and all evils in comparison with these? Hope in God, who did not spare His own Son but gave Him up to the death of the cross for your sins (Romans 8:32)." This, then, is what it means to be confined under the Law according to the flesh, not forever but until the coming of Christ. When you are terrified by the Law, therefore, say: "Lady Law, you are not the only thing, and you are not everything! Besides you there is something greater and better, namely, grace, faith, blessing. These do not accuse me; they do not terrify or condemn me. But they comfort me, command me to have hope, and promise me sure victory and salvation in Christ. Therefore there is no reason for me to despair."

From *Lectures on Galatians* (Luther's Works 26:341–42)

Wisdom Hidden in Mystery

od's cataracts [or "waterfalls"] are the preachers of the Gospel. The Lord has opened them up and has poured down in abundance the rain of saving doctrine. And by the public proclamation of such a one the faithful are multiplied. This is what it means for the deep to call to the deep, that is, one always follows another in the Church, and a saint within calls another saint to the inner things of faith, just as day follows day and night follows night. These are those hidden things which God conceals from the prudent and the wise (Matthew 11:25). This is the wisdom hidden in a mystery (1 Corinthians 2:7).

From *First Lectures on the Psalms*, on Psalm 33
(Luther's Works 10:156)

All Your breakers and Your waves have gone over me.

PSALM 42:7

Suspended

ll *Thy waves* (v. 7) can also be taken in a good sense, namely, that the high waves, that is, the swirling waters of the deep and the flow of living waters, of which [the psalmist] had already spoken, that is, the Gospels, passed over the church and made it glad, as also Psalm 93:4 says: "With the noise of many waters wonderful are the surges of the sea." Hence an old translation reads, "all thy vaulted works," which properly expresses the peculiarity of evangelical teaching; for it does not rest on the earth or on human wisdom, but it arches overhead and takes every understanding captive to the obedience of Christ (2 Corinthians 10:5) . . . . Those are the salutary floods and surges of the Lord, which submerge the flesh and its desires and cause the soul or spirit to swim and carry it suspended.

From *First Lectures on the Psalms*, on Psalm 42
(Luther's Works 10:201–2)

For not in my bow do I trust,
nor can my sword save me.
But You have saved us from our foes
and have put to shame those who hate us.

PSALM 44:6–7

The Busy Hand

Under the surface sign of things at hand God shows His works and wants us to use them but not to trust in them. For while it is true that the busy hand produces riches, nevertheless what Solomon also said is true, that only the blessing of the Lord makes wealthy men, namely, through the busy hand (Proverbs 10:22). For if the busy hand were to be hindered by force, the blessing of the Lord would still enrich. So through the sword He alone gives safety. Nevertheless, the safety of a man is empty, and "my sword [he says] will not save" (Psalm 44:6). But God will save through the sword if it is at hand, and without the sword if it is not available. Hence one must use things, but one must not trust in them. Only in God should one trust, whether that which you may use is at hand or lacking.

From *Lectures on Deuteronomy* (Luther's Works 9:74–75)

For not in my bow do I trust,
nor can my sword save me.
But You have saved us from our foes.

PSALM 44:6–7

Arms Made Ready

 t is indeed a great honor that Jacob has the courage to say that the bows, the arrows, the hands, and the arms are sturdy, firm, and strong [Genesis 49:23–24]. From what source? From the hands of the Mighty One of God, who is the God of Jacob. . . . To be sure, arms must be made ready and all things that are of value for the administration of a kingdom and for accomplishing things in times of peace and war. Surely something must be done. The means that are at hand must be employed. Consultations and deliberations must be held. But one should by no means trust in all these preparations and excellent provisions. No, one should pray: "O Lord, make haste to help me!" (Cf. Psalm 70:2.) "Our help is in the name of the Lord" (Psalm 124:8), for the adversaries are far superior to us in counsel and in strength.

From *Lectures on Genesis* (Luther's Works 8:299)

Changed by Grace

herever the word "song" (*canticum*) is used in psalm titles, it must always be understood that such a psalm is one of joy and dancing and is to be sung with a feeling of rejoicing. For a song and singing spring from the fullness of a rejoicing heart. But a spiritual song, or spiritual melody, is the very jubilation of the heart. So the title means: This psalm is for triumph, or a triumphal song, about Christ and the Church, which are roses or lilies, a spiritual instruction revealed to the sons of Korah, a song of the beloved, Christ and the Church, which are loved by each other. . . . But the ancient translation [of the title] reads, "Unto the end, for those who will be changed." . . . These words want to be understood as referring to the faithful, who have been truly changed by Christ and altered and reborn and begotten again. . . . Therefore all of us are here changed by grace from sin to righteousness, from flesh to spirit, from the letter and shadow of the Law to the life and light of the Gospel, and after this from corruption to incorruption, from disgrace to eternal glory.

From *First Lectures on the Psalms*, on Psalm 45
(Luther's Works 10:208–9)

My heart overflows with a pleasing theme;
I address my verses to the King;
my tongue is like the pen of a ready scribe.

PSALM 45:1

To Be the Pen

ust as a man uses the tongue as a tool with which he produces and forms words, so God uses our words, whether Gospels or prophetic books, as tools with which He Himself writes living words in our hearts. When one has put another's word and the sense of the words into the heart, this is not yet writing, but only the stylus poised over the tablet, which is then reduced to living letters, when God gives the increase and grants it to be efficacious and wise. This is something He can do very swiftly. Therefore, as he who waters and plants is nothing, but God who gives the increase (1 Corinthians 3:7), so he who has the stylus or is the stylus or puts it to the tablet is nothing, but He who writes, namely, the writer writing swiftly, the Holy Spirit. Therefore, O prophet, it is for you to utter and be the pen.

From *First Lectures on the Psalms*, on Psalm 45
(Luther's Works 10:212)

You are the most handsome of the sons of men;
grace is poured upon Your lips;
therefore God has blessed You forever.

PSALM 45:2

Celebrating the King

his is the first sweet and delightful thing in this lyric, which sings about and promises a kingdom with such a King. There will be no imperfections in Him, but a will full of virtues and a mind full of wisdom, with glowing love toward all miserable, damned, and sorrowful sinners. . . . Our King, who is celebrated here, is full of mercy, grace, and truth. In Him love for mankind is to be found and the greatest sweetness; a person who, as we find in Isaiah 42:2, "does not cry in the streets," is not austere and rough, but patient and long-suffering. He exercises judgment against the wicked and blasphemers, and shows mercy toward sinners. Therefore He is a most pleasant and fair King, and there is no one like Him in the whole world. In Him is to be found the highest virtue and the highest love toward God and men. . . . He did not keep company with the holy, powerful, and wise, but with despicable and miserable sinners, with those ruined by misfortune, with men weighed down by painful and incurable diseases; these He healed, comforted, raised up, helped. And at last He even died for sinners.

From *Lectures on Psalm 45* (Luther's Works 12:207–8)

Grace is poured upon Your lips;
therefore God has blessed You forever.

PSALM 45:2

Fountain of Grace

 rom [Christ's] mouth, as from some overflowing fountain, the richest promises and teachings stem, and with these He strengthens and comforts souls. So the things you hear daily about this Christ are what the poet depicts, as you see, however briefly, yet with distinctive words and the loveliest poetry: Grace is on the lips of this King, and not only that, it overflows, so that you may understand how abundantly this fountain of grace flows and gushes forth. As though he said: "Our King has wisdom such as no man has, namely, the sweetest and loveliest wisdom; He helps the penitent, comforts the afflicted, recalls the despairing, raises up the fallen and humiliated, justifies sinners, gives life to the dying. And whatever there is in addition to this, that the Word of salvation accomplishes, that He does in rich abundance." It is, therefore, a sweet and delightful wisdom, worthy of such high praise. Therefore He says in Isaiah 50:4: "The Lord has given Me the tongue of those who are taught," the Lord has given Me a fluent tongue, "that I may know how to sustain with a word him that is weary."

From *Lectures on Psalm 45* (Luther's Works 12:211–12)

Gird Your sword on Your thigh, O Mighty One,
in Your splendor and majesty!

PSALM 45:3

Rendered Invincible

he power of the Word is shown in this, that Christ fights in us with His armament, "with the breastplate of faith and the sword of the Word" (Ephesians 6:16–17). So we strike the enemy on all sides, first by laying bare his deceit and lies in the heretics, then by snatching up and defending our men so that they may persevere in holy faith and life. . . . You see here what kind of king we have. After He has taught us and poured out His promises on us, and by His Word has transferred us into His kingdom (Colossians 1:13), Satan is immediately there and crucifies us. For "all who wish to live a godly life in Christ must bear persecution" (2 Timothy 3:12); similarly, "through many tribulations we must enter the kingdom of God" (Acts 14:22). But our King will not forsake us. He is present and fights in us against the power of tyrants and against the lies of the devil. Indeed He renders us invincible against the lying teachers and secure against the power of tyrants.

From *Lectures on Psalm 45* (Luther's Works 12:216)

Gird Your sword on Your thigh, O Mighty One,
in Your splendor and majesty!
In Your majesty ride out victoriously!

PSALM 45:3–4

Grain and Wine

Not with might, not with physical armament, not with a warlike attack will Christ save His people. He will do this with beauty and delight. He will save not with the savagery of weapons but with majesty and beauty, as we have it in Psalm 45:4. This is what he here [Zechariah 9:17] calls grain and wine: the Gospel, which is Christ's greatest honor and beauty. With this Gospel He attracts hearts which taste that sweetness of the Gospel. You see, the Gospel is the light and ray in which Christ is glorified, because He now has praises, celebration, magnificence, majesty, beauty, and the thousand things the Psalms call by other names when they describe the beauty of Christ.

From *Lectures on Zechariah (Latin)* (Luther's Works 20:104)

In Your majesty ride out victoriously
for the cause of truth and meekness and righteousness;
let Your right hand teach You awesome deeds!

PSALM 45:4

Invisible Progress and Success

ouse yourself. Do not give in to evils, but go forth more boldly against them. Hold on. Do not be disheartened either by contempt or ingratitude within or by agitation and raging without. But think as follows: "When I am weak, I am strongest (2 Corinthians 12:10); when I am suppressed, I rise up, as a palm rises up under its burden." So they thought that we had perished at Augsburg, but there we rose highest of all. Similarly it is in sorrow, when we are the closest to despair, that hope rises the highest. So today, when there is the greatest contempt and weariness with the Word, the true glory of the Word begins. Therefore we should learn to understand this verse as speaking of invisible progress and success. Our King enjoys success and good fortune even though you do not see it. Moreover, it would not be expedient for us to see this success, for then we would be puffed up. Now, however, He raises us up through faith and gives us hope. Even though we see no fruit of the Word, still we can be certain that fruit will not be wanting but will certainly follow; for so it is written here. . . . He is the kind of king who will have success, steadfastness, and victory—if not in this place and time, then at another time and place.

From *Lectures on Psalm 45* (Luther's Works 12:220–21)

June 15

Your arrows are sharp
in the heart of the King's enemies;
the peoples fall under You.

PSALM 45:5

Sure of Victory

So our King is the defender and savior of the miserable, abounding in comfort toward the humble and distressed, completely victorious over His stubborn enemies. And we are really sure of victory if we hold fast to this King. What kind of kingdom would that be if we had to live continually surrounded by enemies, exposed to everyone's plots and weapons, always suffering and hard pressed? There must be some change, and those who have borne with so much must someday gain the victory. Victory is certain if only we persevere, as Paul says in 2 Corinthians 2:14: "I thank God who always causes us to triumph in Christ Jesus." Christians do not succumb to despair and lack of trust, they do not turn from the Word, they do not deny Christ. They persevere in teaching and confessing Him—at times strongly, but at other times feebly. For He is a conquering King and a King of the miserable. He can raise us up even though at times we are weak.

From *Lectures on Psalm 45* (Luther's Works 12:229)

Your throne, O God, is forever and ever.
The scepter of Your kingdom
is a scepter of uprightness.

PSALM 45:6

No Other King or Kingdom

his kingdom is eternal and spiritual. It is adminis-tered by a person who is at the same time God and man, mortal and immortal, one who has passed over from this life to another and rules for life against death, for righteousness against sin, for salvation against dam-nation. Just as none of these features can be applied to any other kingdom except in a weak shadow, so, too, there is no other king who lives forever; they live for a time, and others in turn succeed them. So this that follows, the staff or scepter of equity ["uprightness"], also applies only to the kingdom of Christ. . . . The scepter of this kingdom receives singular praise and commendation: it is straight, not curved or full of knots; that is, it dispenses injustice to no one but exercises justice in the most exact degree.

From *Lectures on Psalm 45* (Luther's Works 12:236)

The scepter of Your kingdom
is a scepter of uprightness.

PSALM 45:6

Altogether Pure

his is a straight scepter, because Christ's teaching and the Laws of His kingdom are altogether straight and pure, namely, that we should believe in Christ and love God and our neighbor. There is no error in this Law, but there is in us; for we do not believe enough, we do not love enough, we are not strong enough in tribulation. And yet, since we are under this shadow of Christ, who loves God and man purely, we enjoy His favor and are regarded as holy also in this life. First, then, there is no error in His Law, no crookedness in His scepter. For the Word is pure, promising grace and teaching men to love God. This is the equity of His scepter. Second, there is no error in us either: first, so far as concerns our Head, Christ, who absorbs our sins; and second, so far as concerns the future life, in which the righteousness will be revealed that we now believe.

From *Lectures on Psalm 45* (Luther's Works 12:239–40)

The scepter of Your kingdom is a scepter of uprightness;
You have loved righteousness and hated wickedness.

PSALM 45:6–7

The Sign among the Peoples

his, therefore, is a remarkable picture of our King Jesus Christ. He sits upon His throne in order to declare the right, to employ Christians, and to sanctify them. Thus they grow from day to day in faith and the righteousness of works. They are purified from offenses, so that lust is diminished, sadness is reduced, despair taken away. All of this He does by the scepter, as [the psalmist] expressly adds, since the fanatical spirits mock the oral Word and the ministry of the Holy Spirit. You must not do that, but follow the authority of the Holy Spirit, who calls the Word by the glorious name "straight scepter." It is the sign and banner that He has raised among the peoples. Christ did not wish to be seen by us visibly. For that reason He has given His scepter, that we may pay attention and hear, for through it the Holy Spirit is active. If we have this scepter, we have enough, since He will give nothing by visible pomp or the external appearance of the kingdom. Rather, He offers His scepter, through which He confers His benefits on us.

From *Lectures on Psalm 45* (Luther's Works 12:247)

From ivory palaces stringed instruments make You glad.

PSALM 45:8

More Than Meets the Eye

ur King Christ does not have a palace made of "clay, wood, or stubble" (1 Corinthians 3:12), such as our people construct, but of ivory. For who would believe that the church at Wittenberg, Kemberg, and other places where Baptism and the Word are, is in God's eyes an ivory palace? Yet it actually is. For Baptism is not something inane; neither is the Word, nor the government of the Church; nor is the comfort of the downtrodden something meaningless. If you wish to judge by external appearances, what do you see here at Wittenberg of value? You see nothing splendid about the church; the city is actually built of clay, and yet it is an ivory palace of Christ. So even the poorest village in which there is a pastor and some believers is a palace of ivory. But in order to see this, you need other than physical eyes. Its value cannot be determined by appearance, by the judgment of the five senses or reason, nor by laws, nor by the arts or philosophy; but according to God's Word—by the fact that the Word is there, Baptism, the Eucharist, divine governance, the consolation of consciences, the fear of God, trust in God, waiting upon God, the imitation of Christ, and the like. You should look around for these things, and when you see them somewhere, do not let external appearance or anything else influence you, but simply conclude: "Here is Christ in palaces of ivory; here Christ dwells."

From *Lectures on Psalm 45* (Luther's Works 12:255)

A Most Beautiful Transformation

[he psalmist] calls the bride "the queen," [Christ's] spouse. She stands as though all in gold. This bride is the Church. . . . This is common usage, that Christ is called the Bridegroom and the Church, the bride, as in Ephesians 5:23ff., and other passages. He calls her through Holy Baptism and the Word of the Gospel, and adorns and clothes her with mercy, grace, and the remission of sins. That is what [the psalmist] means when he says, "She stands at Thy right hand." It is a magnificent compliment, and it is also appropriate that no one be nearer the bridegroom than the bride herself. But the principal thing is that the Church has everything that is Christ's and that two bodies have become one, so that what belongs to the Church is Christ's and in the same way what belongs to Christ is the Church's. . . . What, then, does Christ have? Indeed, eternal righteousness, wisdom, power, truth, life, joy, grace. The Church, therefore, is mistress and queen of mercy, life, salvation, and all things. . . . The Church reigns over death, sin, hell, the devil, and over all the terrors and evils in demons and in men, not by her own strength or merits, but by her Bridegroom, Christ. He has placed all these loveliest ornaments about her neck and has trampled death underfoot for her, has given her life, and by His blood has freed her from all dangers. So she has all these things from her Bridegroom and rightly says to heretics: "Mine is the wisdom"; to the Gentiles: "Mine is the righteousness"; to the Jews: "Mine is worship and piety"; to death: "Mine is life"; to sin: "Mine is the remission of sins"; to the Law: "Mine is liberty"; to fears: "Mine is peace and joy, not by myself or my own strength, but through Jesus Christ, my Bridegroom." This is a most beautiful transformation, that the Church, miserable in the eyes of men, should be so richly adorned in the eyes of God.

From *Lectures on Psalm 45* (Luther's Works 12:259–61)

Hear, O daughter, and consider, and incline your ear:
forget your people and your father's house,
and the King will desire your beauty.

PSALM 45:10–11

Adorned with His Word

he Holy Spirit says: "I will give you most beautiful advice. If you hear Me, it will make you a most lovely maiden. If you wish to be beautiful before God in order that all your works may please Him, so that He may say: 'Your prayer pleases Me, all that you say, do, and think pleases Me,' then you should hear, look, and incline your ear. You will be completely lovely when you hear, look, and forget your earlier righteousness, every law, all human traditions . . . and believe. Then you are beautiful not by your own beauty, but by the beauty of the King, who has adorned you with His Word, who has granted you His righteousness, His holiness, truth, strength, and all the gifts of the Holy Spirit." . . . If you look at Baptism with spiritual eyes you will see that it clothes you with the vestments and adornments of Christ. So the Eucharist clothes you with the adornment of Christ, the Gospel clothes you with the adornment of Christ. How could you wish for a better or more precious adornment than that with which Christ is adorned and adorns you?

From *Lectures on Psalm 45* (Luther's Works 12:278)

The King will desire your beauty.

PSALM 45:11

A Different Kind of Beauty

ur beauty does not consist in our own virtues nor even in the gifts we have received from God, by which we exercise our virtues and do everything that pertains to the life of the Law. It consists in this, that if we apprehend Christ and believe in Him, we are truly lovely, and Christ looks at that beauty alone and at nothing besides. Therefore it is nothing to teach that we should try to be beautiful by our own chosen religiousness and our own righteousness. To be sure, among men and at the courts of the wise these things are brilliant, but in God's courts we must have another beauty. There this is the one and only beauty—to believe in the Lord Jesus Christ. He removes all spots and wrinkles and makes us acceptable to God. This faith is an all-powerful matter and the greatest beauty, besides which there is no beauty. For without and outside Christ we are damned and lost with everything we have and are.

From *Lectures on Psalm 45* (Luther's Works 12:280)

All glorious is the princess in her chamber,

with robes interwoven with gold.

PSALM 45:13

Through God's Eyes

 n [the Church] are all good things, that is, in her is nothing but Christ, nothing but wisdom of faith, life, and glory. She is adorned with these from the soles of her feet to her head, so that no evil and no spot of ugliness is visible in her—but in the sight of God and beyond the perception of men. God sees no wrinkles in her because He sees nothing in her besides His Son, in whom the Church is clothed, from whom she has salvation, life, and glory, which is in Christ. If sin is present, the devil sees it and we feel it, each in his own conscience. But God does not. For on account of His Son, Christ, with whom the Church is clothed, she is altogether beautiful, without spot and wrinkle, because Christ is altogether beautiful and without spot. For that reason the Church, too, clothed by Him and in Him, is in the same condition.

From *Lectures on Psalm 45* (Luther's Works 12:264–65)

God is our refuge and strength,
a very present help in trouble.

PSALM 46:1

A Mighty Fortress Is Our God

A mighty fortress is our God,
A trusty shield and weapon;
He helps us free from ev'ry need
That hath us now o'ertaken.
The old evil foe
Now means deadly woe;
Deep guile and great might
Are his dread arms in fight;
On earth is not his equal.

With might of ours can naught be done,
Soon were our loss effected;
But for us fights the valiant One,
Whom God Himself elected.
Ask ye, Who is this?
Jesus Christ it is,
Of Sabaoth Lord,
And there's none other God;
He holds the field forever.

"A Mighty Fortress Is Our God" (*Lutheran Service Book* 656:1–2)

Offer to God a sacrifice of thanksgiving,
and perform your vows to the Most High.

PSALM 50:14

A Reasonable Sacrifice

he true acts of worship are described in Psalm 50:14 in the words: "Offer to God a sacrifice of thanksgiving and pay your vows to the Most High." External rites serve these and stir you up to praise Him who hears, rescues, governs, and saves so that you trust Him, endure His hand, learn to be mortified and die, and in all these respects show forth a patience worthy of godly men. This is the sacrifice of our body and a reasonable sacrifice (cf. Romans 12:1).

From *Lectures on Genesis* (Luther's Works 6:237)

*Offer to God a sacrifice of thanksgiving,
and perform your vows to the Most High.*

PSALM 50:14

The True Sacrifice of Praise

he sacrifice of praise must be given to God alone. For He has indeed reserved praise and glory to Himself, something that the devil and man have stolen from Him. . . . Then is God rightly worshiped when we completely disparage ourselves and ascribe all praise and glory and whatever is in us to Him. For when we attribute to God what belongs to Him and keep for ourselves what is ours, then we keep nothing, and that very nothing is ours, but everything is God's, from whom we receive it. Therefore such a confession out of a true heart is itself the sacrifice of praise, namely, to confess that everything, whatever we are, is owed to God, and there is absolutely nothing left for ourselves. . . . For if God wished to charge us with what is in us outside of His gifts, then we would be sinners. But we are saved through this, that He does not charge us with our very nothingness, at least not when we acknowledge it. . . . This, then is the true sacrifice of praise, that a person acknowledges his own total abyss and ascribes and confesses as belonging to the goodness of God everything that he is, has, and can do.

From *First Lectures on the Psalms*, from Psalm 50
(Luther's Works 10:232–34)

Hear, O My people, and I will speak . . .
I am God, your God. . . .
Call upon Me in the day of trouble;
I will deliver you, and you shall glorify Me.

PSALM 50:7, 15

Our Power and Victory in Every Trial

t is necessary above all to know for certain that we have the Word. For this is the foundation and basis of our assurance that we are hearers and that God is speaking with us. Concerning this no one should be in doubt; for he who does not know it, or doubts, will surely mumble prayers with the vain repetition customary among hypocrites. But he is unable to pray. But where this foundation, which is the Word of God, has been laid, there prayer is the ultimate help. No, it is not help. It is our power and victory in every trial. Thus God's Word declares: "Call upon Me in the day of trouble; I will deliver you" (Psalm 50:15). And in Isaiah 65:24: "Before they call, I will answer; while they are yet speaking, I will hear." And Gabriel says to Daniel: "At the beginning of your supplications a Word went forth" (Daniel 9:23). For when the heart prays seriously and ardently, it is impossible for those prayers not to be heard by God as soon as one begins to pray.

From *Lectures on Genesis* (Luther's Works 7:369)

Call upon Me in the day of trouble.

PSALM 50:15

The Foundation of Prayer

f it is a true prayer . . . it must rely on the promise of God. For who would be bold enough in his own right to lift up his hands and eyes to God unless he were sure about the will of God? Accordingly, all prayer relies on the command and promise of God, because in the Second Commandment there is the Word of God, which teaches us to pray: "You shall not take the name of the Lord your God in vain" (Exodus 20:7). Likewise: "Call upon Me in the day of trouble" (Psalm 50:15). But after you have prayed, you should know that just as you can have no doubts about the promise, so you should have no doubts about its being heard; for the foundation of the prayer is the promise—and not our will, not our worthiness, and not our merits.

From *Lectures on Genesis* (Luther's Works 4:361)

Have mercy on me, O God.

PSALM 51:1

Our Highest Occasion for Praying

he contrite and fearful are the people of grace, whose wounds the good Shepherd wants to bind up and heal, the Shepherd who gives His life for the sheep (John 10:11). Such people should not give in to the thoughts of their hearts, which persuade them that because of their sins they ought not to pray or hope for grace. With David they should cry out, "Have mercy on me, O God," for such people are well pleasing to God. . . . Look at David here. With his mouth open he breaks out in the words "Have mercy on me, O God." Thus he combines things that by nature are dissimilar, God and himself the sinner, the Righteous and the unrighteous. That gigantic mountain of divine wrath that so separates God and David, he crosses by trust in mercy and joins himself to God. That is really what our theology adds to the Law. To call on God and to say, "Have mercy," is not a great deal of work. But to add the particle "on me"—this is really what the Gospel inculcates so earnestly, and yet we experience how hard it is for us to do it. This "on me" hinders almost all our prayers, when it ought to be the only reason and highest occasion for praying.

From *Commentary on Psalm 51* (Luther's Works 12:317)

Have mercy on me, O God . . .
blot out my transgressions.

PSALM 51:1

Do Not Flee but Pray

I f anyone thinks that prayer should be put off until the mind is clean of impure thoughts, he is doing nothing but using his wisdom and strength to help Satan, who is already more than strong enough. . . . Against it we must maintain the example and teaching of this psalm, where we see that David, viewing his total impurity and his special sin of the flesh, does not flee from God, the way Peter foolishly said in the ship (Luke 5:8), "Depart from me, for I am a sinful man, O Lord." But with trust in mercy [David] breaks out in prayer and says, "Lord, if I am a sinner, just as I am, have mercy on me." Just because our hearts really feel sin, we ought to come to God through prayer all the more.

From *Commentary on Psalm 51* (Luther's Works 12:318)

Have mercy on me, O God,
according to Your steadfast love;
according to Your abundant mercy.

PSALM 51:1

True Theology about the True God

his picture of a gracious and merciful God is a picture that gives life. By it he shields the pronoun "on me," throws wrath into the corner, and says, "God is gracious." This is not the theology of reason, which counsels despair in the midst of sin. David feels sin and the wrath of God, and yet he says, "Have mercy on me, O God." Reason does not know this teaching, but the Holy Scriptures teach it, as you see in the first verse of this psalm. The individual words are purely and chastely placed, but they are the words of the Spirit which have life. From them spiritual men learn to distinguish between sinner and sinner, between God and God, and learn to reconcile the wrath of God or the wrathful God with man the sinner. . . . This is true theology about the true God and the true worship of God. It is false theology that God is wrathful to those who acknowledge their sins. Such a God is not in heaven or anywhere else, but is the idol of a perverse heart. The true God says (Ezekiel 33:11): "I do not want the death of the sinner, but that he might turn from his way and live." This is proved also by the present example of David and his prayer.

From *Commentary on Psalm 51* (Luther's Works 12:321–22)

Have mercy on me, O God,
according to Your steadfast love;
according to Your abundant mercy
blot out my transgressions.

PSALM 51:1

Grace Abounds

A true and penitent heart sees nothing but its sin and misery of conscience. He who still finds any counsel and help in himself cannot in all earnestness speak these words; for he is not yet altogether miserable but feels some comfort in himself, apart from God's mercy. The sense, then, is this: "O God, no man or creature can help or comfort me, so great is my misery; for my affliction is not bodily or temporal. Thou alone, therefore, who art God and eternal, canst help me. Have mercy on me, for without Thy mercy all things are terrible and bitter to me." *According to Thy abundant mercy blot out my transgressions.* These are all words of a true repentance which magnifies and multiplies the grace of God by magnifying and multiplying sin. The apostle says (Romans 5:20): "Where sin increased, grace abounded all the more."

From *Seven Penitential Psalms*, on Psalm 51 (Luther's Works 14:166)

Have mercy on me, O God,
according to Your steadfast love,
according to Your abundant mercy
blot out my transgressions.

PSALM 51:1

Our Only Salvation

ook how beautifully David combines these two things: first, that God is merciful, that is, that He freely blesses us undeserving ones; second, that He gives us the forgiveness of sins, which we accept by faith through the Holy Spirit and His promises. If God did not freely forgive, we should have no satisfaction and no remedy left. Not by our fasting nor by other works, not by angels nor by any other creature, is there salvation. Our only salvation is if we flee to the mercy of God and seek blessing and forgiveness from God, asking Him not to look at our sins and transgressions, but to close His eyes and to deal with us according to His steadfast love and abundant mercy. Unless God does this, we are not worthy of being granted one hour of life or one morsel of bread.

From *Commentary on Psalm 51* (Luther's Works 12:324)

Wash me thoroughly from my iniquity,
and cleanse me from my sin!

PSALM 51:2

The Christian Life

After [David] has asked for the forgiveness of sins as far as their guilt is concerned, and rejoices in God's mercy, he still asks for what remains: that he might be washed from his iniquities; that he might be granted the Holy Spirit, the power and gift that lives within the heart and cleanses the remnants of sin, which began to be buried through Baptism but have not been completely buried. This is the Christian life, as it is marvelously described in Colossians 3:1–3, that we seek the things that are above, as men who are dead to the world and whose life is hid in Christ; and in 2 Corinthians 7:1, that we "cleanse ourselves from every defilement of body and spirit." . . . Let us take care to be washed daily, to become purer day by day, so that daily the new man may arise and the old man may be crushed, not only for his death but also for our sanctification.

From *Commentary on Psalm 51* (Luther's Works 12:329–30)

Wash me thoroughly from my iniquity,
and cleanse me from my sin!

PSALM 51:2

Grace and Gifts

hese are the two parts of justification. The first is grace revealed through Christ, that through Christ we have a gracious God, so that sin can no longer accuse us, but our conscience has found peace through trust in the mercy of God. The second part is the conferring of the Holy Spirit with His gifts, who enlightens us against the defilements of spirit and flesh (2 Corinthians 7:1). Thus we are defended against the opinions with which the devil seduces the whole world. Thus the true knowledge of God grows daily, together with other gifts, like chastity, obedience, and patience. Thus our body and its lusts are broken so that we do not obey them.

From *Commentary on Psalm 51* (Luther's Works 12:331)

For I know my transgressions,
and my sin is ever before me.

PSALM 51:3

Let Christ Come and Console

avid gives this reason for requesting mercy: "because, " he says, "my sin is ever before me." That is, my sin drives me on, it will not give me rest or peace. Neither wine nor bread nor sleep will drive away this feeling of wrath and death. In such danger there is no other remedy left but that the mind set itself against this feeling and say: "Have mercy on me, O God. This is Thy time, the time that requires divine operation and the aid by which Thou dost help and console the sinner." What would it mean to be God if He knew nothing but to kill and to terrify? This is what Satan usually does, along with my sin and my own conscience. But to be God means to be capable of doing something beyond this and to do it, namely, that in such perils He consoles, lifts up, and makes alive, proving that He knows more and can do more than Satan, the Law, and I. If the law has frightened and whipped a hard heart until it has been led to a feeling of sin, let Christ come according to His promise and let Him console and lift up such a frightened one again.

From *Commentary on Psalm 51* (Luther's Works 12:336)

Against You, You only, have I sinned
and done what is evil in Your sight,
so that You may be justified in Your words
and blameless in Your judgment.

PSALM 51:4

Endure the Hand of God

avid fell in a horrible manner on account of his smugness and pride, in order that he might learn what sin is and be able to say from the heart: "Against Thee, Thee only, have I sinned. I see that we are all accused and condemned in Thy Law. But no man understands this. I, however, confess that I am such a great sinner, that I have deserved wrath and am worthy of eternal death; in short, that I am nothing else than sin, so that Thou art justified in Thy sentence and blameless in Thy judgment by others, who claim to be righteous" (cf. Psalm 51:4). Therefore let us learn to cling to the consolation that although guilt gnaws at our conscience and the goad of the Law and death torments us, yet this is not being done for our destruction but rather for our instruction and cleansing, in order that we may come to a knowledge of ourselves and our corruption. Therefore let us endure the hand of God, who cleanses us.

From *Lectures on Genesis* (Luther's Works 7:228–29)

Against You, You only, have I sinned
and done what is evil in Your sight. . . .
Create in me a clean heart, O God,
and renew a right spirit within me.

PSALM 51:4, 10

God's Promise

he Holy Spirit speaks the same way in Psalm 32:5: "I said, I will confess my transgression to the Lord; then Thou didst forgive the guilt of my sin." For the forgiveness of sins, therefore, this confession or knowledge is necessary, that we believe and confess that we are sinners and that the whole world is under the wrath of God. Thus the First Commandment denounces sin by its very promise. God promises: "I am the Lord, your God; that is, I am He through whom salvation will come to you against death and sin." This itself argues that our whole nature is punishable by death and sin. Why else should He promise that He will be God to us? Thus the Word of God—that is, both the Law and the Gospel, or promise—proves with clear and certain arguments that we are sinners and are saved by grace alone. If God promises life, it follows that we are under death. If He promises forgiveness of sins, it follows that sins dominate and possess us. Now, the wages of sin is death (Romans 6:23). Both the threats and the promises all show the same thing. . . . The divine voice and the promise of salvation were addressed to us men, against death, sin, and hell.

From *Commentary on Psalm 51* (Luther's Works 12:340)

Behold, I was brought forth in iniquity,
and in sin did my mother conceive me.

PSALM 51:5

The Nature of Man

ehold, it is so true that before Thee I am a sinner that even my nature, my very beginning, my conception, is sin, to say nothing of the words, works, thoughts, and life which follow. How could I be without sin if I was made in sin and sin is my nature and manner? I am an evil tree and by nature a child of wrath and sin. Therefore as long as this same nature and essence remains with us, we will be sinners and must say: "Forgive us our trespasses" until the body dies and is destroyed. Adam must die and decay before Christ can arise completely, and this begins with a penitent life and is completed through death. Hence death is a wholesome thing to all who believe in Christ; for it does nothing else than destroy and reduce to powder everything born of Adam, so that Christ alone may be in us.

From *Seven Penitential Psalms*, on Psalm 51 (Luther's Works 14:169)

Behold, You delight in truth in the inward being,
and You teach me wisdom in the secret heart.

PSALM 51:6

A Prayer That Never Ceases

he more a godly man feels his weakness, the more earnest he is in prayer. With this wisdom there simultaneously begins continuous prayer. Because the feeling of sin does not cease, sighing and prayer do not cease, asking that this wisdom may be made perfect. . . . The godly always talk as though they were sinners, as indeed they are; but because they are in the truth, they are loved by God and are in grace. This feeling of grace is weaker on account of the flesh. Therefore though they have the forgiveness of sins, they still pray and sigh for the forgiveness of sins. On the other hand, smug sinners say, "I thank Thee that I am not like other men," as that man in Luke (18:11) did. This is the reason why the godly man asks for grace, a man who is just beginning to be godly and has had a taste of this teaching. This taste provokes a greater thirst. The mind is not satisfied with the firstfruits of the Spirit (Romans 8:23), but would rather have the fullness, as Paul says: "Not as though I had already attained or were already perfect; but I follow after so that I may apprehend just as I also am apprehended" (Philippians 3:12). David acts the same way here; as though he were saying: "I know that Thou lovest that truth which Thou hast begun in me. Only make me to grasp it more certainly, and not to doubt."

From *Commentary on Psalm 51* (Luther's Works 12:358–59)

July 11

Purge me with hyssop, and I shall be clean;
wash me, and I shall be whiter than snow.

PSALM 51:7

The Stain of Sin Removed

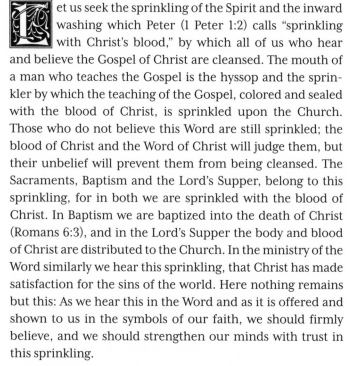et us seek the sprinkling of the Spirit and the inward washing which Peter (1 Peter 1:2) calls "sprinkling with Christ's blood," by which all of us who hear and believe the Gospel of Christ are cleansed. The mouth of a man who teaches the Gospel is the hyssop and the sprinkler by which the teaching of the Gospel, colored and sealed with the blood of Christ, is sprinkled upon the Church. Those who do not believe this Word are still sprinkled; the blood of Christ and the Word of Christ will judge them, but their unbelief will prevent them from being cleansed. The Sacraments, Baptism and the Lord's Supper, belong to this sprinkling, for in both we are sprinkled with the blood of Christ. In Baptism we are baptized into the death of Christ (Romans 6:3), and in the Lord's Supper the body and blood of Christ are distributed to the Church. In the ministry of the Word similarly we hear this sprinkling, that Christ has made satisfaction for the sins of the world. Here nothing remains but this: As we hear this in the Word and as it is offered and shown to us in the symbols of our faith, we should firmly believe, and we should strengthen our minds with trust in this sprinkling.

From *Commentary on Psalm 51* (Luther's Works 12:363)

Let me hear joy and gladness.

PSALM 51:8

The Hearing of Gladness

his verse is an outstanding testimony to the adornment of the ministry of the Word or of the spoken Word. Because [David] asks for the hearing of gladness, he clearly shows that the Word is necessary for consoling minds, whether it is brought by a brother or whether the Spirit suggests a word that once was heard. . . . This is the doctrine for which we bear not only the name "heresy" but punishment, namely, that we attribute everything to hearing or to the Word or to faith in the Word—these are all the same—and not to our works. Yes, in the use of the Sacraments and in confession we teach men to look mainly at the Word, so that we call everything back from our works to the Word. The hearing of gladness is in Baptism, when it is said: "I baptize you in the name of the Father and of the Son and of the Holy Spirit" (Matthew 28:19); "He who believes and is baptized will be saved" (Mark 16:16). The hearing of gladness is in the Lord's Supper, when it is said, "This is My body, which is given for you" (Luke 22:19). The hearing of gladness is in confession or, to call it by its more proper name, in absolution and the use of the Keys: "Have faith. Your sins are forgiven you through the death of Christ." . . . We call men back to the Word so that the chief part of the whole action might be the voice of God itself and the hearing itself.

From *Commentary on Psalm 51* (Luther's Works 12:369–70)

July 13

Let me hear joy and gladness;
let the bones that You have broken rejoice.

PSALM 51:8

The Most Effective Medicine

We must believe that our God is "the Father of mercies and of all comfort" (2 Corinthians 1:3). We must believe that "the Lord takes pleasure in those who fear Him, in those who hope in His steadfast love" (Psalm 147:11). We must know that He wants us to hope and that unless we hope, we shall undergo the punishment of eternal damnation. Why would He command us to hope unless He wanted to forgive us? Why would He surrender His only-begotten Son to such a shameful death if He did not want us to be saved through faith in Him? These statements and others like them are the true "sprinkling" and most effective medicine, with which the humbled bones are healed and the conscience strengthened. Those who doubt this will of God and look at their own unworthiness, at the fact that in holiness they are not equal to Paul and Peter—they can never have a quiet heart. . . . You should draw the conclusion that David drew earlier: "I would rather be a sinner than that God should be a liar. When I hope for mercy, I do so with confidence in His Word, which is preached about Christ."

From *Commentary on Psalm 51* (Luther's Works 12:373)

Restore to me the joy of Your salvation,
and uphold me with a willing spirit.

PSALM 51:12

Righteous, Sanctified, Restored

his is now the third gift of the Holy Spirit that [David] asks to be conferred upon him. It is surely a fine sequence that the prophet follows; as though he were to say: "I am already righteous by the grace of God, because I am sure of the forgiveness of sins. Then I am also sanctified, for I walk in the obedience and holiness of the Lord's commandments, and this gift of the Spirit is growing daily. Now a third still remains, that there come a courageous and strong mind, which will confess this justifier and sanctifier before the world and will not let itself be driven away from confession by any dangers." For this reason we have rendered this verse in German in such a way that he appears to ask for a mind that is "happy" and despises all dangers. "Happiness" here properly means constancy or a fearless mind that is not afraid of the world or Satan or even death. Such a mind we see in Paul, when he says with a happy, exulting, and full spirit (Romans 8:35): "Who shall separate us from the love of God?" It seems to me that in this passage David is asking for the same thing, that he might be able to confess his God freely, despising all the dangers of the world.

From *Commentary on Psalm 51* (Luther's Works 12:382–83)

Restore to me the joy of Your salvation,
and uphold me with a willing spirit.

PSALM 51:12

What Is Done Willingly Remains Firm

 hat is, [uphold me] with the Holy Spirit; He makes free and willing men, who do not serve God out of painful fear or improper love. For all who serve out of fear are not firmly established as long as the fear lasts. In fact, they are forced; they serve with resentment. If there were no hell and punishment, they would not serve at all. Even those who serve God out of love of reward or some good thing are not firmly established. For if they know of no reward or if the good thing does not materialize, they stop. All these have no joy in God's salvation. Nor do they have a clean heart or a right Spirit. They are lovers of themselves more than of God. Those, however, who serve God with a good and honest will are firm in their service of God, whether things go this way or that way, are sweet or sour. They are established and made firm by God with a noble, free, princely, and unconstrained will. . . . What is done because of force does not last, but what is done willingly remains firm.

From *Seven Penitential Psalms*, on Psalm 51
(Luther's Works 14:172–73)

My tongue will sing aloud of Your righteousness.

PSALM 51:14

A Joyful Announcement

his belongs to the proclamation of the Word; as if [David] were to say: "When I have thus been absolved before the world and justified before Thee and before men, then with my tongue I can extol, that is, joyfully announce and preach Thy righteousness, that is, Thy grace, by which Thou dost forgive sins and have mercy." . . . Remember that the righteousness of God is that by which we are justified, or the gift of the forgiveness of sins. This righteousness in God is pleasant, because it makes of God not a righteous Judge but a forgiving Father, who wants to use His righteousness not to judge but to justify and absolve sinners.

From *Commentary on Psalm 51* (Luther's Works 12:392)

O Lord, open my lips,
and my mouth will declare Your praise.

PSALM 51:15

Faith Opens the Mouth

his properly belongs to the Church, because the mouth of the whole Scripture has now been opened and the praise of Christ is publicly proclaimed. But it is opened by faith, without which it is closed and silent, as it is written: "I have believed, therefore have I spoken" (Psalm 116:10). For faith opens the mouth especially toward God (thus we are now speaking) and concerning God speaking in truth.

From *First Lectures on the Psalms*, on Psalm 51
(Luther's Works 10:242)

For You will not delight in sacrifice,
or I would give it;
You will not be pleased
with a burnt offering.

PSALM 51:16

Everything Is His

So there is nothing left for us to do for God but to thank Him. Whatever we are, live, and have is a gift of God, as Romans 11:35 says, "Who has given Him something first?" When we do everything we can, we do nothing but give back what we have received. What is so special about that? Here the self-righteous answer: "We want to merit something and to testify to free will." But that is to give His own back to God as though it were not His but ours. Even reason denounces as wicked and foolish the notion that someone who is generous not with his own property but with someone else's is doing anything special. What we should have done was to give glory to God by acknowledging that whatever we have or can do we possess by His blessing, since it is He who confirms us with His Spirit, who opens our mouth and fills it with His praise.

From *Commentary on Psalm 51* (Luther's Works 12:397)

The sacrifices of God are a broken spirit;
a broken and contrite heart, O God,
You will not despise.

PSALM 51:17

A God of the Humble and Troubled

 he present verse of this psalm sets forth this knowledge very pleasantly, that God is the kind of God who does nothing for any other purpose than to regard and love the contrite, vexed, and troubled, and that He is a God of the humble and the troubled. If anyone could grasp this definition with his heart, he would be a theologian. God cannot be grasped in His majesty and power. Therefore this definition opens the will of God to us, that He is a God not of death but of life, not of damnation but of salvation, not the enemy of the humble and the damned but their lover and helper—simply that He is the God of life, salvation, quiet, peace, and all comfort and happiness. Therefore the prophet comforts all the contrite that no more pleasing sacrifice can be brought to God than that we fear and tremble and in this trembling believe that God is kindly disposed and gracious.

From *Commentary on Psalm 51* (Luther's Works 12:403–4)

A broken and contrite heart, O God,

You will not despise.

Psalm 51:17

Nothing Else but Grace and Favor

his is a description or definition of God that is full of comfort: that in His true form God is a God who loves the afflicted, has mercy upon the humbled, forgives the fallen, and revives the drooping. How can any more pleasant picture be painted of God? Since God is truly this way, we have as much of Him as we believe. Then this verse simply rejects all other acts of worship and all works and simply calls us back to trust alone in the mercy and kindness of God, so that we believe that God is favorably disposed to us even when we seem to ourselves to be forsaken and distressed. . . . This theology must be learned through experience. Without experience it cannot be understood that the "poor in spirit" (Matthew 5:3) should know that they are in grace when they most feel the wrath of God, that in despair they should keep their hope in mercy, and in smugness they should keep their fear of God. As another passage says (Psalm 147:11): "The Lord takes pleasure in those who fear Him, in those who hope in His steadfast love." According to this verse, God is by definition nothing else than grace and favor, but only to the humble and afflicted.

From *Commentary on Psalm 51* (Luther's Works 12:406)

Do good to Zion in Your good pleasure;
build up the walls of Jerusalem.

PSALM 51:18

Fortified in Knowledge

 his is to build the walls so that they are firm, if in this way men learn to trust in the mercy of God and to receive grace. Those who have once begun, grow daily more and more. It is not enough just to begin in this knowledge. But because after they have received grace, Satan rages against the pious with all his ministers, angelic and human, therefore it is necessary to stand in battle and to have your mind fortified and confirmed more and more. Thus, as Satan does not stop attacking, so He also does not stop defending and fortifying, He who keeps Israel (Psalm 121:4). This verse contains a petition that grace might be bestowed and kept. Here, too, he attributes everything to the kindness of God, not to his own merits or efforts. He asks God to preserve the knowledge of this grace "according to His good pleasure" and to build the walls. That is, he asks for minds to be firm and well fortified in this knowledge so that in the time of battle they might stand up against the devil.

From *Commentary on Psalm 51* (Luther's Works 12:408)

O God, save me by Your name,
and vindicate me by Your might.

PSALM 54:1

Good Strife and Bad Peace

hrist] gained the upper hand over the devil and the yoke of his burden, not with bustle and worldly power but in the name of the Lord, so that, as in the case of Midian, the demons would kill and destroy themselves (Isaiah 9:4), for He sent a sword on earth and came to set a man against his father (Matthew 10:34–35). And so a good strife comes in order that a bad peace may be disrupted. This is what the prophet has in mind when he says (Isaiah 9:4): "Thou hast overcome the yoke of his burden, as in the day of Midian," for there the enemies were slain without the sword and the shedding of blood, simply by the sound of the trumpets (Judges 7:22). And the reason is: "Unto us a Child is born" (Isaiah 9:6). This is "humility," namely, in the name of the Lord. We must not attempt to be saved by our own powers or by the world's resources, but in humility, that is, in the name of the Lord, being fully aware of the fact that we possess absolutely nothing of salvation in ourselves, so that we may not trust in our bow, and our sword will not save us.

From *First Lectures on the Psalms*, on Psalm 54
(Luther's Works 10:250)

Vindicate me by Your might.

Psalm 54:1

Strength in Weakness

hat is the strength of God by which He saves us? It is that which is a stumbling block to the Jews and folly to the Gentiles. It is weakness, suffering, cross, persecution, etc. These are the weapons of God, these the strengths and powers by which He saves and judges us and distinguishes us from those who think otherwise. For according to the apostle, in 1 Corinthians 1:25, "the weakness of God is stronger than men, and the foolishness of God is wiser than men." ["The Gospel is the power of God unto salvation to everyone who believes" (Romans 1:16).] For this the world does not know, that patience, humility, cross, and persecution are strength and wisdom. Hence it is judged on this point and by its ignorance is distinguished from the saints, to whom Christ crucified is strength and wisdom; for through the cross and suffering that is both theirs and His they triumph over every force of the devil. Therefore this is truly God's power, and yet it is the weakness of men. For He has chosen what is weak to confound what is strong.

From *First Lectures on the Psalms* (Luther's Works 10:250)

Behold, God is my helper;
the Lord is the upholder of my life.

PSALM 54:4

When You Least Expect It

 ven if a man is persecuted, God is his helper. Man is openly persecuted, but God helps immediately and secretly. This is something the ungodly do not see. Only he whom God helps sees it. For man is out in the open, but God is invisible. Therefore He helps invisibly, and especially then, when it is least expected, that is, especially when God has apparently abandoned him to the hands of men. The nearer man is present outwardly, inflicting harm, the nearer God is present inwardly, providing help, so that in this way He might triumph over the devil by His own strength and by the patience of His saints. . . . Thus the apostle says (2 Corinthians 12:9–10): "For strength is made perfect in weakness," and "when I am weak, then I am strong." Again, "I will gladly boast of my weaknesses that the strength of Christ may dwell in me." . . . Consequently, *strength* at this place [Psalm 54:1], though it could be taken to mean uncreated power, is properly understood of that strength of God by which God strengthens and firms up His saints in adversities.

From *First Lectures on the Psalms* (Luther's Works 10:251–52)

Cast your burden on the Lord,
and He will sustain you.

PSALM 55:22

Let Him Care

 et us believe, hope, wait, pray; let us listen to the Word and cling to it. For this is what God wants when He says: "Cast your burden on the Lord, and He will sustain you" (Psalm 55:22). He will care for you. Do not fear. Likewise in Philippians 4:4–6: "Rejoice in the Lord always: again I will say: Rejoice. Let all men know your forbearance. The Lord is at hand. Have no anxiety about anything, but in everything by prayer and supplication with thanksgiving let your requests be made known to God." Let Him care. We are too stolid and wretched to be able to endure that mass of cares and worry about our affairs for even one moment. Therefore it is best to trust in God, even though we cannot be without tears, sorrow, and pain. What can we do against this? Our flesh is such that it is impossible for it not to sob, weep, grieve, and complain. . . . But let us sustain ourselves with the Word and faith, and let us not doubt that it has already been determined by God that He wants to turn these pains, troubles, and brief crosses . . . into everlasting and supreme joy. With this confidence and hope we shall very easily lighten our troubles and cares. "He will act" (Psalm 37:5).

From *Lectures on Genesis* (Luther's Works 8:47)

Men of blood and treachery
shall not live out half their days.

PSALM 55:23

Rely Not on Yourself

estruction comes promptly to the ungodly. They will be "like the grass on the housetops, which withers before it grows up" (Psalm 129:6). And the ungodly are like thorns on a branch, because the thorn dies when it is still in fresh sap. These comparisons show that the ungodly come to naught in the midst of a plan, when they are absorbed in their supreme and most eager endeavor, just like premature fruits that are very promising but dry up before the harvest comes. . . . Therefore note well that the ungodly always boast of themselves, for they are the proud crowns, the flowers *of glorious beauty, etc.* In that boasting they persist, they put forth much effort, they plan diligently for the future, but they "shall not live out half their days" (Psalm 55:23), that is, they will not accomplish half of what they boast with excessive certainty. On the contrary, they will perish in the midst of their effort. So you see our tyrants still self-confidently trying much but always fading out as they rely on their own ideas. For those, however, who hold fast to Christ and His Word every undertaking and plan will happily endure.

From *Lectures on Isaiah* (Luther's Works 16:220–21)

You have kept count of my tossings;

put my tears in Your bottle.

Are they not in Your book?

PSALM 56:8

God Hears Your Cry

e must not assume that God is disregarding our blood. We must not assume that God has no regard for our afflictions. "Our tears, too, He gathers into His bottle," as Psalm 56:8 says. And the cry of the blood of the godly penetrates the clouds and heaven until it arrives at God's throne and urges Him to avenge the blood of the righteous (Psalm 79:10). Just as these words have been written for our comfort, so they have been written to fill our adversaries with terror. What, in your opinion, is more awe-inspiring for those tyrants to hear than that the blood of those whom they have slain cries and incessantly accuses them before God? God is indeed long-suffering, especially now near the end of the world. Therefore sin reposes for a longer time. Vengeance does not follow immediately. But it surely is true that God is most profoundly outraged by this sin and will never allow it to go unpunished.

From *Lectures on Genesis* (Luther's Works 1:288–89)

In God, whose word I praise,
in the LORD, whose word I praise,
in God I trust; I shall not be afraid.
What can man do to me?.

PSALM 56:10–11

Where Our Hope Lies

hy is [the psalmist] not afraid? Because he hopes in God. On the contrary, one who puts his hope in man or gold, what is there left for him but to fear what man may do to him, namely, by taking away gold, friendships, honors, and other human goods? . . . To praise the words [of God] is to preach and hear them gladly, not indeed on their own account or because they come from a man (since every man is a liar and speaks lies), but in God, that is, because the words of God are both true and righteous, I will not be ashamed of them. But why do we not do this? Because we have put our trust in man and human affairs, which must necessarily perish, if you have proclaimed the words of God. Therefore we are afraid that man may do us some harm. This man, however, can fear no one but God, since he puts his hope in God.

From *First Lectures on the Psalms*, on Psalm 56
(Luther's Works 10:260–61)

God has spoken in His sanctuary.

PSALM 60:6 (RSV)

God Alone Should Speak

ut those who believe and whom the Holy Spirit touches through the Word know and receive the Holy Spirit, even though this is not at all apparent to the world. Therefore it is a different word and a far different government from that of a man. Beyond question it is the Word of God that speaks through us and through which He is powerful in the Church. He does all things with the Word alone, illumines, buoys up, and saves; for it is a Word of promise, grace, eternal life, and salvation. Concerning this efficacy of the Word the world knows nothing. Yet just as in the Gospel Christ casts out demons by means of the Word, so the minister says to the sinner: "I absolve you from all your sins." And this is the way it happens. For it is not the word of a man, at whose voice the devil would by no means flee. . . . But when the minister pronounces absolution, liberation from the devil and from sin is sure to follow. If the Holy Spirit grants you grace to believe, there He drives out Satan and death with one word. . . . We want to hear God alone [in the Church], as is stated in Psalm 60:6: "God has spoken in His sanctuary"; that is, in this assembly of the called and the baptized God alone should hear and speak. But where God is not heard, from that place you should flee as far as you can.

From *Lectures on Genesis* (Luther's Works 8:271)

God has spoken in His sanctuary.

PSALM 60:6 (RSV)

The Most Precious Gem

f we knew of a church somewhere in the world where God's voice could be heard, how we would run off to it! And yet we could hear nothing other than what we hear at home in our own church from the pastor. Among the other blessings and gifts of God that he has received, David counts this as the foremost blessing and highest jewel: that God has given him a kingdom in which the Word of God is taught, as he says in Psalms 60 [:6] and 108 [:7]: "God is speaking in His sanctuary; therefore, I am glad." We, too, can make the same boast and say that God has given us the most precious gem, His dear, holy Word. Therefore, the holy Christian Church is a beautiful and glorious thing, because there we are able to hear what God is speaking and requires of us: that we should repent, be baptized in His name, and believe in His Son, Jesus Christ, and demonstrate our faith with Christian fruits, be obedient to God, and serve our neighbor. Whoever touches a Christian believer, touches the apple of God's eye [Zechariah 2:8]. Whoever believes and does thus shall be God's house and dwelling place.

From *Sermons on John 20* (Luther's Works 69:405–6)

[God] only is my rock and my salvation, my fortress;
I shall not be greatly shaken.

PSALM 62:2

A Rare Soul Sings Such a Song

avid] calls God his "Rock" or his "Refuge" because he sets the sure and certain confidence of his heart on Him. He calls Him his "Salvation" because he does not doubt but believes that God will help him with happiness and salvation, though Saul and all men should forsake him and refuse to give him anything, even a place to stay. He calls Him his "Defense" because he hopes and is sure that God will defend him against all evil, though Saul and all his sycophants should seek to destroy and kill him. What a fine soul it is that can sing such a song to God! But also what a rare soul it is!

From *Four Psalms of Comfort*, on Psalm 62 (Luther's Works 14:234)

Trust in [God] at all times, O people;
pour out your heart before Him;
God is a refuge for us.

PSALM 62:8

God Can Take It

 f you are lacking something, well, here is good advice: "Pour out your heart before Him." Voice your complaint freely, and do not conceal anything from Him. Regardless of what it is, just throw it in a pile before Him, as you open your heart completely to a good friend. He wants to hear it, and He wants to give you His aid and counsel. Do not be bashful before Him, and do not think that what you ask is too big or too much. Come right out with it, even if all you have is bags full of need. Out with everything; God is greater and more able and more willing than all our transgressions. Do not dribble your requests before Him; God is not a man whom you can overburden with your begging and asking. The more you ask, the happier He is to hear you. Only pour it all out, do not dribble or drip it. For He will not drip or dribble either, but He will flood you with a veritable deluge. "God is a Refuge for us," our Hiding Place, He and no one else. All the others are too puny for us to pour out our hearts before them.

From *Four Psalms of Comfort*, on Psalm 62
(Luther's Works 14:237–38)

If riches increase, set not your heart on them.

PSALM 62:10

Always Cling to God Alone

t is a great thing and the work of a rich spirit not to forget God when affairs prosper, and to conduct yourself, with Paul, as if you had nothing, to use the world as if you did not use it (1 Corinthians 7:30–31), to know how to endure want and to abound, to know how to be low and to be high (Philippians 4:12), and, with the prophet, not to attach the heart to wealth when it abounds, and not to become vain (Psalm 62:10) but to cling to God alone.

From *Lectures on Deuteronomy* (Luther's Works 9:95)

O God, You are my God; earnestly I seek You;
my soul thirsts for You; my flesh faints for You.

PSALM 63:1

Sleepers and Seekers

he watch is twofold, the body's and the soul's. The soul keeps watch when it does not sin but earnestly and speedily does the works of light. Romans 13:11: "It is now the hour for us to rise from sleep." This watch begins with the light, that is, at the spiritual daybreak of faith, by which we are enlightened by Christ when the sun of righteousness arises through good admonition in the soul. Ephesians 5:14: "Rise, O sleeper." On the contrary, to act lukewarmly is to sleep. And such people do not know how to thirst for the Lord or for righteousness. *How many ways my flesh thirsts for Thee!* Augustine explains: The flesh needs many things even for this life, and this, too, it seeks from God, because not only spiritual things but also earthly things are to be sought from no one but God. But this is expressed in a very strong way, for he does not say, "I thirst for Thy gifts," but "for Thee," so that even the flesh is understood as thirsting for spiritual things, namely, God's glorification.

From *First Lectures on the Psalms*, on Psalm 63, where the comments follow the Latin translation, which reads: "O God, my God, to Thee do I watch at break of day. For Thee my soul hath thirsted; for Thee my flesh, O how many ways!" (Luther's Works 10:302)

Because Your steadfast love is better than life,
my lips will praise You.

PSALM 63:3

How Precious Is the Grace of God

ee how greatly he esteems and magnifies the mercy of God. For in the judgment of all there is nothing more precious than life. Of all things it is especially sought, and so are all things for its sake, so that life is commonly called a noble thing. But here he says that God's mercy is "better," not than gold, silver, purple, and jewels, nor only "one life," but better than "all lives" that anyone could have and contemplate. For the plural "lives" embraces all. From this it is clear how precious we should consider the grace of God, so that we ought to despise even a thousand lives for it and undergo a thousand deaths for it. But alas, how many there are who do not only not despise one life or one death, but not even one sickness or health for its sake, yea, rather choose one denarius and sometimes one word than to keep that mercy! Therefore, if it is better than lives, we are surely taught here to keep it in such a way that, if necessary, we would be prepared to lose all riches, honors, and pleasures and to undergo every reproach, poverty, and affliction, as the kind of people who should despise lives and deaths for its sake.

From *First Lectures on the Psalms*, on Psalm 63
(Luther's Works 10:305–6)

My mouth will praise You with joyful lips,
when I remember You upon my bed,
and meditate on You in the watches of the night.

PSALM 63:5–6

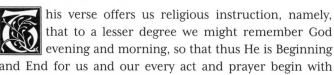

Beginning, Middle, and End

his verse offers us religious instruction, namely, that to a lesser degree we might remember God evening and morning, so that thus He is Beginning and End for us and our every act and prayer begin with Him and come to a close in Him, as the Church prays and the holy fathers teach; indeed, that He also be the middle. "From Him and through Him, or with Him, and to Him are all things" (Romans 11:36). From Him, as to the beginning; through Him, or with Him, as to the middle; and to Him, as to the end, all our activities should be done and completed. And so "evening and morning and at noon we will declare" (Psalm 55:17), that is, at the end, the beginning, and the middle. . . . Note, however, that he attributes remembrance to the evening and meditation to the morning, and thereby in a striking way shows us the difference. For since the vexation and the tickling of the flesh are wont to be aroused upon the bed for the idle . . . remembrance is necessary, and not a perfunctory recall of God, but one must remain and go to sleep fixed on the meditation of God, so that it might somehow last also during sleep.

From *First Lectures on the Psalms*, on Psalm 63
(Luther's Works 10:304–5)

Praise is due to You, O God, in Zion. . . .
O You who hear prayer,
to You shall all flesh come.

PSALM 65:1–2

When You Gather in My Name

 salm 65] calls Him a "hearer of prayer" because our Lord God's proper work is to hear prayers and help those who cry to Him. Therefore, it says, "All flesh shall come to You." No other house in the world had borne the name "a house of prayer," except for the temple in Jerusalem. If anyone lived far from Jerusalem or was unable to travel there quickly, he knelt down and simply faced the temple and made his prayer toward Jerusalem [cf. Daniel 6:10]. . . . But the true Church has been established for prayer. We also have here in Wittenberg our temple, where we gather to hear Christ's Word, receive Baptism, the Supper, and Absolution. And Christ Himself is also here, as He says in chapter 18 [:20] of Matthew: "Wherever two or three are gathered in My name, there I am in the midst of them." And the Lord Christ should be sought nowhere except where such a group gathers, where the Gospel is preached purely, and where people have the Sacraments and the power of the Keys in the proper understanding and practice. Then it is certain that Christ is there. Apart from that, He has no certain place or location. This is true, for the temple is now as wide as the world. For the Word is being preached and the Sacraments are being administered everywhere.

From *Sermons on Matthew 18–24* (Luther's Works 68:88, 93)

August 7

Thou crownest the year with Thy goodness;
and Thy paths drop fatness.

PSALM 65:11 (KJV)

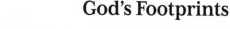

God's Footprints

his means that the saints, through whom and in whom Christ works and dwells, are His tracks, as He says, Leviticus 26:11–12: "I will dwell in them and walk among them and be their God, and they will be My people." Furthermore, in Ezekiel 43:7: "The place of My throne and the place of the soles of My feet, where I dwell in the midst of the children of Israel forever." Again, Psalm 132:7: "We will adore in the place where His feet stood." Therefore works of strength are the going and passing of God. When we therefore accomplish them in the body, God is imprinting His footprints on us. For through such works it is recognized that God is in us, as the passing of a man is known by his footprints. Therefore the footprints of truth, wisdom, and righteousness, which God is in us, become apparent through the works of such things in our body. And so the earth is His footstool, on which His footprints are impressed. The soul, however, is His throne, because it is heaven. Therefore such tracks drip with fatness, that is, they are flooded with spiritual joy from above, since every good work gladdens the conscience and the soul.

From *First Lectures on the Psalms*, on Psalm 65
(Luther's Works 10:315–16)

I cried to Him with my mouth,
and high praise was on my tongue.

PSALM 66:17

The Majesty of His Name

e theologians commonly mention the holy name of God so irreverently, especially in our arguing and even in our praying, because we do not know how to extol with our tongue. And we argue so boldly about the Trinity of Persons, even though their three names are exceedingly formidable and should never be uttered without a trembling of the heart. We argue about the formal and real distinction the way a cobbler argues about his leather. I believe that we would be better instructed by God inwardly if we would take these so holy names into our mouth with humility and reverence than when we move ahead foolhardily through our subtleties. For thus the saints, when they have taken God's name into their mouth, are inwardly so stunned by the majesty of Him whom they have mentioned openly that they repent, as it were, for having taken His name into their mouth. This is what it means properly to extol with the tongue.

From *First Lectures on the Psalms*, on Psalm 66
(Luther's Works 10:322)

Blessed be God, because He has not rejected my prayer
or removed His steadfast love from me!

PSALM 66:20

While You Speak, He Hears

herefore let us persuade ourselves without any hesitation that God is ever so ready and prompt to hear our prayer and to grant what we ask for, as Psalm 66:20 praises Him: "Blessed be God, because He has not rejected my prayer or removed His steadfast love from me!" And the name of God that is suitable to the highest degree and proper is Hearer of Prayer. Indeed, it is just as proper as the familiar name Creator of heaven and earth. And God not only hears a prayer that is offered without specifying particulars; but let us maintain that even at the very moment a prayer is uttered that which is asked for is being done or has been done, just as very many ever so pleasing words of the psalms testify, such as "To Thee they cried, and were saved" (Psalm 22:5), where simply no particular at all is added. Consequently, the one who cries out is here; God, who hears is there. Just cry out, and you will be heard, as Psalm 34:5 urges: "Look to Him, and be radiant; so your faces shall never be ashamed." And from this source Isaiah has taken the very beautiful promise (65:24): "Before they call, I will answer; while they are yet speaking, I will hear."

From *Lectures on Genesis* (Luther's Works 4:267)

God shall arise, His enemies shall be scattered;
and those who hate Him shall flee before Him!

PSALM 68:1

Five Times Christ Rises

od, that is, Christ, rises, first, when He becomes incarnate, for then He began to stand and take on the form of a servant, so that He who before then had rested in the bosom of the Father might serve us and fight for us. Psalm 12:5: "I will now arise, says the Lord." Second, when He rises from the dead, as here. Third, in a tropological sense, when a person's dead faith comes back to life in the soul, namely, when he is converted to repentance by faith in Christ. For as Christ is crucified, so He also rises, sleeps, wakes, acts, and rests in us. Fourth, as often as He offers help in accomplishment. Psalm 3:7: "Arise, O Lord, save me, O my God!" So blessed Augustine explains it. Fifth, at the Last Judgment.

From *First Lectures on the Psalms*, on Psalm 68
(Luther's Works 10:324)

As smoke is driven away, so You shall drive them away;
as wax melts before fire, so the wicked shall perish before God!

PSALM 68:2

Fire and Wind

ere we find two beautiful similes. Smoke is dissipated by the wind, wax is melted by fire. This is an allusion to the Holy Spirit, who is a fire and a wind (Luke 3:16–17). . . . This wind and this fire came from heaven to earth after Christ's resurrection and now converts the world through the Gospel. For such great enemies, who presume to contend against heaven and earth, it must be a disgrace to be compared to smoke and wax. Smoke rises, flutters about freely in the air, and acts as if it wanted to blind the sun and to storm heaven itself. But actually what does it amount to? A mere breath of air will dissipate this arrogant smoke, and no one knows what has become of it. Similarly, all the enemies of the truth plot pretentiously and rage furiously; but in the end they fare the way the smoke does against the wind and the sky. . . . Wax is heavy and hard, comparable to stone or wood; but, faced by fire, it flows away like water, yes, it is consumed and disappears. Likewise all enemies of the truth flourish at first. In the beginning they seem more solid than the Rock, Christ Himself (1 Corinthians 10:4). But when they encounter the fire of the divine Word and Spirit (Jeremiah 23:29; Luke 3:16), that is the end for them—a merciful end if they choose, an unmerciful one if they refuse.

From *Commentary on Psalm 68* (Luther's Works 13:3–4)

Sing to God, sing praises to His name;
lift up a song to Him who rides through the deserts;
His name is the LORD; exult before Him!

PSALM 68:4

Highway to Heaven

ince we do not have Christ in our midst today physically, but are only walking in faith, we cannot sing praises to His person or address His person in song. But we sing praises to His name; this we praise, this we address, this we preach and confess. . . . This relates to all the sermons of the sweet Gospel which proclaim God's grace, honor, and praise. . . . But the Gospel and the proclamation of God's name in Christ do construct a solid highway, for faith furnishes a good foundation and dries out every foul marsh of the wicked flesh. And now Christ rides on them; that is, He performs in them His works, which are love, joy, peace, kindness, meekness, chastity (Galatians 5:22). Let us note the word "ride." He does not stand still; for the life in faith implies progress, a walk or journey toward heaven into another life.

From *Commentary on Psalm 68* (Luther's Works 13:4–5)

Father of the fatherless and protector of widows
is God in His holy habitation.

PSALM 68:5

Seen by Eyes of Faith

Because of your faith, you may be forced here on earth to leave father, friend, life, goods, and honor. You may have to become poor and wretched orphans and widows, suffering violence and injustice at the hands of all. Then you will find comfort in the knowledge that the Lord of creation is the Father of such orphans and the Avenger of such widows, that He is not distant, but near you, and that you need not seek Him in Jerusalem or Rome. He resides in the midst of His Christians; there He is surely to be found. But He is not content just to dwell there. No, He also wants to be a God among them, a God to whom all hearts may flee, who freely gives all, does all, and is able to do all; in brief, who is all that you should have in a God. But this calls for faith. For the Father, the Judge, God, is present invisibly. His dwelling is holy; that is, it is set apart and can be seen only with the eyes of faith. If you believe that He is your Father, your Judge, your God, then this is what He is.

From *Commentary on Psalm 68* (Luther's Works 13:6–7)

August 14

Rain in abundance, O God, You shed abroad;
You restored Your inheritance as it languished.

PSALM 68:9

Gospel Raindrops

his is to signify that the preaching of the New Testament, since Christ's true exodus from this world, will far excel that of the old Law. For while it rained sparsely there, it is to rain in abundance here; while it descended only on one spot there, here it will be diffused over all parts of the world; while it affected only one nation there, Israel, here a general shower will be dispersed over all, Gentile and Jew. The Gospel will not be confined to one country and one nation as the proclamation of the Law was. Those drops were released by the heavens, too, by the angels through Moses, in God's stead, as St. Paul declares in Galatians 4. But this rain Thou, O God, wilt distribute Thyself. "Free rain" [cf. Psalm 67:10 Vulgate] could also be interpreted to mean that the teaching of the Gospel is free and that it engenders free hearts, which are no longer bound to externals but live freely by faith. That is the Christian liberty of which Psalm 110:3 speaks: "Thy people will be spontaneous."

From *Commentary on Psalm 68* (Luther's Works 13:10)

Your flock found a dwelling in it;
in Your goodness, O God, You provided for the needy.

PSALM 68:10

Thy Loving-Kindness

ince the members of Christ's flock are subjected to much suffering for their faith's sake and are humbled and oppressed and despised by all, God manifests His loving-kindness toward them so that after much humiliation they taste and experience ever more how good, loving, and kind God is. Thus the many abasements and sufferings teach the simple believers to become ever better acquainted with God, to trust Him and believe in Him and thereby grow strong and rich and established in their confidence in God's kindness. This is what the psalmist means when he says: "In Thy goodness, O God, Thou wilt provide for the humbled." That is: "Through his humiliation and suffering, Thy goodness, O God, will find a way to him. He will now surrender his own goodness and no longer count it gain, solely intent upon collecting a treasure for himself in Thy goodness." This is nothing else than a growth in faith (Romans 5:3–4). To this the flock of Moses, the works-righteous, and the disciples of the Law will never attain; for it must be effected by faith and the free rain. Thus man prepares nothing but evil for himself. All the good accruing to him comes from God.

From *Commentary on Psalm 68* (Luther's Works 13:11–12)

The Lord gives the word;
the women who announce the news are a great host.

PSALM 68:11

Ready for Battle

he psalmist uses a martial term: "great is the host," not a rabble but a host armed and arrayed for battle. Here we find an intimation that the Word of God does not generate peace but strife on earth. This is borne out by Christ's words in Matthew 10:34: "I have not come to bring peace on earth, but a sword." The soldiers and the warfare of the New Testament are not of a secular but of a spiritual nature. And the weapons are not sword and armor, steed and mount, but solely the Word of God, as St. Paul declares, 2 Corinthians 10:4: "For the weapons of our warfare are not physical, but have divine power to destroy strongholds." Therefore, although the psalmist uses the military term "hosts," he also calls them "evangelists," whose weapons are the Word and its proclamation. It is clear that the Gospel alone conquers the world for the faith.

From *Commentary on Psalm 68* (Luther's Works 13:12)

Our God is a God of salvation;
and to GOD, the Lord, belongs escape from death.

PSALM 68:20 (RSV)

Snatched from Death

t would have been bootless if He had assumed our burden and conquered death only for Himself. But as matters stand, He presented us with His victory, conquering sin and death in our behalf, so that we, who were held captive by the evil spirit and lived in sin and death without any God and Lord, henceforth would have our own Lord and God, who reigns over us in such a manner that through Him we were saved and escaped death. What more fervent wish does mankind entertain than deliverance from death? And now our God has become just such a Lord and God, who satisfies this ardent longing of all men for escape from death and for salvation. As this verse sets forth, His kingdom means nothing else than accomplishing our salvation and being a God who snatches us from death.

From *Commentary on Psalm 68* (Luther's Works 13:22)

Our God is a God of salvation,
*and to G*OD, *the Lord, belong deliverances from death.*

PSALM 68:20

The Departure of Death

 here is a difference between "the Lord of life" and "the Lord of the departure of death," for this is said more specifically concerning the future immortality and incorruption. . . . The "departure of death" is a going out of death altogether and a going into the total life. This is what it means for death to be swallowed up, not just to be bitten, but to be swallowed up in victory and to be left altogether behind the back. This is now going on in the spirit, but in the future it will also happen in the body, and so the Lord Jesus is truly the God of life, and not of life only, but also of the departure of death, that is, of immortal life without the admixture of death or mortality, but life pure and simple. Thus we may go out of death, and death itself may depart, that is, be done with. For the departure is the end. The Lord is the End and Finisher of death. Yet at the same time redemption is given expression by it. For the Lord of life is understood as the Creator of life. But the Lord of the departure of death is the Recreator of the life that has fallen into death. So Psalm 65:8: "Thou wilt make the outgoings of the morning and the evening joyful," that is, "the fact that the spirit and the flesh go out from death is a sweet message, and through it Thou wilt make Thy faithful ones joyful."

From *First Lectures on the Psalms*, on Psalm 68
(Luther's Works 10:337–38)

Your procession is seen, O God,
the procession of my God, my King, into the sanctuary.

PSALM 68:24

My God and My King

od's "processions" represent His work, which is steadfast love and faithfulness. Thus we read in Psalm 25:10: "All the paths of the Lord are steadfast love and faithfulness." However, it requires great skill to recognize God's work and to let Him work in us, so that all our work will in the end be God's and not our own. This is the proper celebration of the Sabbath, to rest from our own works and to be full of God's works. All this is effected in us through faith, which teaches that we count for naught and our work no less. This is what the psalmist has in mind when he says: "Thy processions are seen and recognized." And the words "my God, my King" point to Christ, who is our King according to His human nature and who is God from eternity. No one can say "My God and my King" unless he regards God with the eyes of faith, not only as a God, not only as a King, but as his God and his King, as the God and King of his salvation. Neither is it possible to recognize the ways and works of God in the absence of that faith. Faith renders Him my God and my King, and brings me to a realization that all my works are, after all, not mine but God's. . . . Those who utter these words, "My God and my King," in holiness are truthful and sincere; they are the real believers.

From *Commentary on Psalm 68* (Luther's Works 13:25–26)

August 20

Awesome is God from His sanctuary;
the God of Israel—He is the one who gives
power and strength to His people.

PSALM 68:35

God's Holy Dwelling Place

veryone, therefore, really ought to stand in awe of [God's saints] and honor them, since they form God's holy dwelling place. For the word "saints" refers to a holy place and dwelling here. The holy Christians make up the holy dwelling place of God in the New Testament, where God is no longer confined to cities and buildings as He was in the Old Testament. These Christians are sanctified far more perfectly than Solomon's temple, sanctified with the Holy Spirit Himself, and anointed with the living oil of God's grace. Whoever touches them also touches the apple of God's eye (Zechariah 2:8). This assurance is given us to console and fortify us in the days of persecution. Whatever persecution is visited on us, whom they despise, is really inflicted on God, who will deal terribly with them. The appellation "the God of Israel" signifies that our God is none other than the one whom the Israelites once had. It is Christ, whom the Israelites once possessed and of whom we now also say: He who does these things is no longer only Israel's God but the God of the whole world.

From *Commentary on Psalm 68*, where the comments follow the Latin translation, which reads: "God is wonderful in His saints: the God of Israel is He who will give power and strength to His people." (Luther's Works 13:36–37)

Save Me, O God!
For the waters have come up to My neck.
PSALM 69:1

Christ in Our Place

ave Me. This general word gives expression to all misery. Therefore [Christ] seeks to be set free from all of them. It is to be noted, however, that Christ always has a simple response to us for our double request. . . . Since [Christ] was innocent even of the punishment, His punishment was for our sin. Hence when He Himself prays to be freed from punishments, He is at the same time praying that we might be freed from sins and punishments, since He would have no punishments if it were not for our sins and our punishments. Thus the psalm is speaking about Him and about us at the same time, and it must be read with the most devoted love for Christ. Let us, I say, understand our sins and His punishment at the same time, expressed in the same words. Hence the *waters* are the very punishments and sufferings of Christ, but at the same time they are our iniquities.

From *First Lectures on the Psalms*, on Psalm 69
(Luther's Works 10:354)

O God, You know My folly;
the wrongs I have done are not hidden from You.

PSALM 69:5

Our Highest Comfort

he Holy Spirit is speaking in the person of Christ and testifying in clear words that He has sinned or has sins. These testimonies of the psalms are not the words of an innocent one; they are the words of the suffering Christ, who undertook to bear the person of all sinners and therefore was made guilty of the sins of the entire world. Therefore Christ not only was crucified and died, but by divine love sin was laid upon Him. . . . And this is our highest comfort, to clothe and wrap Christ this way in my sins, your sins, and the sins of the entire world, and in this way to behold Him bearing all our sins. . . . For God has laid our sins, not upon us but upon Christ, His Son. If they are taken away by Him, then they cannot be taken away by us. All Scripture says this, and we confess and pray the same thing in the Creed when we say: "I believe in Jesus Christ, the Son of God, who suffered, was crucified, and died for us." This is the most joyous of all doctrines and the one that contains the most comfort. It teaches that we have the indescribable and inestimable mercy and love of God.

From *Lectures on Galatians* (Luther's Works 26:279–80)

Let not the flood sweep over Me,
or the deep swallow Me up,
or the pit close its mouth over Me. . . .
According to Your abundant mercy, turn to Me.

PSALM 69:15–16

Draw Me Out, Set Me Free

e magnifies His mercy with us. But those who do not occupy themselves with such reflection consider His mercy of little value, in opposition to them Jonah 2:8 says: "Those who are vain forsake their own mercy." For he himself said with such deep emotion (Jonah 2:3): "I cried to Thee out of the belly of hell." . . . Thus all the prayers of the Psalms which are uttered in the person of Christ as being in hell, are also uttered in the person of the saints, as descending to hell in their mind and heart. Thus "the wicked shall be turned into hell, all the nations that forget God" (Psalm 9:17). For that reason whoever does not die with Christ and descend to hell will never rise and ascend with Him. Therefore He prays here, "Draw Me out, set Me free." All these are the most earnest prayers also of those who are occupied with meditating on hell, just as they are the prayers of Christ who was literally in hell.

From *First Lectures on the Psalms*, on Psalm 69
(Luther's Works 10:372)

Answer me, O LORD, for Your steadfast love is good;
according to Your abundant mercy, turn to me.

PSALM 69:16

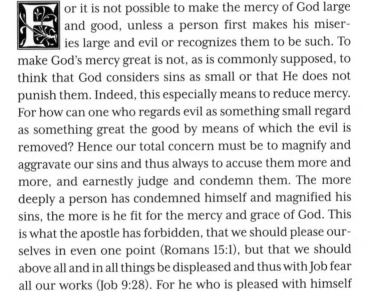

Fit for Mercy and Grace

or it is not possible to make the mercy of God large and good, unless a person first makes his miseries large and evil or recognizes them to be such. To make God's mercy great is not, as is commonly supposed, to think that God considers sins as small or that He does not punish them. Indeed, this especially means to reduce mercy. For how can one who regards evil as something small regard as something great the good by means of which the evil is removed? Hence our total concern must be to magnify and aggravate our sins and thus always to accuse them more and more, and earnestly judge and condemn them. The more deeply a person has condemned himself and magnified his sins, the more is he fit for the mercy and grace of God. This is what the apostle has forbidden, that we should please ourselves in even one point (Romans 15:1), but that we should above all and in all things be displeased and thus with Job fear all our works (Job 9:28). For he who is pleased with himself cannot stand in the fear of God and be without presumption.

From *First Lectures on the Psalms*, on Psalm 69
(Luther's Works 10:368)

Make haste, O God, to deliver me!
*O L*ord*, make haste to help me!*

Psalm 70:1

Pray with All Your Heart

herefore this psalm, whose opening words we recite so often day and night, is to be commended to all priests, so that they will not mumble it so coldly and perfunctorily, but help the Church of God with this prayer with all their heart. . . . First, against the vices and sins of the past, lest they lead you to despair. Second, against the reviling of the lust of the flesh and its works. Third, against the attractions of the world and the promptings of the devil, lest they prevail over you, but that you may persevere in hope and faith, in grace and union with Christ. Say: "Lord God, be pleased to deliver me." For this prayer is the shield, spear, thunderbolt, and defense against every attack of fear, presumption, lukewarmness, security, etc., which are especially dominant today. . . . Then, so that you might be able to prevail over them, and this quickly, to destroy such evil impulses, add: "Lord, make haste to help me." For haste is necessary to drive them away, especially in our age of defects, security, and lukewarmness.

From *First Lectures on the Psalms,* on Psalm 70
(Luther's Works 10:391–92)

May all who seek You rejoice and be glad in You!
May those who love Your salvation say evermore,
"God is great!"

We, Not Me

he Lord is magnified by regarding His blessings as great. Second, by fearing His great wrath, that thus He might be grandly loved and grandly feared. And in these two things we must make progress without end. Therefore he says, "Let the Lord always be magnified." Third, by asking great and many things from Him. Therefore in praying no one should pray for himself alone or of himself alone, nor should he pray for some one gift, but prayer should be made for all that is good and for all men. Otherwise it would mean to narrow His goodness and enclose it for one man. Hence He taught us to pray, "Forgive us our sins" (Matthew 6:12). He says "us," which means all, and all things, which are nevertheless countless and exceedingly great. Therefore no one should pray only for himself.

From *First Lectures on the Psalms*, on Psalm 70
(Luther's Works 10:393–94)

*In You, O L*ORD*, do I take refuge; let me never be put to shame!*
In Your righteousness deliver me and rescue me;
incline Your ear to me, and save me!
Be to me a rock of refuge, to which I may continually come.

PSALM 71:1–3

Save Me, O God

irst, one who has not yet lost hope in mammon and all the world and himself cannot *hope* in God. . . . Second, whoever does not hope in God who justifies the ungodly cannot be delivered in God's righteousness or be rescued. . . . Then follows *and rescue me*, namely, from this body, or with regard to the body. For even when the soul has been delivered through righteousness, we are still held through the body in the dangers and the captivity and exile of this life. Third, no one can say *and save me* except one who understands and acknowledges himself to be weak and sick and condemned. Therefore those who consider themselves saved and who are pleased with their own health in the flesh, in the world, and in riches do not pray, even if they have uttered these words. Fourth, having now been delivered, saved, and justified, there remains that the person be sent into battle and probation. But here he needs as his protector Him who was his Savior, for He who has begun is the One who also completes it (Philippians 1:6). Therefore he says, *Be Thou unto me a God, a protector* (v. 3), namely, from attacks.

From *First Lectures on the Psalms*, on Psalm 71
(Luther's Works 10:395–96)

August 28

Be to me a rock of refuge, to which I may continually come;
You have given the command to save me,
for You are my rock and my fortress.

PSALM 71:3

My God and My Protector

ote the remarkable construction of the statement. He does not say, "Be unto me merely a protector" or "merely a God," but both at the same time. He is embattled by great danger, and the matter of this battle is so difficult that he cannot survive unless God is the protector. For the strength by which the world is overcome is a divine strength, and one cannot stand by any protection except the divine. But how shall he who has made flesh his arm say this word? Therefore he must first forsake all and turn to God alone. Then follows *and a fortified place* where I may steadfastly defend myself, so that I who have already been saved by Thee in hope may also be saved in reality. For salvation in hope is in vain unless one arrives at the reality. But for this purpose God the protector and a fortified place are necessary, so that what is hoped for may not be lost or driven out by temptation.

From *First Lectures on the Psalms*, on Psalm 71, where the comments follow the Latin translation, which reads: "Be Thou unto me a God, a protector, and a place of strength: that Thou mayst make me safe." (Luther's Works 10:396)

But I will hope continually
and will praise You yet more and more.

PSALM 71:14

In the Good Times and the Bad

 ut I will always hope, even when they seek evil for me. Hope is easier in good times but more difficult in bad times. Therefore only a saint always hopes, always blesses, like Job. The next words express the same truth: *I will add to all Thy praise*, as if to say: "I will praise Thee not only in good times, when there is material for total praise, but also in bad times," when there appears to be no material for praise, except for those who live in hope and in the present evil and visible things see and hope for invisible things at the same time. One who does not see such things, but sees only the present, cannot praise God except in good times, for he does not know what evil is and what it is for. Therefore he cannot add to all praise like the one who hopes. Such a one knows that these things happen not only not unjustly but even serve a useful purpose, which those people do not realize.

From *First Lectures on the Psalms*, on Psalm 71
(Luther's Works 10:398)

Your righteousness, O God,
reaches the high heavens.
You who have done great things,
O God, who is like You?

PSALM 71:19

Reaching the Heart and the Heavens

 n this verse at last the correct distinction between divine and human righteousness is depicted. For the righteousness of God reaches up to the heavens of heavens and causes us to reach. It is righteousness even to the highest, namely, of reaching the highest. Not so the human righteousness, but rather it reaches down to the lowest. This is so because he who exalts himself will be humbled, and he who humbles himself will be exalted. But now the whole righteousness of God is this: To humble oneself into the depth. Such a one comes to the highest, because he first went down to the lowest depth. Here he properly refers to Christ, who is the power of God and the righteousness of God through the greatest and deepest humility. Therefore He is now in the highest through supreme glory.

From *First Lectures on the Psalms*, on Psalm 71
(Luther's Works 10:401–2)

My feet had almost stumbled,
my steps had nearly slipped.
For I was envious of the arrogant
when I saw the prosperity of the wicked.

PSALM 73:2–3

The Talent of God's Grace

ow few are there even today whose feet are not moved when they see the prosperity of sinners. When one looks at them in their riches, display of luxury, and gluttony, he stops and looks with open mouth. Indeed, in the presence of some spectacle we stand and gape, and meanwhile forget our own affairs. He is an exceedingly rare person who goes his way with eyes and ears closed. But these things, too, are for many a cause of lukewarmness, because when they look at the corrupt habits of others, they regard themselves as better than those people by far, because they themselves are not like other men. And so, by the very fact of pleasing themselves they become abominable to God, failing to consider that perhaps those people, soon to be converted, will be much better than they. Meanwhile they themselves have buried the talent of God's grace in the ground.

From *First Lectures on the Psalms*, on Psalm 73
(Luther's Works 10:417–18)

My flesh and my heart may fail,
but God is the strength of my heart
and my portion forever.

PSALM 73:26

A Gracious God

s it not great and deplorable wretchedness that we fear and shun Him concerning whom Holy Scripture so often asserts that He has become our Refuge from generation to generation? Indeed, if father and mother forsook us and cast us off, He would receive those who have been cast off, as Psalm 27:10 states: "My father and my mother have forsaken me, but the Lord will take me up." Therefore if all creation were to declare nothing else than that you are lost, cursed, and damned, you would nevertheless have to say with Psalm 73:25–26: "Just as long as I have Thee, my flesh and my heart may fail, but God is the strength of my heart and my portion forever." What do I care if only I have a gracious God?

From *Lectures on Genesis* (Luther's Works 7:335–36)

*In the hand of the L*ord *there is a cup with foaming wine,*
well mixed, and He pours out from it,
and all the wicked of the earth shall drain it down to the dregs.

PSALM 75:8

Pure Truth and Prideful Hearts

ll who want to study in the Bible and sacred letters should with extreme diligence take note of this verse for themselves: *In the hand of the Lord there is a cup of pure wine* (v. 8). That is to say, Scripture is not in our power nor in the ability of our mind. Therefore in its study we must in no way rely on our understanding, but we must become humble and pray that He may bring that understanding to us, since it is not given except to those who are bowed down and humble. . . . Thus it happens to all the proud and stubborn who rely on their own puffed-up idea that God tips the truth and the pure wine away from them toward others and leaves them the dregs, as long as they are ignorant. . . . The pure truth cannot stand at the same time with the pride of the heart. Even if such a person would speak the truth, he no longer speaks it truly, because he does not speak it humbly. Therefore he does not speak truth, for he does not speak it how, to whom, when, where, and as much as, he should. Hence, whenever one of these is missing, it is no longer pure wine, but wine mixed with the dregs of some carnal passion. Therefore the Lord takes it away from him.

From *First Lectures on the Psalms*, on Psalm 75
(Luther's Works 10:461–62)

September 3

In Judah God is known;
His name is great in Israel.

PSALM 76:1

Worship and Magnify Him

hus Christ was *known in Judah* (v. 1) in a threefold way. First, because the saints of the Old Testament had the knowledge and religion of the one true God. Second, and more properly, through the personal presence of the flesh, where He was known and appeared also to the senses. And so this psalm could also be applied to the Feast of the Epiphany, for there He who was born was also made manifest in the flesh, and there He became well-known for His whole life through miracles and teachings. In Titus we read: "The humanity of our Savior God has appeared." Third, and most properly, because then the revealed faith in Christ, the light of the Gospel, truth and righteousness, began to be manifested through the sending of the Holy Spirit. And this latter was and is the manifestation of Christ in the spirit, as the former was His manifestation in the flesh. The latter alone is saving. While the former did not benefit all to whom it was made, the latter is salvation for all to whom it appears. And that the psalm speaks above all about the latter is clear from what follows: *And His name is great in Israel.* The name of God is great wherever He is, and He is everywhere. But it is not called great except where it is known to be great, namely, in the mind and heart of one who worships and magnifies Him.

From *First Lectures on the Psalms*, on Psalm 76 (Luther's Works 11:6)

From the heavens You uttered judgment;
the earth feared and was still.

PSALM 76:8

His Mighty Deeds Save

hou hast made Thy judgment to be heard from heaven, that is, the judgment (namely, the Gospel) by which He shows that all are carnal and that whatever is of the flesh is damnable. For through His own resurrection Christ conquered death, flesh, and every corruption. And taking on new life, He condemned the old, and thus He rose for judgment. Thus Romans 1:18 says: "The wrath of God is revealed from heaven against all ungodliness." For thus the prince of this world has been judged (John 16:11), and "now is the judgment of the world" (John 12:31). Therefore now follows: *The earth trembled and was still.* For they were stung, and they ceased to be wise after the flesh, and the tumult of the flesh was still, as Acts 2:37 reports: "Brethren, what shall we do?" Thus Isaiah 1:16 says: "Cease to act perversely." Through such a judgment, then, He saved all the meek of the earth but condemned the proud. Nevertheless, He did not cause this judgment to be heard for the purpose of condemning them, but of saving them. However, since they refused to be meek, they perished.

From *First Lectures on the Psalms*, on Psalm 76 (Luther's Works 11:4)

In the day of my trouble I seek the Lord;
in the night my hand is stretched out without wearying;
my soul refuses to be comforted.

PSALM 77:2

A Most Suitable Time for Prayer

his is the trouble of remorse and the total wretchedness of this life, as suggested by blessed Augustine on this passage. For the remorseful man understands his wretchedness and sees that he is in the midst of trouble and trial, since in fact the life of man on earth is trial and warfare (Job 7:1). But this salutary knowledge in a wonderful way makes a man remorseful and turns him away from earthly things and turns him toward God. Therefore he says: *I sought the Lord with my hands lifted up to Him in the night.* The Hebrew reads: "My hand is stretched forth in the night and is not silent." Whether this statement about the night is taken spiritually or literally, it is true, for the night is the most suitable time for praying and recollecting and praying in remorse.

From *First Lectures on the Psalms*, on Psalm 77 (Luther's Works 11:19)

I will remember the deeds of the Lord;
yes, I will remember Your wonders of old.

PSALM 77:11

Remember Them All

The works of God are threefold. In a general way, there are all the works of creation. These have been shown to all people so that they might remember them, give thanks and know God, and thus serve their Creator. Indeed, this is the apostle's argument in Romans 1:19f., especially with regard to the Gentiles. Hence even in the old law the saints often refer to these works and bless the Lord in them. Spiritually, there are the wonderful works shown to the people of Israel in Egypt, for these are the ones the Lord wanted remembered especially, although He later did many other works. These properly concern the Jews that in them they might give thanks to God because of the figure of things to come. Most particularly, there are the spiritual works of redemption and justification, for these above all have been committed to all Christians. The works of glorification, however, are subsumed under these, because they have not yet been done, so that they can be remembered only in Christ, the Head. These will indeed be the most wonderful. But in all of these we must remember not only the good things He offered but also the evils He brought to the evil, so that we may derive hope and love from the good things and fear and hatred of sin from the evils.

From *First Lectures on the Psalms*, on Psalm 77
(Luther's Works 11:10–11)

September 7

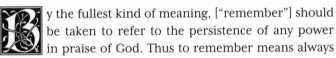

The Intellect, the Will, the Hand

y the fullest kind of meaning, ["remember"] should be taken to refer to the persistence of any power in praise of God. Thus to remember means always to praise, give thanks, tell others, bless, not only with the tongue as in the physical synagogue but with the whole heart, with the tongue, and with the whole life. So the intellect remembers when it keeps busy meditating on these things; the will remembers when it keeps on loving and praying; the hand remembers when it is constantly active. For if it would remember this only once and with one stroke, it is not memory, but recollection. . . . To remember the works of God is not a bare contemplation of them but always to thank Him in them, and thus through them to place one's hope in God, fear Him, love Him, seek Him, and to hate evil and flee sin. He who acts thus shows that he is truly remembering the works of God and not forgetting them. But he who does otherwise certainly shows that he has forgotten.

From *First Lectures on the Psalms*, on Psalm 77
(Luther's Works 11:11–12)

I will ponder all Your work.

PSALM 77:12

God's Work and Strength

od's work and His strength is faith. This makes people righteous and produces all virtues; it chastises, crucifies, and weakens the flesh, so that it should not have its own work or strength but that the work of God should be in it. And thus it saves and strengthens the spirit. But when this happens, then all who do this become God's work and God's strength allegorically. And so the Church is God's work and strength. The world, however, is weak and worthless, and, as in the flesh, so also in the world there is no work of God, for the reason that it is separated from the Church and the faithful people. But if they persevere in this, they will finally arrive at the final destiny of the evil and the eternal judgment, while the believers will arrive at the final destiny of the good.

From *First Lectures on the Psalms*, on Psalm 77
(Luther's Works 11:12–13)

I will . . . meditate on Your mighty deeds.
You have made known Your might among the peoples.

PSALM 77:12, 14

What Is Greater?

Almost the same thing is said in Psalm 111:6: "He will show forth to His people the power of His works." This is faith in Christ, for we preach Christ crucified, the power and wisdom of God (1 Corinthians 1:23f.), Christ, that is, faith in Christ. It accomplishes these great things. What, indeed, is greater than conquering the whole world and its prince? What is greater than overcoming all good and evil things in this life? What is greater than crushing eternal death? Than for the soul to rise from sins and become a daughter of God, an heir of the heavenly kingdom, a brother of Christ, an associate of angels, a friend of the Holy Spirit? These are incalculable and so wonderful and truly great that the ancient miracles are barely shadows and figures of these. Therefore every man is ignorant of this power, but Christ the Lord has declared it to His people. This is truly the power of God which does the works of God. Therefore the strength of the works is His. For this is your victory which conquers the world, namely, your faith (1 John 5:4).

From *First Lectures on the Psalms*, on Psalm 77
(Luther's Works 11:28–29)

You are the God who works wonders;
You have made known Your might among the peoples.

PSALM 77:14

Spiritual Power

hus He has made His power known (v. 14). How? By showing the people that the power of God is not in the flesh and earthly might but rather that the weakness according to the world is pleasing to Him, for His power is spiritual. This power conquers and works spiritually. He chooses the weak to shame the strong (1 Corinthians 1:27). For He has made known to all that His delight is not in the legs of man nor in the strength of the horse (Psalm 147:10). But such people as are powerful and rich, hale and strong do not do the works of God, because theirs is the strength of the world. It is rather the poor and weak, the lowly and despised, who act in His strength.

From *First Lectures on the Psalms*, on Psalm 77 (Luther's Works 11:13)

You with Your arm redeemed Your people,
the children of Jacob and Joseph.

PSALM 77:15

In the Midst of God's Wonders

e includes both [the literal and spiritual children of Jacob and Joseph], because he recounts the ancient miracles in order to prophesy the new ones in them. But who will see to it that we, too, will not be unfeeling in the midst of God's wonders, as they were? And who believes that we are in so many holy things today? The Lord does miracles everywhere. But since they are spiritual, they are not heeded. Certainly there are few who are mindful of the works of the Lord, who meditate on His wonders and exercise themselves in and speak about all His works. . . . But as I have said, he recounts the old and prophesies the new at the same time. For he saw that as the wonderful works of God in ancient times did not come about by the work of men, so he has in a much larger measure come to understand that all the works of God by which He redeems us and triumphs come about apart from the power of men. If the symbolic things were done by God, how much more the real and spiritual? So that all should abstain from boasting and confess to God. Hence, when Psalm 114 has recounted the works of God, there follows (Psalm 115:1): "Not to us, O Lord, not to us, but to Thy name give glory, for Thy mercy and Thy truth's sake."

From *First Lectures on the Psalms*, on Psalm 77
(Luther's Works 11:29–30)

Your footprints were unseen.
You led Your people like a flock.

PSALM 77:19–20

Veiled

ust as divinity was veiled under the flesh of weakness, so [Christ's] works were veiled in the weakness of suffering. These works were especially the casting down of the devil, victory over the world, destruction of hell, the gaining of heaven, the sanctification of the church, and the killing of the flesh, which are utterly divine works. Who would believe that the cross and suffering would achieve such incalculable results? Therefore His footsteps were not known, nor did any man see His way which He then walked. And neither the world nor the devil understood what He was doing. Nevertheless, this does not mean that He was therefore not the same God who anciently led the people in open strength, but it means that He then administered the letter and now administers the spirit of the letter, which was hidden in the letter.

From *First Lectures on the Psalms*, on Psalm 77
(Luther's Works 11:34)

They should set their hope in God
and not forget the works of God,
but keep His commandments.

PSALM 78:7

The Creature and the Creator

or this reason the Lord commanded the Gospel to be preached, that men might learn to believe and hope in God, to love heavenly things and despise the earthly, and that we might always have in memory the works which He did for us in the flesh. They increase hope and faith in a wonderful way. One who has forgotten and has no interest in such great things that the Lord has done for us, one who regards them as small and does not constantly give thanks, he, it is true, neither believes nor hopes in God and has truly forgotten His works. But he puts his hope in other things, namely, the creature, serving the creature rather than the Creator, "who is blessed forever! Amen" (Romans 1:25). If he had regard for the works of Christ and valued them and believed them to be true, he would undoubtedly understand that they had been set forth for him as an example and as a testimony of things to come, and he would certainly try to imitate Him by believing and hoping in Him and by despising all earthly things as He did.

From *First Lectures on the Psalms*, on Psalm 78 (Luther's Works 11:45)

They should not be like their fathers . . .
a generation whose heart was not steadfast,
whose spirit was not faithful to God.

PSALM 78:8

A Heart Set Right by Faith

A heart is set aright when it is turned from self to the Lord. This is the true direction, and it happens through faith and hope. The heart cannot be directed toward the Lord except by faith, because the Lord is a spirit, both invisible and incomprehensible. Therefore there is need for faith, which reaches out to Him. But these people do not set their heart aright. They distort it and bend it away from the Lord toward themselves, toward the flesh, toward the world, toward the creature. And there are as many bendings as they have desires and things desirable. They direct the eye and the flesh but not the heart. And why did they not set their heart aright? He says: "Their spirit was not faithful to God." This is what I said, for without faith this setting aright does not take place. In a devious way they are tossed to and fro on the roundabout way of every wind. Faith is the shortcut by which one comes quickly to peace and salvation. This is the direct way.

From *First Lectures on the Psalms*, on Psalm 78
(Luther's Works 11:47–48)

They did not keep God's covenant,
but refused to walk according to His Law.
They forgot His works
and the wonders that He had shown them.

PSALM 78:10–11

Counterfeit Faith

Nothing so provokes God as unbelief, for every such person accuses God of lying. For they doubt and do not believe what God attests by His word and deed, and so they regard Him as false and lying. If they believed that Christ is truthful in His word and deed, by which He condemned all the things of the world and showed the spiritual and heavenly, they would certainly accept His words and works and follow Him and forsake the world. But now they either do not believe, or if they say they believe, they do not in fact believe. Therefore it is truly a rebellious and stubborn generation, irritating and unbelieving. The Jews were the first to do this. They believed neither Christ's nor the apostles' word and work. Then the heretics do likewise. . . . They, too, are a stubborn generation through their pride and unbelief. Third, all the evil and proud do this, as I have sufficiently said, because they do not believe with the whole heart but live by a counterfeit faith, because they do not remember the works of the Lord nor seek His commandments. They hear in a superficial way and later fall away.

From *First Lectures on the Psalms*, on Psalm 78
(Luther's Works 11:46–47)

September 16

*How often they rebelled against Him in the wilderness
and grieved Him in the desert!*

PSALM 78:40

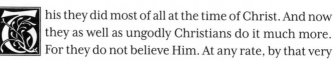

The Idolatry of Unbelief

his they did most of all at the time of Christ. And now they as well as ungodly Christians do it much more. For they do not believe Him. At any rate, by that very fact they tempt and deny Him, and so charge Him with lying. Nothing so provokes God as unbelief, for this means denying God directly and thus committing idolatry. Since they do not believe God's truth, they do not believe God either. He who does not believe that what God says is true at the same time does not believe that God exists, since God is truth and truthful. Oh, what wretches we are! How persistently we do what this verse says! This is clear from Psalm 95:7–9: "Today, if you will hear His voice, harden not your hearts, as in the provocation, etc." Therefore everyone who hears the voice of the Lord and still hardens his heart against it, lest he truly believe in his heart, is as in the provocation according to the day of temptation in the wilderness. This now happens not ten times, but as he says, "How often did they provoke Him."

From *First Lectures on the Psalms*, on Psalm 78
(Luther's Works 11:71–72)

O God, the nations have come into Your inheritance;
they have defiled Your holy temple.

PSALM 79:1

Extreme Supplications

 God, the heathen (that is, vices and evil thoughts) *have come into Thy inheritance* (that is, into my soul and flesh, which were sanctified to Thee, so that Thou mightest dwell in this possession, after sins had been driven out from there). *They have defiled Thy holy temple* (that is, soul and body, for our members are the temple of the Holy Spirit). This prayer vehemently moves and challenges and affects the Hearer, the Lord. . . . In these short words the Lord is reminded of the same thing that others say in explicit words: "Lord Jesus Christ, be mindful of Thy death and Thy blood poured out for me." And all other extreme and most vehement supplications are included here, if the words are properly broken up and chewed or pondered. How can you beseech the Lord in a more exalted way than if you call His inheritance to His attention? Having heard this one word, He will immediately remember how much He suffered for it and how much it cost Him.

From *First Lectures on the Psalms*, on Psalm 79 (Luther's Works 11:90)

I relieved Your shoulder of the burden.

PSALM 81:6

Snatched from Burdens

his is an interchange (*hypallage*), for he should have said, "He removed the burdens from His back." Yet in a mystical sense it is expressed in a most fitting manner, because in this way God removes Him [Christ] from the burdens, not as though the burdens were not there, but so that He is not where the burdens are. He shifted Him and not the burdens. For the burdens, that is, sins, are in the world, but He abandons them as He snatches the righteous man from them and likewise from their penalties. First, however, He removed Christ from them when He raised Him from the dead, and then all who belong to Christ.

From *First Lectures on the Psalms*, on Psalm 81, where the comments follow the Latin translation, which reads: "He removed His back from the burdens." (Luther's Works 11:107)

But My people did not listen to My voice;
Israel would not submit to Me.
So I gave them over to their stubborn hearts,
to follow their own counsels.

PSALM 81:11–12

No Greater Wrath

ow much God is vexed by such guilt He shows here by saying that He will withdraw His hand and let the people go their own way, as Psalm 81:12 also says, "I gave them over to their stubborn hearts." But what could be greater wrath than when He permits us to act according to our own conceits, takes His Word from us, and permits men, yes, even the devil, to be our masters? What else can one have then but sects and disunity in teaching? Later, outward disunity with strife and rebellion follows from this disunity in teaching.

From *Lectures on Zechariah (German)* (Luther's Works 20:313–14)

God has taken His place in the divine council;
in the midst of the gods He holds judgment.

PSALM 82:1

A Divine Ordinance

oses calls [rulers] gods because all the offices of government, from the least to the highest, are God's ordinance, as St. Paul teaches (Romans 13:1). . . . Now, because this is not a matter of human will or devising, but God Himself appoints and preserves all authority, and if He no longer held it up, it would all fall down, even though all the world held it fast—therefore it is rightly called a divine thing, a divine ordinance. And such persons are rightly called divine, godlike, or gods; especially is this so when, beside the institution itself, we have a word or command of God for it, as among the people of Israel, where the priests, princes, and kings were appointed by the oral command and word of God. From this we see how high and how glorious God will have rulers held, and that men ought to obey them as His officers and be subject to them with all fear and reverence, as to God Himself. Whoever resists them or is disobedient to them or despises them, whom God names with His own name and calls "gods," and to whom He attaches His own honor— whoever, I say, despises, disobeys, or resists them is thereby despising, disobeying, and resisting the true Supreme God, who is in them, who speaks and judges through them, and calls their judgment His judgment.

From *Commentary on Psalm 82* (Luther's Works 13:44)

God stands in the congregation of God
and is Judge among the gods.

PSALM 82:1 (according to Luther's translation)

A Regard for God from All

bserve that [the psalmist] calls all communities or organized assemblies "the congregation of God," because they are God's own. . . . Such communities are God's work, which He daily creates, supports, and increases, so that they can sit at home and beget children and educate them. Therefore this word is, in the first place, a great and pleasant comfort to all those who find themselves situated in such a community. It assures them that God accepts them as His work and His creation, cares for them and protects and supports them, as we can, in fact, see with our own eyes. . . . In the second place, it is a terrible and threatening word against the wicked, self-willed gods or rulers; for it tells them that they are set over not wood and stone, not swine and dogs (about which God has given no commandments), but over the "congregation of God." They ought to fear, lest the wrong they do be done against God Himself. For the congregations are not their own. . . . But He is, and wills to be, in them; and they are to be called His congregation. On both sides, then, everything will go well, in the fear of God and in humility. Subjects will have regard for God and gladly be obedient for His sake, and rulers will also have regard for God and do right and keep peace for His sake.

From *Commentary on Psalm 82* (Luther's Works 13:46–47)

Arise, O God, judge the earth;
for You shall inherit all the nations!

PSALM 82:8

The Kingdom of Christ

Worldly government will make no progress. The people are too wicked, and the lords dishonor God's name and Word continually by the shameful abuse of their godhead. Therefore [the psalmist] prays for another government and kingdom in which things will be better, where God's name will be honored, His Word kept and He Himself be served; that is the kingdom of Christ. . . . That is to say: He is Lord in all the world, for no empire has spread so far among the heathen as has the kingdom of Christ; and this verse cannot be understood as meaning any other than Christ. This God is a God by nature, to whom it is not said: "I have said that Thou art God"; but: "Arise, O God, and judge the earth." For Christ practices aright the three divine virtues mentioned above. He advances God's Word and the preachers of it; He makes and keeps law for the poor; He protects and rescues the miserable. . . . Thus we see that, over and above the righteousness, wisdom, and power of this world, there is need for another kingdom, in which there is another righteousness, wisdom, and power. For the righteousness of this world has an end, but the righteousness of Christ and of those who are in His kingdom abides forever.

From *Commentary on Psalm 82* (Luther's Works 13:72)

O God, do not keep silence;
do not hold Your peace or be still, O God!

PSALM 83:1

A Not-So-Quiet God

 hat is, "do not be quiet, do not be hidden, but begin to be manifested, and by word and deed show Yourself to be God." But the fact that he says "do not keep silence" shows that he is speaking about Christ's glorification in this life. For [in the first advent] it was not yet manifested to the eyes, but only to the ears, that Christ is God. Hence he does not say "do not be hidden" but "do not keep silence," that is, "bring it about that the proclamation of You as God is not silent but is preached publicly and as much as possible." Thus now our God comes manifestly not to the eyes but to the ears. Why? Because there follows: "Our God comes and does not keep silence" (Psalm 50:3). For He is not silent, but He speaks throughout the world in His preachers and manifests Himself to all for hearing.

From *First Lectures on the Psalms*, on Psalm 83
(Luther's Works 11:118–19)

How lovely is Your dwelling place,

O L̲ᴏʀᴅ of hosts!

Pᴀᴜᴍ 84:1

The Spiritual Things Inside

he dwelling places of Christ are His churches throughout the world, which are altogether one dwelling place. . . . He is here not speaking about physical dwelling places made of stone and wood nor about houses of this kind which are indifferent to the good and the evil. Rather, he is speaking of spiritual things that are in them. They are "lovely," first, to God and angels and men. So the ungodly ones are lovely to the devil and the wicked. They also hate and persecute the former, the lovely ones, when they should be hating the latter, and yet they feel sorry for and grieve over them. [The person who loves the tabernacles of the Lord is one who finds joy and delight in being present at the gathering of the people, participating in songs of praise, giving thanks for being made worthy to be among such saints.]

From *First Lectures on the Psalms*, on Psalm 84
(Luther's Works 11:136–37)

Blessed are those who dwell in Your house,

ever singing Your praise!

PSALM 84:4

God Alone We Praise

ince we receive everything from God, there is nothing that we can render Him but praise, and praise to Him alone. For a person cannot praise God only unless he understands that there is nothing in himself worthy of praise but that all that is worthy of praise is of God and from God. But since God is eternally praiseworthy, because He is the infinite Good and can never be exhausted, therefore they will praise Him forever and ever.

From *First Lectures on the Psalms*, on Psalm 84
(Luther's Works 11:144)

Blessed are those whose strength is in You,
in whose heart are the highways to Zion.

PSALM 84:5

The Power and Wisdom of God

hey are those to whom the Lord Christ is Help and Strength, which comes about through their faith in Him, as 1 Corinthians 1:23–24 says: "We preach Christ to those who are saints as the Power and Wisdom of God." For in Christ they are strong and manly and blessed through faith. . . . Hence he wants to say that he who is in the faith and spirit serves God out of the heart freely and joyfully and walks in His ways. Because the ways are in his heart, that is, in his affection and his will, they please him, and he loves them, for he walks in them out of love and from the bottom of his heart. On the contrary, those who are under the Law and the letter, since they do not have the spirit and grace, act out of coercion and unwillingly, out of fear and not from the heart, because they would prefer to neglect what should be done and to do what should not be done, if the choice were up to them. Therefore a hatred of the commandments is in their heart. But these very commandments have been outlawed from their heart, and they observe them only in a physical way and in the sight of men. The spiritual people, however, do it in the sight of God, because the ways are in their heart and please them. And this they do not have of themselves, but by the help of God, for "blessed is the man whose help is from Thee, or whose strength is in Thee."

From *First Lectures on the Psalms*, on Psalm 84 (Luther's Works 11:145)

September 27

Blessed are those whose strength is in You . . . .
They go from strength to strength;
each one appears before God in Zion.

PSALM 84:7

The Greatest Power

ow will one who has doubts and is uncertain in faith have substance, how will he ascend [cf. Psalm 83:6–7 Vulgate]? Therefore he says that the upward paths are disposed in a place which he had, however, previously fixed. Thus Christ says in the Gospel "only believe" (Luke 8:50), "believe" (Mark 11:24), "take heart (Mark 6:50), "all things are possible for him who believes" (Mark 9:23). The greatest power is in the faith that must be established. Therefore our psalm says at the end, "blessed is the man who trusts in Thee" (v. 12). But this is not to set a place. It is rather to set one's feet in a place. Hence to set a place is to choose something fixed on which a man may rest in faith and hope; that is, on nothing temporal, which cannot be established but is forever in flux. Rather, it is to choose what is fixed for eternity, namely, the Word of Christ, which remains forever, because it has been established.

From *First Lectures on the Psalms*, on Psalm 84
(Luther's Works 11:149)

For a day in Thy courts
is better than a thousand elsewhere . . .

PSALM 84:10

Never-Ending Day

his is the day of grace and the time of fullness and of faith. It is one continuous day, because it knows no night. For His righteousness remains forever and ever.

From *First Lectures on the Psalms*, on Psalm 84 (Luther's Works 11:151)

*For the L*ORD *God is a sun and shield:*
*the L*ORD *will give grace and glory:*
no good thing will He withhold from them that walk uprightly.

PSALM 84:11 (KJV)

The Giver and Preserver

his, too, the Lord loves, for this is truth, to humble oneself and know oneself. And then He will give grace and glory, for He gives His grace to the humble (1 Peter 5:5) and exalts the humble and lowly (Luke 1:52). If He will give, however, He will give to those who do not have, but are lowly; not to those who have, who are also proud and try to confer and bestow glory on themselves. They do not look to the Lord, the Giver of grace and glory, but rather get the jump on Him by snatching it from His hands. Therefore God will also remove glory and grace from them, because they do not have in them the truth and mercy which He loves and by which He may be moved to grant grace. . . . He gives and preserves His grace to the humble, that is, the fact that He is Sun and Shield; Sun, by illuminating with the rays of His grace; Shield, by protecting with His power and preserving the grace He gave.

From *First Lectures on the Psalms*, on Psalm 84
(Luther's Works 11:149–50)

September 30

Restore us again, O God of our salvation,

and put away Your indignation toward us!

PSALM 85:4

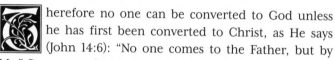

Converted to the Truth

herefore no one can be converted to God unless he has first been converted to Christ, as He says (John 14:6): "No one comes to the Father, but by Me." Consequently the prophet, who sees that many, indeed almost all, of his people could go astray, be offended, and be turned away from Christ, prays that they might be converted. And that happens through the knowledge of Christ or God incarnate. . . . Therefore it is extremely necessary for us now to be converted, lest we offend against the truth which meets us in marvelous ways, so that we could not turn to it anywhere unless God is gracious to us and turns our face toward recognizing it by turning away His wrath from us, so that we do not turn our back to it and are thus turned away from it. . . . If we are converted to the truth, God's wrath is turned away from us.

From *First Lectures on the Psalms*, on Psalm 85
(Luther's Works 11:157)

Let me hear what God the Lord will speak,
for He will speak peace to His people, to His saints.

PSALM 85:8

The Hearing of Faith

he Word of God is perceived only by hearing. It is the nature of the Word to be heard. . . . Therefore, for the Lord Himself to speak is to give out and manifest His Word, but as something to be heard. Thus God the Father has spoken to us, that is, He has shown us the Son, His Word, in the hearing of faith. And this is the Gospel of God which He had promised before through the prophets, one of whom is here saying, "I will hear what He will speak." And this speaking, this showing of the Word, this proclamation of the Gospel He accomplished by the ministry of the apostles and their successors, for in them He has spoken to the whole world.

From *First Lectures on the Psalms*, on Psalm 85
(Luther's Works 11:160)

Mercy and truth are met together.

PSALM 85:10 (KJV)

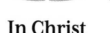

In Christ

 ruth, in a way that I think fits better to the theme, is called the faithful setting forth of what was promised over against reduction and omission of what was promised. Thus Christ is the Truth, because He showed forth the promise made to the fathers concerning Him, so that God might be true in His promises, since the salvation which He promised has been given. Hence Lyra well explains it when he says, " 'Mercy and truth have met each other,' that is, they have come together in one Person. For by the mercy of God the Word took on flesh for the purpose of fulfilling the truth of the promise made to the fathers of the Old Testament concerning the incarnation of the Son of God." For the fact that He promised us the Son was the sheer mercy of God. And so He Himself, in His coming, is Mercy, that is, the result of God's mercy which He promised. But the fact that God sent Him was the truth and faithfulness of God. And so He is Himself the Truth, that is, the realization of the truth of God offering the promise. Therefore what God the Father promised was Mercy; and what He sent was Truth. And so they are wonderfully mingled and brought together. . . . And both are in Christ.

From *First Lectures on the Psalms*, on Psalm 85
(Luther's Works 11:165)

Truth shall spring out of the earth;
and righteousness shall look down from heaven.

PSALM 85:11 (KJV)

Justified by His Coming

herefore, because truth has sprung up from the earth, we have the result that righteousness looks down on us from heaven. For the fact that Christ came and was born was sheer promise and not merit. And by this very thing we are now justified, namely, by His coming. It is not so that we first became righteous and deserving, and by this fact God was truthful, that He sent Him. Otherwise truth would spring out of heaven and righteousness would look up from the earth, which is the greatest possible perversion. . . .

Therefore Christ came to earth that He might lift us up to heaven. He came to us where we are that He might lead us to Himself where He is. But it is the promise that was responsible for His coming to us. Therefore truth springs up from the earth, for it had been promised that He would come to us. And so truth has been fulfilled. But it is His righteousness, which is in heaven, that is responsible for our coming to Him. And thus through truth He comes to us, and through righteousness we come to Him. Hence there is a marvelous mixture. Therefore those who did not want to be in heaven were not justified. For righteousness did not spring up from the earth, but it stays in heaven and looks down from heaven, choosing and imparting itself only to the elect.

From *First Lectures on the Psalms*, on Psalm 85
(Luther's Works 11:170–71)

October 4

Lord, You have been our dwelling place
in all generations.

PSALM 90:1

Place of Refuge

his introduction, too, breathes life and is relevant to the sure hope in the resurrection and life eternal. He calls the eternal God our Dwelling Place, or, if I may speak more precisely, our Place of Refuge, to which we may flee and where we may feel secure. If God is our Dwelling Place—and God is Life—and we are residents in that Dwelling Place, it necessarily follows that we are in life and will live eternally. That all this is a perfectly good and entirely valid inference we know because of the First Commandment. Who would call God a Dwelling Place of the dead? Who would think Him to be a tomb or a cross? He is Life. And so also those will live whose Dwelling Place He is. . . . Of course, Moses expressed himself in this way intentionally. He meant to show that our every hope is most firmly grounded in God and that those who pray to this God have this assurance: they are not needlessly afflicted in the world, and they will not die, since God is their Place of Refuge and the Divine Majesty, so to speak, their Dwelling Place, in which they can rest securely throughout eternity.

From *Commentary on Psalm 90* (Luther's Works 13:83–84)

You return man to dust. . . .
We are brought to an end by Your anger;
by Your wrath we are dismayed.

PSALM 90:3, 7

Created for Life

he death of human beings is a genuine disaster. Man's death is in itself truly an infinite and eternal wrath. The reason is that man is a being created for this purpose: to live forever in obedience to the Word and to be like God. He was not created for death. In his case death was ordained as a punishment of sin; for God said to Adam: "In the day that you eat of this tree, you shall die" (Genesis 2:17). The death of human beings is, therefore, not like the death of animals. These die because of a law of nature. Nor is man's death an event which occurs accidentally or has merely an aspect of temporality. On the contrary, man's death, if I may so speak, was threatened by God and is caused by an incensed and estranged God. . . . Therefore it comes to man as shocking news to hear that he, who had been created as a good and perfect being for life and who was to have his dwelling place in God, is now destined for death. Man fell from his former blessed estate through sin. It is this truly awful revelation which Moses wishes to communicate to us when he studiously portrays God as an enraged God. He does it in order to terrify smug and impenitent sinners.

From *Commentary on Psalm 90* (Luther's Works 13:94)

You have set our iniquities before You,
our secret sins in the light of Your presence.
For all our days pass away under Your wrath.

PSALM 90:8–9

A Knowledge of Sin

od afflicts us with various disasters, not to punish us, although this really is a punishment. But He takes no pleasure in it. What, then, does He mean by sending so many troubles, vexations, sicknesses, etc.? He does this in order that you may be led to a knowledge of your sin. He knows that you cannot make satisfaction, and He does not return evil in accordance with our merits; for we deserve nothing else than death and hell. But the sin that clings to our nature is hidden from our eyes, and He brings it to light, as the prayer of Moses puts it: "Thou hast set our iniquities before Thee, our secret sins in the light of Thy countenance" (Psalm 90:8). This means: "Thou art aware of the evils that are ours. We do not see them. In Thy sight we are impure and most horribly polluted." To us, however, the deformity and foulness of depraved nature are unknown. Therefore God uses powerful and bitter remedies to make it manifest and to cleanse it. If He is to sweep out the evil, He must take a broom and sharp sand, and He must scrub until blood flows. . . . Indeed, we must even fall most horribly, in order that we may recognize our wretchedness and weakness.

From *Lectures on Genesis* (Luther's Works 7:228)

Who considers the power of Your anger,
and Your wrath according to the fear of You?

PSALM 90:11

What God Has Prepared

It is as if he were saying: "No one knows how great the strength of Your wrath is, and no one can withstand it, no one can escape it, no one can turn it aside, unless You will reveal to them what comes about through faith and spirit." But this happens in this way, that from the wrath of gentleness by which He corrects, since it is so great, as is evident in the martyrs, one gathers how great is the wrath of severity and in which way it condemns. Therefore, in order that they may know this, the wrath of gentleness must supervene and they must be corrected. So St. Peter draws the conclusion in 1 Peter 4:17–18: "But if the judgment of God begins with us, what will be the end of those who do not believe the Gospel? And if the righteous man will scarcely be saved, where will the sinner and the ungodly appear?" For as "eye has not seen, nor ear heard, neither has it entered into the heart of man, what God has prepared for those who love Him" (1 Corinthians 2:9), so has eye not seen, nor ear heard, neither has it entered into the heart of man what God has prepared for those who hate Him.

From *First Lectures on the Psalms*, on Psalm 90
(Luther's Works 11:205)

So teach us to number our days
that we may get a heart of wisdom.

PSALM 90:12

The Beginning of Deliverance

rom the beginning of his prayer to this point Moses stressed the truth that another life succeeds this life—however, not just another life, but a life either of wrath or of grace. For otherwise it would be meaningless to call upon a King who dwells beyond this life, yes, even beyond this world, if there were no other life and no other world. . . . Therefore Moses prays that the Lord would teach us to number our days. This is not to be understood in the sense that he wishes to know the day or hour of his death, but that he and all human beings might truly consider how miserable and tragic life is, that it vanishes like a shadow, and that one must spend eternity subject either to wrath or to grace. . . . Therefore, O God, preserve us in the wisdom Thou hast taught us, that is, preserve us in Thy fear. For the "beginning of wisdom" (Proverbs 9:10), or the highest wisdom, is the "fear of God," to know God's wrath and, as a result, to live and to perform everything we do with humble hearts. . . . We should cling to the truth that it is not a damnable thing to feel God's wrath, but that this feeling is the beginning of deliverance, which cannot be gained without constant prayer. This feeling is a singular gift of God, which reason does not grasp or understand. Otherwise Moses would not plead with so much fervency that this wisdom be given.

From *Commentary on Psalm 90* (Luther's Works 13:126, 128, 129–30)

*Return, O L*ORD*! How long? Have pity on Your servants! . . .*
Let Your work be shown to Your servants,
and Your glorious power to their children.

PSALM 90:13, 16

The Forms of God

rembling consciences, which do not see [God's] work of glory, fear Him and imagine Him to be the devil; for they cannot picture Him as having a lovely form or costume. They arm Him with swords and lightning, as though, in reality, nothing in heaven or on earth were more repulsive and more horrible than an incensed God. As such a God He did appear on Mount Sinai (Exodus 19:18). As such a God Moses also depicted Him above. But in the passage before us Moses prays that God might reveal another form of Himself, one which we can behold with pleasure and over which we can rejoice. Such a form God truly has when we behold Him in the person of Christ. In Christ He is consummate Grace, Life, Salvation, Redemption. In Christ we see the glorious God, God clothed in His glorious and gracious works. And so Moses prays: "Show Thyself to us miserable and condemned sinners in this form." This is the chief part of his petition. In it he prays for remission of sins, righteousness, and life eternal. But he prays for these gifts in such a way that we might have assurance and that our heart might not in the least degree doubt these matters. Because this petition cannot be realized except in Christ.

From *Commentary on Psalm 90* (Luther's Works 13:137)

Let the favor of the Lord our God be upon us,
and establish the work of our hands upon us.

PSALM 90:17

Friendly and Kindly Disposed

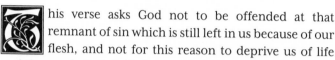his verse asks God not to be offended at that remnant of sin which is still left in us because of our flesh, and not for this reason to deprive us of life and the remission of sins but rather to remain friendly and kindly disposed toward us. It also asks that we might remain friendly and kindly disposed toward Him. To show forth God in His glory does not mean to show how He is in Himself apart from us but to show that He is friendly toward us and glorious and filled with joy over us. And this our God, so Scripture says, rejoices over us when we are persuaded that He is not incensed at us but is our kind and lovable Friend. But this is an exceedingly essential petition, because "our flesh is weak" (Matthew 26:41), our heart trembles, and our conscience experiences the worst possible fears. . . . Therefore this petition is at the right place, for it causes us to say: "O Lord, Thou hast given us Thy Son. Preserve unto us this gift. We often sin in word, often in deed, more often in thoughts. All this impairs our joy. Whether, therefore, we sin, whether we are careless and ungrateful: continue nevertheless to be our God. Be a God who is kind and gracious. Therefore grant that we may be kept in the joy and peace of the Holy Spirit."

From *Commentary on Psalm 90* (Luther's Works 13:138)

He shall cover thee with His feathers,
and under His wings shalt thou trust:
His truth shall be thy shield and buckler.
Thou shalt not be afraid for the terror by night;
nor for the arrow that flieth by day.

PSALM 91:4–5 (KJV)

Surrounded on All Sides

 is truth will encompass you with a shield. This is faith or the spirit of the letter, and the true understanding of Scripture, not a shadow or a figure. Therefore this truth will abound in such a way that it will encompass you on every side. You will be rich and full of spiritual understanding, so that you will lack nothing in any grace, as 1 Corinthians 1:5 says: "In every way you were enriched." Therefore *You will not fear the terror of the night nor the arrow that flies by day nor the trouble that stalks in darkness nor the invasion nor the noonday devil.* . . . In these words I understand nothing else than the corruptions of the truth and faith and of the integrity of spiritual understanding which he described above. . . . From these no one can be safe, except he whom truth has surrounded on all sides, whom the pinions of Christ overshadow, and to whom it is granted to have hope under His wings, that is to say, except the one who is guarded in the faith of the truth by faithful pastors, bishops, and teachers against these wolves who come in sheep's clothing (Matthew 7:15).

From *First Lectures on the Psalms*, on Psalm 91 (Luther's Works 11:215)

October 12

A thousand may fall at your side,
ten thousand at your right hand,
but it will not come near you. . . .
For He will command His angels concerning you
to guard you in all your ways.

PSALM 91:7, 11

By God's Command

He who holds firmly to this promise and meanwhile diligently does his duty in his place, which he knows has been assigned to him by God, even if some dangers or obstacles are put in his way, nevertheless has no doubt about a happy issue and favorable outcome but is convinced in his heart that all the angels will come flying from heaven to help and defend him rather than that any godly undertaking in accord with the Word of God should be in vain and useless. What you undertake on the strength of His Word must succeed, even though there were to be no angel remaining in heaven. In this the sacred accounts are therefore superior to the histories of the heathen; for in the former everything happens by God's command, but in the latter it happens by chance and by the plans of men.

From *Lectures on Genesis* (Luther's Works 4:107)

He will command His angels concerning you
to guard you in all your ways.

PSALM 91:11

Protected by the Angels

hrist says (Matthew 26:53): "Do you think that I cannot appeal to My Father, and He will at once send Me more than twelve legions of angels?" Accordingly, when we are under the protection of God, there is no doubt that we are also under the safekeeping and guardianship of the angels, who are present with those who are encountering dangers in life and who conduct the dead to the place of peace and rest. For David says (Psalm 91:11): "He will give His angels charge of you, etc.," and likewise (Psalm 34:7): "The angel of the Lord encamps around those who fear Him." These things should admonish and stir us up gladly to hear and love the Word but even more gladly to believe the Word in this confidence, that we are covered by the protection of the angels.

From *Lectures on Genesis* (Luther's Works 6:41–42)

You will tread on the lion and the adder;
the young lion and the serpent
you will trample underfoot.

PSALM 91:13

Fear Not

hrist has called us and has tied us with a most pleasing bond to His vineyards, that is, to His spiritual gifts, with which He fills us, so that we fear none of all the things that can harm us. Would that we truly understood and impressed on our hearts the divine promises, namely, that our sins have been forgiven us, that death and the devil have been conquered, and that hell has been destroyed, as this is gloriously proclaimed in Psalm 91:13: "You will tread on the lion and the adder, the young lion and the serpent you will trample underfoot"! He who firmly believes this imbibes these promises, feeds most pleasantly on these vines, and is lord over death.

From *Lectures on Genesis* (Luther's Works 8:251)

You will tread on the lion and the adder;

the young lion and the serpent

you will trample underfoot.

Psalm 91:13

The Strength of the Christian

et us remain in the purity of Christian faith, in order that we may be children of Abraham, Isaac, and Jacob, not according to the flesh but rather according to the spirit. For if I believe the promise of God, I am certain that my life is pleasing to God and is superior to all the orders, since it makes a heavenly man, a conqueror of death, an heir of eternal life, and one who tramples the devil underfoot, as is stated in Psalm 91:13: "You will tread on the lion and the adder, the young lion and serpent you will trample underfoot." This is the strength and particular power of Christians.

From *Lectures on Genesis* (Luther's Works 8:167–68)

How great are Your works, O LORD!
Your thoughts are very deep!

PSALM 92:5

The Wisdom of God

Who would know that those who are humiliated, afflicted, rejected, and killed visibly, are at the same time exceedingly exalted, consoled, taken up, and made inwardly alive, unless he were taught by the Spirit through faith? And who would think that those who are visibly exalted, honored, strengthened, and made alive, are in the same degree wretchedly cast down, despised, weakened, and killed inwardly, unless the wisdom of the Spirit taught him? Thus it pleased God through the foolishness of the cross (1 Corinthians 1:21) to save the believers and by the wisdom of salvation to condemn the unbelieving. This is because by such wisdom they did not know God in the wisdom of God, for they could come out of such wisdom into the wisdom of God and thus know God. For as the things which the flesh savors for itself are good, so the things which the spirit savors for itself are much better. Of which they ought to have acknowledged these as a figure and a thing signified, and because they were unwilling, they are now compelled under their opposite to acknowledge God in the wisdom of God.

From *First Lectures on the Psalms*, on Psalm 92
(Luther's Works 11:231)

The wicked sprout like grass. . . .
The righteous flourish like the palm tree.

PSALM 92:7, 12

Withering Grass and Blooming Palm

hy? Because the palm blooms all the time, in summer as well as in winter, while the grass does not bloom throughout the summer, and there is none at all in the winter. So the righteous in this life always bloom in spirit, both in adversity and in prosperity, and after this, forever, because the spirit is life eternal. The ungodly, however, bloom only in prosperity, but not even throughout that period. Death and adversity take him away because he has only the life of the flesh.

From *First Lectures on the Psalms*, on Psalm 92
(Luther's Works 11:233)

O Lord, God of vengeance,
O God of vengeance, shine forth!
Rise up, O judge of the earth;
repay to the proud what they deserve!
Psalm 94:1–2

A Prayer for the Pious

his psalm is clearly a prayer that is common to all the pious children of God and members of His spiritual people, to be prayed against all their persecutors. Therefore it can be prayed from the beginning of the world to its end by all pious and devout people, be they Jews, Christians, or patriarchs. For they all have to suffer from the two groups of persecutors about whom this psalm complains: first, the tyrants, who use force to persecute the body on account of the Word; secondly, the false teachers, heretics, and sectarians, who use lies and mockery to persecute the soul. For this reason we, too, may pray this psalm in our day against both groups. . . . Here "God of vengeance" means "the one who takes vengeance." For the Scriptures give Him His names on the basis of His works. But because no one but God can do such works, no one but God is entitled to the names that are based on such works. No one but God can give comfort, hope, patience, and the like; thus also no one but God can punish sin and avenge evil.

From *Four Psalms of Comfort*, on Psalm 94
(Luther's Works 14:243–44)

The LORD will not forsake His people;

He will not abandon His heritage;

for justice will return to the righteous,

and all the upright in heart will follow it.

PSALM 94:14–15

The Plans of the Wicked

his makes it clear that this psalm is speaking about the plans of the wicked against the people of God. For God cannot forsake His own; this is certain, as he says here. Therefore it is impossible for the wicked to accomplish what they set out to do. It must fail, as certainly as God is God. Only there must first be days of trouble, in which one must be still and patient while the wicked begin their campaign and then come to naught. As Psalm 91:8 also says, "You will look with your eyes and see the recompense of the wicked." If you are killed before seeing it in this life, you will come back to life and see it in the life to come. But the living will see it even in this life. For those who believe it, then, this verse comforts the pious and emboldens them mightily, while it pronounces a fearful judgment on the tyrants and the heretics. For this is the certain outcome, in spite of thousands upon thousands of popes, emperors, princes, scholars, and heretics piled on top of one another, just as the following verse also says: *For justice will return to the righteous, and all the upright in heart will follow it.*

From *Four Psalms of Comfort*, on Psalm 94 (Luther's Works 14:252)

When I thought, "My foot slips,"
Your steadfast love, O Lord, held me up.

PSALM 94:18

Failings, Fallings, Forgiveness

ut a confession of humility saves and helps. And, indeed, in these verses the outcome and function of temptation is beautifully expressed. For against the wicked no one except the Lord helps; if He did not help, the soul of any tempted person would dwell in hell. And yet He does not help in such a way that He does not permit a man to fall, so that he may acknowledge his weakness and not think that he has stood by his own strength. Therefore, if you have not stood perfectly, give thanks that you did not perish altogether, and ask for pardon for that in which you have failed, so that in this way you may acknowledge the strength of the Lord who helps you and has mercy on, and forgiveness for, that same weakness of yours, as was shown in the case of St. Peter in Matthew 14:30–31. And in 2 Corinthians 1:9 we read: "We had in ourselves the sentence of death, but that was to make us rely not on ourselves but on God who raises the dead." Therefore let the foot be moved, and so let a multitude of griefs come . . . so that also the sweet consolation of mercy may come.

From *First Lectures on the Psalms*, on Psalm 94
(Luther's Works 11:248)

When the cares of my heart are many,
Your consolations cheer my soul.

Psalm 94:19

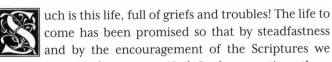

In the Meantime

Such is this life, full of griefs and troubles! The life to come has been promised so that by steadfastness and by the encouragement of the Scriptures we might have hope (cf. Romans 15:4). In the meantime, these two are mingled, steadfastness, or encouragement, and tribulation. . . . Accordingly, the Word must be learned, and a person must exercise himself in it and get to know these continuous alternations which are customary in the life of the saints and of all believers who wish to please God. Paul says (2 Timothy 3:12): "All who desire to live a godly life in Christ Jesus will be persecuted." In Acts 14:22 we read: "Through many tribulations we must enter the kingdom of God." "But God is faithful, and He will not let you be tempted beyond your strength" (cf. 1 Corinthians 10:13), however different it appears to human reason and however much every temptation seems to be beyond measure and intolerable. Thus Paul says of himself in 2 Corinthians 1:8: "We were so utterly, unbearably crushed that we despaired of life itself," but there is no need for you to fear that you will be burdened by God beyond measure, because the statement stands firm: "God is faithful, etc."

From *Lectures on Genesis* (Luther's Works 6:99)

But the Lord has become my stronghold,
and my God the rock of my refuge.
He will bring back on them their iniquity
and wipe them out for their wickedness;
the Lord our God will wipe them out.

PSALM 94:22–23

Waiting It Out

et them preach, rage, and slaughter all they please! I am safe against them and mightily defended, for God is my Stronghold. Our teaching must abide, their fiction must pass away; for God is our Stronghold. Therefore we shall remain safe against them both here and hereafter, for our God is our Refuge; He makes us bold and secure. Not only that, but as a God of vengeance He will also destroy them, as the next verse says: *He will bring back on them their iniquity and wipe them out for their wickedness; the Lord our God will wipe them out.* Here is the ultimate and certain judgment: God will not let their wickedness go unnoticed but will wipe them all out in their wickedness, and their wickedness will stop. And this will be done by "our God," whose Word we speak and whom they do not regard as God at all. . . . Whoever believes this and is instructed by God can be patient and permit the wicked to rage, for he considers their end and waits it out.

From *Four Psalms of Comfort*, on Psalm 94 (Luther's Works 14:256)

For the LORD is a great God,
and a great King above all gods.

PSALM 95:3

Love, Trust, and Rejoice in Him

n order to stimulate love for Christ and hatred for earthly things, and likewise hope and joy in Him and fear and sadness for the world, [the psalmist] says: "For the Lord is a great God and a great King above all gods." . . . Here is the Lord of heaven and earth, not now a David or a Solomon, who were little kings, and thus the kind of kings and lords who might nevertheless be servants under other gods, namely, angels, but One who is Lord alone and over all gods. Why, then, do you not love, trust, and rejoice in Him? For men naturally rejoice, if they can boast of a great king. Thus if you fear the greatness of the enemy and tyrant, behold, fear not, he will not harm you at all, he will take nothing from you, and you will lose nothing, for He is a great Lord and a great King above all gods. Therefore He can give you everything and safeguard from the enemies all that has been given. What then? Why do you not love, trust, and rejoice? Indeed, why do you not hate, fear, and grieve that you are not under this King?

From *First Lectures on the Psalms*, on Psalm 95
(Luther's Works 11:254)

October 24

*Ascribe to the L*ORD *glory and strength!*
*Ascribe to the L*ORD *the glory due His name;*
bring an offering and come into His courts!

PSALM 96:7–8

God before Your Eyes

As long as confession remains in the heart, so long also beauty; as long as humility remains, so long also grace. It will remain, however, if you remain in the presence of God, that is, if you will always have God before your eyes, to whom you are always incomparable. Indeed, if it remains, you, too, will remain in His presence. But if you descend or ascend to a view of yourself, that is, in order to become something and a spectacle in your own eyes, then confession and beauty have perished. . . . Therefore do not go out with the wicked servant from the face of the Lord and from His presence (Matthew 18:28), but "come into His presence" (Psalm 100:2).

From *First Lectures on the Psalms*, on Psalm 96
(Luther's Works 11:264)

King of the Universe

his is the truest joy. Who would not rejoice over the fact that the tyrant has been cast out and the legitimate heir and lord reigns over him? This means: "Indeed, these are Thy judgments, O Lord, on account of which the daughters of Judah have rejoiced, that 'now is the judgment of the world; now shall the prince of this world be cast out' (John 12:31), and the Savior of the world reigns over us."

From *First Lectures on the Psalms*, on Psalm 97
(Luther's Works 11:267)

*Know that the L*ORD*, He is God!*
It is He who made us, and we are His.

PSALM 100:3

⁂

A Good Reminder

he psalm (100:3) states: "The Lord made us, and not we ourselves." Why does the Holy Spirit put us in mind of this, as though no one actually knew it? Truly, the entire world has need of this teaching. For all who are presumptuous about their works do not know that they were made by the Lord; and they need to be reminded that they were made by the Lord. Otherwise they would humble themselves before their Creator and not be presumptuous about their own powers, because whatever they have, they have from God. Thus ignorance of the act of creation makes us presumptuous. So does God's exceedingly great friendliness toward us. Therefore it is necessary for God to put a lawgiver over us, as Psalm 9:20 expresses it, and to kill us along with Ishmael, in order that Paul's statement (cf. Ephesians 2:8–9) may stand firm: "Through faith and not by works, through grace and not through our merits" we are what we are, even naturally and according to the body and the flesh, and to a far greater extent supernaturally and according to the spirit, so that we should simply say: "O God, have mercy on me!"

From *Lectures on Genesis* (Luther's Works 4:62)

I will sing of steadfast love and justice;
to You, O Lᴏʀᴅ, I will make music.

Pꜱᴀʟᴍ 101:1

Knowledge of Self and God

 any indeed have both mercy and judgment, but they do not sing of them to the Lord. Who is there who does not have good things from God? Again, who does not have his own evils and the things he does not want? But they do not praise God in these; of the good things they do not confess to God that they are unworthy of them, nor of the evil things that they are worthy of them. And so they murmur judgment for themselves rather than singing to the Lord. To sing is to confess and praise God with joy and to take pleasure and be delighted in God, since He is righteous in judgment, because He chastens and is merciful, because He grants good things. Thus "the daughters of Judah rejoiced, because of Thy judgments, O Lord" (Psalm 97:8). . . . Hence also the Lord thus governs the Church and any righteous man through knowledge of self and knowledge of God; for if we know ourselves, we easily sing of judgment; but if we know God, we easily sing of mercy. For we know God through His blessings, ourselves through our evils. Therefore whenever blessings come to us or we consider those already given, the believer at once says, "All these are from the mercy of God." And with this attitude he lifts up his voice to God and praises Him, and he does not bend it back on himself or boast about these things before men.

From *First Lectures on the Psalms*, on Psalm 101
(Luther's Works 11:282–83)

October 28

I will sing of steadfast love and justice;
*to You, O L*ORD*, I will make music.*

PSALM 101:1

Spiritual Blessings and Temporal Troubles

t follows that in this life both, namely, mercy and judgment, are present only in the saints. In hell there will be only judgment, in heaven only mercy, but here both at the same time. Therefore ascribe spiritual blessings, yes, everything, to the mercy of God and praise the Lord in them, but impute bodily evils and the temporal troubles of this life to yourself as proper and due. Regard the former as undeserved and as given purely by grace, and so you will not be proud in the former case nor despair in the latter. You will not become vain and puffed up in the former nor timid and sad and downcast in the latter, so that through mercy and judgment you may come from judgment without mercy to mercy without judgment. Amen. Therefore the words are most aptly placed, since mercy precedes so that judgment may become singable. Mercy is sung before judgment, otherwise it would be a judgment to be lamented if mercy had not been there before.

From *First Lectures on the Psalms*, on Psalm 101
(Luther's Works 11:284)

I will not set before my eyes anything that is worthless.
I hate the work of those who fall away;
it shall not cling to me.

PSALM 101:3

Firm Faith

hus it is clearly discernible in David's psalms how diligently he guarded himself and warned others. For instance, Psalm 1:1: "Blessed is the man who does not walk in the counsel of the ungodly." For this purpose he also composed especially Psalm 119. . . . It is as if he said: "It is a great thing for a person to have the true doctrine of God and a desire to hear His Word. But it is just as great for a person to be able to continue in it and to keep it pure and fine against Belial and his servants, who are always opposing it." As St. Peter warns us (1 Peter 5:8–9): "Be sober, be watchful. Your adversary the devil prowls around like a roaring lion, seeking someone to devour. Resist him, firm in your faith." Here you hear that there must not be a milk faith, which merely begins to serve God, but a firm faith, which can resist Belial and his wicked works.

From *Commentary on Psalm 101* (Luther's Works 13:178)

*Hear my prayer, O L*ORD*;*
let my cry come to You!
Do not hide Your face from me
in the day of my distress!
PSALM 102:1–2

A Prayer and a Cry

N o one can pray this prayer except one who is poor in spirit and has begun to loathe the vanity of the world and the goods of the flesh and to long for spiritual blessings. . . . Therefore, as he sees them having their own property while he is still lacking his and is being put off, he says: *O Lord, hear my prayer, and let my cry come to Thee.* The intellect makes the prayer, but the feeling makes the cry, for the latter desires, but the former shows what it should desire, and how and whence, etc. . . . And what does my prayer and my cry want? *Turn not Thy face away from me* (v. 2). Behold, here you have how this prayer is, for he prays not only in spirit but also with the mind. . . . Therefore he here seeks his good things, which are the very face of Christ, and he has the mind and the spirit in his prayer at the same time, for he understands what he prays, and he knows what he desires. In this petition every good thing is sought.

From *First Lectures on the Psalms*, on Psalm 102
(Luther's Works 11:295)

Do not hide Your face from me
in the day of my distress!

PSALM 102:2

Cry for Help

t has often been said what the face of the Lord signifies, namely, the spirit itself in contradistinction to the letter, which is the back, as Psalm 80:3 says: "Show us Thy face, and we shall be saved"; Psalm 4:6: "The light of Thy countenance, O Lord, is signed upon us"; and Psalm 89:15: "They shall walk in the light of Thy countenance." But in that light and face all good things are comprehended, because it is nothing else than knowing Jesus Christ. And to know Him is to know and have everything. The face is the knowledge of the Lord, which is now in us by faith, but then by sight. Hence the meaning is: "Do not turn away from me the Spirit and faith and spiritual blessings, as You do with those who love vanity and seek lying. Therefore, turn away from me, if it pleases You, riches, glory, health, and whatever the flesh can have in this life: Only do not turn Your face away from me."

From *First Lectures on the Psalms*, on Psalm 102
(Luther's Works 11:299–300)

Incline Your ear to me;
answer me speedily in the day when I call!
PSALM 102:2

Hear My Prayer

e prays that his evils might be removed, saying: *In whatever day I am in trouble, incline Thy ear to me.* For we do not yet possess our good things in reality, but in faith and hope, and therefore it is necessary to be in tribulations and evils. For if those blessings were here in this life, we would not have evils. But we do not have those blessings now; and we still hope for those others. Nothing is left but that we have these evils. However, lest we fail in these, we cry to the Lord that He would not forsake us in tribulation. Indeed, he also says; *In whatever day I shall call upon Thee, hear me speedily.* For he would not bear it, unless He helped quickly.

From *First Lectures on the Psalms*, on Psalm 102
(Luther's Works 11:296)

November 2

He has broken my strength in midcourse;
He has shortened my days.

PSALM 102:23

Oppressed with Christ

his is the way it goes in Christ's kingdom according to the outer man. He breaks, punishes, and humbles His beloved saints and permits them to be tortured here in time that they may be strong and powerful, not outwardly but inwardly. The world, however, which He raises up and strengthens in its way here in time, He will humble in the end. Therefore the prophet and the spiritual people comfort themselves with the thought that they are oppressed with Christ temporally here on earth, but not at the Last Day.

From *Seven Penitential Psalms*, on Psalm 102 (Luther's Works 14:186)

November 3

For as high as the heavens are above the earth,
so great is His steadfast love
toward those who fear Him.

PSALM 103:11

The Grace of God

 e certainly know that we are poor sinners, but here we must not look at what we are and do, but at what Christ is and has done and still does for us. We are not speaking about our nature, but about the grace of God, which is so much more than us, "as high as the heavens are above the earth, as far as the sun's rising is from its setting" (Psalm 103 [:11–12]). If you think it is a big thing that you are God's child, do not think it is a small thing that God's Son was born of a woman, born under the Law, so that you could become such a child [of God]. What God does is altogether something great, which gives us great joy and courage and makes spirits undaunted, which are afraid of nothing and can do everything.

From the *Church Postil*, sermon for the Sunday after Christmas on Galatians 4:1–7 (Luther's Works 75:392–93)

For He knows our frame;
He remembers that we are dust.

PSALM 103:14

The Potter and the Vase

ven though we do not fully understand, we should believe our Creator when He declares something about us. He knows what sort of frame or dust we are (Psalm 103:14), we do not. Just as the vase of a potter may have acquired a crack through a blow or some other way and does not know it has a crack, whereas the potter knows and sees it, so also we do not fully know our faults. Therefore let us confess our infirmity and reverently say: "O Lord, I am Thy clay, Thou art my former and potter (Isaiah 64:8). Therefore because Thou dost declare that I am a sinner, I agree to Thy Word. I freely acknowledge and confess this wickedness hiding in my flesh and my whole nature. That Thou mightest be glorified, let me be confounded. That Thou mightest be righteous and the Life, let me and all men be sin and death. That Thou mightest be the highest good, let me and all men be the lowest evil. I acknowledge and confess this, being instructed in this by Thy promises and Thy Law, not by my reason, which would like to cover up this wickedness or even decorate it. But I am more concerned that Thy glory increase." Whoever confesses his sin in this way, prays this verse with sound mind: "Against Thee only have I sinned and done that which is evil in Thy sight, so that Thou art justified in Thy sentences."

From *Commentary on Psalm 51* (Luther's Works 12:342)

November 5

O Lord, how manifold are Your works!
In wisdom have You made them all;
the earth is full of Your creatures.

Psalm 104:24

The Church Militant

These can be understood as referring to the visible works, but they should not be so understood absolutely, except in respect to the invisible things, which he makes clear because according to the works of creation not only the earth but also heaven is filled with the possession of Christ, yes, also hell, for all things are His, made by Him. But the Church Militant, about which the psalmist is speaking, is only on earth, because it rules in the midst of enemies (Psalm 110:2). And of this possession and inheritance of Him all the earth is full, namely, the Church spread throughout the world. And these are the works that are great and done in wisdom, because the Church has been built by the Word of the Gospel, which is the Word of the wisdom and power of God, as is also the visible world, made by the Word and wisdom of God from the beginning.

From *First Lectures on the Psalms*, on Psalm 104
(Luther's Works 11:341)

He had sent a man ahead of them,
Joseph, who was sold as a slave.

PSALM 105:17

A Sending for Life

God is called the Sender, and indeed a Sender for salvation, when He allows the very fine youth Joseph to be sold and killed, and his father to be most wretchedly disturbed and afflicted. This way of speaking is neither Greek nor Latin nor Hebrew. But it is a wonderful and unheard-of manner of sending. Accordingly, we see how gentle, pleasant, and winsome the Holy Spirit is. He calls that horrible tearing away of a son from his father and that sad cross by which both are nearly killed a sending for life. And it is a designation that is completely true and most pleasing to God. Therefore it should also please us, for it is a word and doctrine of salvation. For this is the way Joseph, on rising from the dead, was accustomed to speak after he had seen the plan of the Lord and the back of God, namely, what He meant with the very grievous trial, and that He is accustomed to be at the side of His own in the greatest disasters, in hatred, in fratricide, in being sold, in prison, in disgrace, and in all misfortunes. And these things should be placed before the church of God, in order that by such examples the godly may be stirred to faith and patience, and learn to believe in God, the almighty Father, the Maker of heaven and earth. With God we can lose nothing when we believe, but every loss is a hundredfold gain.

From *Lectures on Genesis* (Luther's Works 8:34)

*Praise the L*ORD*!*
*Oh give thanks to the L*ORD*, for He is good,*
for His steadfast love endures forever!

PSALM 106:1

God Is Faithful and Just

his psalm teaches the true praise of divine goodness, namely, that to confess one's own evil to God
is to give thanks to the Lord, for He is good. Hence
the hypocrites who confess themselves to be righteous
necessarily deny goodness. For goodness forgives sins which
they do not have. Therefore God does not have goodness for
them, but only righteousness and power. But it is dreadful
to provoke God's righteousness and power. Therefore let us
strive rather to provoke His goodness.

From *First Lectures on the Psalms*, on Psalm 106
(Luther's Works 11:345)

Let them thank the L<small>ORD</small> for His steadfast love,
for His wondrous works to the children of man!

P<small>SALM</small> 107:8

Give Thanks to God Alone

his is a wonderful verse and full of perfect instruction, in the first place, that the blessings of God upon us are by pure mercy and not deserved. Therefore he puts "mercy" first and does not say "our redemption," but "His mercy," for the purpose of showing that nothing of that was from us, but from God alone. Therefore it immediately follows that a man should not boast of them or be superior to others and not give credit to himself but to the Lord, who has done these mercies to us. If they are the mercies of the Lord, they should give thanks to no one but the Lord. If they do not give thanks to Him, however, they are not His mercies, and so they are taken away from Him, indeed, they already are neither His nor mercies, but cruelties. For as sin, when it is ascribed to oneself through confession, becomes righteousness, so grace, attributed to oneself through arrogance, becomes iniquity.

From *First Lectures on the Psalms*, on Psalm 107
(Luther's Works 11:349)

With my mouth I will give great thanks to the LORD;
I will praise Him in the midst of the throng.
For He stands at the right hand of the needy one,
to save him from those who condemn his soul to death.

PSALM 109:30–31

Our God Saves

We would say it this way: O Lord God, who would not praise and laud Thee before the whole world and everywhere for helping the poor so graciously and for toppling and punishing the proud and haughty tyrants so mightily? Or, as it continues: *For He stands at the right hand of the needy, to save him from those who condemn him to death.* May God be praised forever and every day for taking the side of the poor and lowly instead of exalting the bigwigs and haughty tyrants, as they suppose that He will! He saves; yes indeed, He saves not only from occasional needs but also from those who condemn Him to death, judge and sentence Him as a heretic and a deceiver. For here this word "condemn" refers to those who occupy an office and condemn; in other words, to the secular government. Let us be sure, then, that the secular government will never be completely Christian, but that the vast majority will always persecute Christ, His Word, and those who are His. . . . But it happens to them that they waver and are put down from their thrones (Luke 1:52), one after another.

From *Four Psalms of Comfort*, on Psalm 109
(Luther's Works 14:276–77)

The Lord says to my Lord: "Sit at My right hand."

PSALM 110:1

Lord of All

his Lord Christ sits above at the right hand of God, having a kingdom of life, peace, joy, and redemption from all evil, not a kingdom of death, sorrow, and misery. Therefore it must follow that His own will not remain subject to death, anxiety, fear, spiritual conflict, and suffering. They will be snatched from death or the grave and all misery. They will live with Him beyond sin and evil after He has made them alive again in body and soul. He illustrates this in His own person. He became a human being and condescended to the miserable level of our present nature in order to begin His kingdom in us by personally sharing all human weakness and trouble. For this reason He also had to die. But if He was meant to be a Lord and King of all creation, sitting at the right hand of God, He could not remain under the conditions of death and suffering. By God's power He had to break through death and the grave and everything else, so that He might seat Himself at the place where He can work all these things in us and grant them to us.

From *Commentary on Psalm 110* (Luther's Works 13:240–41)

November 11

The LORD says to my Lord: "Sit at My right hand,
until I make Your enemies Your footstool."

PSALM 110:1

The Enemy of Our Enemies

bserve this for your comfort: here these enemies are never called our enemies, or those of Christendom, but enemies of the Lord Christ. . . . For this reason He must deal with them as enemies who attack His person. Everything that happens to the individual Christian, whether it comes from the devil or from the world, such as the terrors of sin, anxiety and grief of the heart, torture, or death, He regards as though it happened to Him. . . . Though we may feel the terrors of sin, anxiety and grief of heart, torture, and death, we are to remember that these are not our enemies but the enemies of our Lord, who is of our flesh and blood. We are to view Him as the Enemy of our enemies. In this comfort we are to direct them away from ourselves to Christ: "Do you not know the Lord who sits above at the right hand of God? God has already judged you and pronounced you the footstool of Christ. Go to Him and see what you can do. You can tear and bite me, and I must let you attack me and scratch me. But you shall gain nothing from me, because my Lord has been placed above you. He can and will trample you down."

From *Commentary on Psalm 110* (Luther's Works 13:262–63)

The LORD says to my Lord: "Sit at My right hand. . . .
You are a priest forever.

PSALM 110:1, 4

A Most Amazing Conclusion

avid drew . . . the following conclusion: This Seed is the Son of God and the equal of God, and He is the kind of king who sits at the right hand of the Father. In the second place, the promise states that He will not only rule but will also bless. At the same time, therefore, He will be a Priest. For not only royal authority but also a priesthood is dealt with, and the name and office of priest embrace the foremost benefits of Christ. Therefore David, enlightened by the Holy Spirit, adds an oath, not in regard to royal authority but in regard to the priesthood: " 'The Lord has sworn and will not change His mind.' 'You are a priest forever,' etc." [Psalm 110:4]; that is, my Lord will sit at the right hand of God, but in such a manner that He will not only rule but will also bless. This is the excellent knowledge David had about Christ, the Seed who was to come from his tribe and flesh; and he undoubtedly realized and was exceedingly glad that such outstanding glory and honor were being heaped upon him in preference to other kings when Nathan brought him the promise (Psalm 132:11): "Of the fruit of your body will I set on your throne." Hence he concluded that this promise was being channeled into his body and seed, and that the Son of God would be born from his offspring.

From *Lectures on Genesis* (Luther's Works 4:173)

The LORD sends forth from Zion
Your mighty scepter.

PSALM 110:2

Recognizing His Kingdom

ou can see, therefore, how the dominion of this King works. In His invisible essence He sits at the right hand of God; but He rules visibly on earth and works through external, visible signs, of which the preaching of the Gospel and the Sacraments are the chief ones, and through public confession and the fruits of faith in the Gospel. These are the true marks whereby one can really recognize the kingdom of the Lord Christ and the Christian Church: namely, wherever this scepter is, that is, the office of the preaching of the Gospel, borne by the apostles into the world and received from them by us. Where it is present and maintained, there the Christian Church and the kingdom of Christ surely exist, no matter how small or negligible the number of the flock.

From *Commentary on Psalm 110* (Luther's Works 13:272)

The LORD sends forth from Zion Your mighty scepter.
Rule in the midst of Your enemies!

PSALM 110:2

The Power to Preserve

he fact that Baptism, the Sacrament of the Altar, preaching, faith, the Holy Scriptures, and the confession of the name of Christ continue in the world up to the present time should be proof plain enough for anyone that this kingdom of Christ is being maintained and preserved solely by divine and almighty power. If this were not so, the devil would have been too mighty and strong for it. . . . But as long as there is one baptized Christian upon the earth, as long as one pulpit remains, yes, as long as the name of Christ remains known anywhere despite the devil's furious wrath and rage, this is due solely to the exalted and heavenly power of this Lord. Thus this article of doctrine, that He sits at the right hand of God with power, is not merely part of the Creed but finds confirmation in general experience. This again powerfully demonstrates the fact that this Christ is the genuine and true God and that He has the power to preserve His kingdom in spite of this mighty evil spirit and in spite of sin and death. . . . For the Father says here that Christ is to rule as God in His own right above and against all the might of His enemies, whether they be in heaven, on earth, or in hell—not through the help or protection of another but by means of the Word or the scepter He is to send out.

From *Commentary on Psalm 110* (Luther's Works 13:282–83)

November 15

Your people will offer themselves freely
on the day of Your power.

PSALM 110:3

His Spontaneous People

here is no other rule or criterion by which a person can conclude who God's people or the Church of Christ is except this only: it is a little flock of those who accept this Word of the Lord and who teach and confess true doctrine against those who persecute them, even though they must suffer for it. . . . He calls this people "spontaneous," that is, a people whose spontaneous, "willing," desire and love is to obey and be subject to this Lord without hypocrisy. It is their determination not to allow themselves to be torn from Him but to remain His own, regardless of the offensive example of the majority in the world—the wise, the educated, the holy, those who call themselves, and want to be, God's people but deny Him and blaspheme and rage against His Word. Nor do these loyal people permit any power, threats, terror, persecution, and suffering, whether it comes from the world or from the devil himself, to frighten them or to lead them into apostasy. In sum, they cling to Christ, regardless of whether the consequences are good or evil, and refuse to be offended or hindered by them, but hold them in contempt and overcome them. Firm and steadfast, they abide with this Lord, even if it should happen that they must stand alone on earth against all other men and forfeit everything they have, such as possessions, honor, friends, freedom, and life itself.

From *Commentary on Psalm 110* (Luther's Works 13:286–87)

November 16

Your people will offer themselves freely
on the day of Your power.

PSALM 110:3

Genuine and True Service

hen people learn to know Christ through the Gospel, when they believe that they obtain God's forgiveness of their sins through Christ and become acceptable to God for Christ's sake, the right service of God develops as a consequence within the heart. Where such a faith exists, the Holy Spirit also works in the heart, as we have said before, so that a man develops such a desire and love for God that he wants to obey Him. Such a man begins to fear God with all his heart, he trusts Him under all conditions of his life, he calls upon Him in all his needs, he is steadfast in the confession of His Word, by his life he praises God before all the world, and for His sake he suffers and bears whatever God is pleased to send him. Such are genuine and true forms of service, and they please God very well because they are done with faith in Christ. They proceed from within the heart, which has now become "a new creation" in Christ, as St. Paul calls it in Galatians 6:15. . . . Therefore the old form of worship stopped of itself when Christ came to create a new form of service and new servants of God through the Gospel. This does not consist in external conduct or behavior or in lifeless types; instead, it lives in the heart and produces a genuinely new being.

From *Commentary on Psalm 110* (Luther's Works 13:293–94)

November 17

The Lord has sworn and will not change His mind,
"You are a priest forever after the order of Melchizedek."

PSALM 110:4

A Protected Priesthood

We are to be sure and certain that this Christ, born, according to the Scriptures, of the lineage of David, is truly the King and Priest promised in the Scriptures. We alone, who believe in Him, have the true faith, worship, and priesthood. We are the true Church, or people of God. No other faith or religion or worship is valid before God than that which belongs to Christ and His Church. In addition, though we may be persecuted and damned on account of this priestly office and faith, and both the devil and the world rage and storm against it and seek to suppress it, we are to have the comfort that He who said this, and took an oath on it, will protect this priesthood and preserve it so that the gates of hell (Matthew 16:18) will not overcome it.

From *Commentary on Psalm 110* (Luther's Works 13:307–8)

The Lord has sworn and will not change His mind,
"You are a priest forever after the order of Melchizedek."

PSALM 110:4

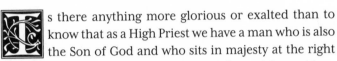

Our Mediator and Advocate

I s there anything more glorious or exalted than to know that as a High Priest we have a man who is also the Son of God and who sits in majesty at the right hand of God? If we had the power to make a wish, could we possibly desire anything greater or better than to have with God a Mediator and Advocate of this stature? Now we are told that God Himself ordained this Christ—indeed, He confirmed it, as we said before, with a sublime oath—to be such a High Priest and to sit at the right hand of the Father especially for the purpose of preventing us from falling into any sort of wrath or disgrace, provided that we continue to believe in Him. We are to look to Him for comfort, help, and the undiluted, everlasting grace of the Father. How can the Father possibly refuse to hear this Priest, His own beloved Son? How can He refuse Him anything He asks for? And Christ asks for nothing else than that which benefits us—grace and mercy for us! Therefore we are certain that when we ourselves pray in His name, God is pleased and will hear us out. Why should anyone have any further doubts or fears? Why not draw near to His throne of grace with joyful confidence, as it is written in Hebrews 4:16, rejoice with all our hearts in this High Priest, and find our comfort in Him?

From *Commentary on Psalm 110* (Luther's Works 13:322)

November 19

You are a priest forever.

PSALM 110:4

Ordained for the Sake of Sinners

hrist's priestly office is the true and precious comfort for us poor and sinful people, as well as for all other burdened hearts. By this we see and hear that His kingdom on earth is not made up of superlative saints who are completely free from sin or perfectly holy. It is the function of the most exalted office which He exercises before God to deal with those who have weaknesses, frailties, and sins, and who therefore possess a shy, burdened, and disturbed conscience. He will not reject them or deal with them severely, measure for measure, with the threats and terrors of wrath and damnation. On the contrary, He seeks to attract and invite them in the most friendly, gentle, and pleasant manner to come to Him and to seek and expect comfort and help from Him. . . . Therefore a priest is ordained for the sake of sinners. Their cause is his. It is his task to stand between God and sinners in order to reconcile them and to plead as the sinners' advocate. . . . God made Christ a Priest for us so that we should seek and find comfort and help against sin in Him; for He is the One who gave Himself as our Sacrifice. This He did in order to reconcile us to God, to restore us to His grace, and to bestow spiritual power on us through His intercession, so that we can be rid of our sins and attain everlasting righteousness, holiness, and eternal life (1 Peter 2:24).

From *Commentary on Psalm 110* (Luther's Works 13:321)

The Lord is at Your right hand;
He will shatter kings on the day of His wrath.

PSALM 110:5

His Enemies Will Not Stand

he prophet has his own way of speaking here. He does not say Christ will do this, but "the Lord at Thy right hand." He retains that sweet and beautiful picture of the Christ of grace and comfort, who sits on high for us and does not think of revenge or punishment. But as St. Peter says in his First Epistle (1 Peter 2:23): "He committed Himself to Him that judges righteously." On the cross He did not threaten or curse His crucifiers (Luke 23:24) but made intercession for them with tears and loud cries (Hebrews 5:7). This is what He does even now. As the previous verse has it, He remains always and eternally our dear and faithful Priest. Yet the Father will not reckon it to their credit nor leave Christ's enemies unpunished, who refuse to have Him as their Priest. For He sits at the right hand of the Father, that exalted, eternal Power and Majesty, who will shortly put an end to their defiance and raging against Christ. Now, since they want to be enemies, they shall indeed have an enemy in Him; and He is the kind of enemy against whom they can do nothing. When He hits them, they will be utterly smashed and will lie in the dust.

From *Commentary on Psalm 110* (Luther's Works 13:341)

November 21

Praise the Lord!
I will give thanks to the Lord with my whole heart.

PSALM 111:1

From the Heart

or genuine Christians it is their real accomplishment and the highest service of God when they praise God and do so out of their whole heart. No other man on earth can reach that accomplishment. True, the world is full of hypocrites who say with their mouth: "I thank the Lord." But it does not come from their heart. As St. Paul says (1 Corinthians 12:3), no one can call Jesus Lord except by the Holy Spirit. Whoever would thank God must sincerely realize and confess that the thing for which he offers thanks is purely God's grace and gift. No one can recognize the gifts of God by his own reason; but the Holy Spirit must show it to our heart, as St. Paul teaches (1 Corinthians 2:12): "We have received the Spirit of God, that we might understand the gifts bestowed on us by God."

From *Commentary on Psalm 111* (Luther's Works 13:363–64)

Praise the Lord!
I will give thanks to the Lord with my whole heart.

PSALM 111:1

The Folly of Serving Two Masters

 ome want to serve two masters (Matthew 6:24), love and have both at the same time, God with half a heart and the world and the flesh with half a heart. And so they limp on both sides, worshiping Baal and the Lord at the same time (1 Kings 18:21). Others do not even confess God with half a heart, but only with the mouth, about whom Isaiah 29:13 says: "This people honors Me with the lips, but their heart is far from Me" (cf. Matthew 15:8). Others, finally, confess with someone else's mouth and not their own. Themselves inactive toward the good, they want to be saved by the merits of others and perish in their own foolish security. . . . Therefore above all things it is necessary to confess to the Lord with one's own heart.

From *First Lectures on the Psalms*, on Psalm 111
(Luther's Works 11:371–72)

November 23

*Great are the works of the L*ORD.

PSALM 111:2

The Church of the Faithful

hese works are the new creatures created in Christ through the Holy Spirit, as Psalm 8:3 says: "When I look at the heavens, the work of Thy fingers." And since they are spiritual works, their greatness is spiritual also. And these are the apostles, the martyrs, and all the faithful in the whole Church. They are indeed great, not physically or before the world, but in virtues and wisdom before God, and wonderful in that they are weak, foolish, and outcast and humble before men. These works of the Lord are small, yes, nothing in the eyes of the world, which does not know the Spirit and His greatness. Therefore the "great works of the Lord" are the Church of the faithful.

From *First Lectures on the Psalms*, on Psalm 111
(Luther's Works 11:374)

He has caused His wondrous works to be remembered;
the Lord is gracious and merciful.

Psalm 111:4

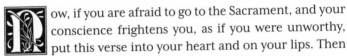

A Sincere Invitation

Now, if you are afraid to go to the Sacrament, and your conscience frightens you, as if you were unworthy, put this verse into your heart and on your lips. Then you must hear and feel how sincerely He calls and invites you. He is here and is waiting for you with hands and heart wide open, for you to take and receive grace and mercy. He does not want you to flee and shy away from Him but to flee to Him and with full confidence go to Him. Here he is called nothing but this: *the gracious and merciful Lord. . . .* This verse expresses not merely the fruit and benefit of the Sacrament—that it is a gracious and merciful institution in which one should seek and find grace and mercy—but it also exalts the remembrance of Christ. What is the suffering of Christ but pure grace and mercy, offered, given, and imparted to us through the Sacrament? It is grace that He shows us all His benefits and by His blood brings us from sin to righteousness, from death to life, from the devil to God. It is mercy that He unceasingly forgives our sin and spares and endures our ingratitude and all wickedness in which we are still bound as long as we live in the flesh. All this He earned for us, once and for all, by His suffering, and daily offers and gives us by His remembrance and Sacrament, actually driving us to it with sweet and gentle words.

From *Commentary on Psalm 111* (Luther's Works 13:374–75)

The works of His hands are faithful and just.

PSALM 111:7

Fitted for Every Good Work

od has certain works that are all His own. . . . They are the works which He Himself performs and which are called "the works of His hands," as a potter with his own hands fashions a piece of pottery. This is our Lord's workmanship, and we are His clay or loam. He is the carpenter, and we are His lumber. The product is the dear holy cross, which must follow the teaching of the Gospel. Here He hews and works on us, planes and saws, that He may put to death the old man in us together with his learning, wisdom, and righteousness, and all his vices, thus making us perfect, His new creation. . . . Thus Christians become experienced and skilled, able to advise and help in all matters. Thus they become bold and equipped to fight against the devil and sin. Thus they are fitted for every good work. In short, thus faith is exercised, the Gospel is fortified, and Christians become a righteous product and a new creature of God. This is a work which we endure from God and do not do ourselves. Therefore it is correctly called the work of His hands; and this is to be proclaimed continually among Christians so that they follow Christ in His suffering and become like Him. He, too, was shaped and prepared in this manner, not merely that He might redeem us from the devil, but also as an example which we should follow, as St. Peter says (1 Peter 2:21), and to which we should be conformed (Romans 8:29).

From *Commentary on Psalm 111* (Luther's Works 13:378–79)

He sent redemption to His people;
He has commanded His covenant forever.
Holy and awesome is His name!

PSALM 111:9

Living under Grace

od is to be praised because He has not based His gracious covenant of the forgiveness of sin on our merit but on His Word, and because He still commands that it should stand firm and eternal, not falling when we sin, nor becoming valid when we are pious. It stands by itself on the command of God, so that every moment we must go to Him and constantly obtain forgiveness of sin. For since there is endless sin in our flesh as long as we live on earth and there is no end of blundering and erring, we must surely have an eternal and everlasting forgiveness for it. Then we can live not under wrath because of sin, but under grace because of forgiveness. Behold, this is His eternal covenant, which He steadfastly maintains and which does not waver, so that our heart may be sure its sin will not condemn it. For this we should praise and thank Him in all the churches.

From *Commentary on Psalm 111* (Luther's Works 13:383–84)

The fear of the LORD is the beginning of wisdom;
all those who practice it have a good understanding.
His praise endures forever!

PSALM 111:10

Earnestly and Reverently Listen

I f one would begin to become wise, one must fear God. One must truly regard it as God's Word; then everything can be learned easily. This is the one mistake, that many people hear God's Word, which is the pure wisdom of God, but learn nothing from it, because they regard it as a word, but not as the Word of God. They think they have mastered it as soon as they have heard it. But if they regarded it as God's Word, they would surely think: "Well, then, God is wiser than you and will say something great. So let us earnestly and reverently listen, as one ought to listen to a god." Behold, then the heart is beginning to become wise; for it earnestly desires to hear God's Word. God can teach such people anything through His Word. . . . Thus the prophet would teach us in this verse that we should hear His Word with fear and earnestness. Then we shall become wise and understand His psalm. To fear God is the same as to fear and honor His Word, for without God's Word we can have no God. . . . He who lives according to the Word of God has eternal glory and honor, and his praise will have no end; for he is adorned with the name of God, which is eternal, and he is decorated with divine glory, which has no end.

From *Commentary on Psalm 111* (Luther's Works 13:385–87)

Praise the LORD!
Blessed is the man who fears the LORD,
who greatly delights in His commandments!

PSALM 112:1

Fearing God

 o fear God is true worship, as he says in the psalm immediately before this (Psalm 111:10): "The fear of the Lord is the beginning of wisdom." It is really nothing else than to keep God in sight. Whoever does this has enough for time and eternity. For he keeps His Commandments, gives God His honor, exalts God as He should be exalted. Then God cannot but exalt him in turn, as He says (1 Samuel 2:30): "Those who honor Me I will honor, and those who despise Me shall be lightly esteemed." We know from experience that this is true. If we fear and honor God, then the way is prepared for us to become rich and blessed and to have enough. Such a person can rightly use riches and fame and pleasure. But the children of the world cannot do this. They meddle into God's business and seek only their own advantage. Those who fear God, however, do not lay hold of possessions without His will. That is the difference between those who fear God and those who do not fear Him.

From *Commentary on Psalm 112* (Luther's Works 13:396–97)

Light dawns in the darkness for the upright;
He is gracious, merciful, and righteous.

PSALM 112:4

Three Titles of God

he prophet gives God three titles because of the three things he has ascribed to Him, as said above: "Gracious, merciful, and righteous." He is gracious, for He forgives where we have sinned. He is merciful, for He spares us so that we still live, and He supplies what we lack. Thirdly, He is righteous, so that we have success in what we do. That is the meaning of "gracious, merciful, and righteous." Our situation is this that we are conceived and born in sin. To this applies the fact that He is gracious. Then I say: "Farewell, sin, you shall not harm me!" And while my life as it continues is not perfectly good, the merciful Lord will bear with it. He is also righteous; for everything I do must be good and right, even if it is not as perfect as it ought to be. If the heart is thus disposed toward God and knows that this is what it has in God, what can a man lack? He knows that God is satisfied with him, that He will forget the past and will gild the future. And whatever he does, be it good or not, must be righteous and have value before Him. . . . All this, as you have heard, is intended to teach us how to conduct ourselves before God.

From *Commentary on Psalm 112* (Luther's Works 13:406)

It is well with the man who deals generously and lends;
who conducts his affairs with justice.

PSALM 112:5

Simply No Comparison

righteous man, however, who fears God and stands in awe of Him, looks upon God as the one who beholds all his words, works, and thoughts. In turn, he is also kind and merciful to his neighbor, as God has been gracious and merciful to him. And how does he prove his mercy? By treating his neighbor as God has treated him. As God has pardoned his sin, so he pardons and remits everything his neighbor does to him. This is an easy thing for me to do if I look into the Fountain and into the Well from which so much has flowed for me. If I realize and feel in my heart what God has pardoned and forgiven me, I am willing to pardon and forgive my neighbor whatever he has done against me. I will not keep books on him but will forgive him freely from my heart as I call to mind: "If God has forgiven and pardoned you for so many great sins, what does what your neighbor has done against you amount to? There is simply no comparison!" For one sin against God is greater than if all the world were to sin against a man. Sin must not be measured on the basis of what it is or of how great it is but on the basis of who it is that has been offended and insulted by the sin. Now, God is infinitely greater than all men. And when I realize what God has done to me, I will do likewise to my neighbor; but if I do not realize this, then I will not do it to my neighbor either.

From *Commentary on Psalm 112* (Luther's Works 13:407)

December 1

He is not afraid of bad news;
*his heart is firm, trusting in the L*ORD.

PSALM 112:7

A Special Skill

is heart is equipped against any misfortune. No matter what adversity may come, he ignores it. His heart is firmly set to trust in God, not in honor and goods, power and favor before the lords, nor in those who may give or lend to him. He will not be shaken if he falls into disgrace, for he trusts in Him who offers him a method by which he may rise upward. But there are so few who want to rise. It is a special skill for someone to know how to trust in God. Even if the whole world defiles him and he remains in disgrace, he will ignore it and let one, two, or a hundred years pass and remember: "God knows about it, and He will direct it well." Thus he is content, in good spirits, and unafraid. Why? Because he has that trust and fears neither death nor shame, knowing that God will rescue him.

From *Commentary on Psalm 112* (Luther's Works 13:416)

December 2

Who is like the L\ORD\ our God?
He raises the poor from the dust
and lifts the needy from the ash heap.

PSALM 113:5, 7

Blessed Is He Who Understands

[G]od] is not neutral as He looks, but He looks in order to raise up. And this is the nature of the true Creator, to make everything out of nothing. Therefore He raises no one except him who is not raised up but prostrate and downcast. Nor does He lift up anyone but the one pressed down, so that unless there is nothing of raising and lifting in that person, but complete degradation and suppression, He does not raise nor lift up. But although we are in truth all cast down and depressed, yet He does not lift and raise up all, but only those who acknowledge themselves to be downcast and depressed. Those who regard themselves as lifted up and standing are held to be and are lifted up and standing before God, though in truth they are most wretchedly degraded and pressed down. "Blessed is he who understands concerning the needy and the poor" (Psalm 41:1), that is, also the one who understands himself to be such a one. And Christ brought this new rule of humility, which had formerly been unknown. Therefore he says, "Who is like the Lord our God, etc.?"

From *First Lectures on the Psalms*, on Psalm 113
(Luther's Works 11:391–92)

I believed, even when I spoke,
"I am greatly afflicted";
I said in my alarm,
"All mankind are liars."

PSALM 116:10–11

Put Not Your Trust in Man

iterally this means: "In this affliction I learned that I must not trust in any man, because I, too, who said, 'I believed,' could fall from the truth of the faith." Unless God comes to one's assistance, the one who is truthful by confession quickly becomes a liar in suffering by the denial of the faith, as if to say: "This cup teaches that unless a person calls on the Lord, relies on the Lord, he himself will in no wise stand, because he is a man and will fall." Therefore it is the Lord who helps in consternation and in persecution, not man.

From *First Lectures on the Psalms*, on Psalm 116
(Luther's Works 11:402)

What shall I render to the Lord
for all His benefits to me?
<small>PSALM 116:12</small>

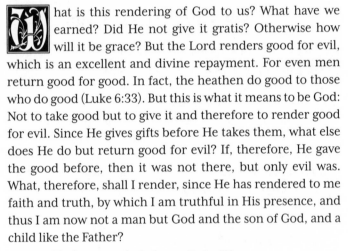

An Excellent and Divine Repayment

What is this rendering of God to us? What have we earned? Did He not give it gratis? Otherwise how will it be grace? But the Lord renders good for evil, which is an excellent and divine repayment. For even men return good for good. In fact, the heathen do good to those who do good (Luke 6:33). But this is what it means to be God: Not to take good but to give it and therefore to render good for evil. Since He gives gifts before He takes them, what else does He do but return good for evil? If, therefore, He gave the good before, then it was not there, but only evil was. What, therefore, shall I render, since He has rendered to me faith and truth, by which I am truthful in His presence, and thus I am now not a man but God and the son of God, and a child like the Father?

From *First Lectures on the Psalms*, on Psalm 116
(Luther's Works 11:403)

I will lift up the cup of salvation
and call on the name of the Lᴏʀᴅ.

Pꜱᴀʟᴍ 116:13

Thy Will Be Done

The text can be so arranged that the meaning is: "I see that if I want to hold fast to faith in Christ, to His Word and grace, it is necessary for me to be humbled exceedingly; yet, because this benefit and retribution of God pleases me more than this suffering displeases me, if this cup cannot pass away unless I drink it for the sake of His Word, well and good, the Lord's will be done. Nevertheless, because of such suffering I will not fall away from the Word, I will not be ungrateful, I will not give in, but I will in every way strive to be grateful, even in the midst of sufferings, lest I be like the one about whom it is said, 'He will praise you when you do well to him' (Psalm 49:18). But as for me, seeing that the gifts of God are so great that I do not know what I should render, I will nevertheless think of rendering, even if I must drink the cup, for He could perhaps withdraw it or He seemed to be able to do so, so that I might either not accept the gifts of God or not be thankful for what was received. Therefore, that I may be altogether thankful, I will even accept the cup, for it is salutary. And lest I trust in myself, I will call on His name. And thus not only when He does good to me but even in the midst of sufferings I will pay my vows, etc."

From *First Lectures on the Psalms*, on Psalm 116
(Luther's Works 11:404)

December 6

*Precious in the sight of the L*ORD
is the death of His saints.
PSALM 116:15

The Great Consolation

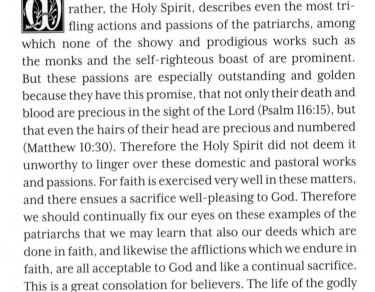

e see, moreover, with what great care Moses, or rather, the Holy Spirit, describes even the most trifling actions and passions of the patriarchs, among which none of the showy and prodigious works such as the monks and the self-righteous boast of are prominent. But these passions are especially outstanding and golden because they have this promise, that not only their death and blood are precious in the sight of the Lord (Psalm 116:15), but that even the hairs of their head are precious and numbered (Matthew 10:30). Therefore the Holy Spirit did not deem it unworthy to linger over these domestic and pastoral works and passions. For faith is exercised very well in these matters, and there ensues a sacrifice well-pleasing to God. Therefore we should continually fix our eyes on these examples of the patriarchs that we may learn that also our deeds which are done in faith, and likewise the afflictions which we endure in faith, are all acceptable to God and like a continual sacrifice. This is a great consolation for believers. The life of the godly appears to be an idle life and without any fruit and worth. But this is our great glory, that we know that our tears and each of the drops that fall from our eyes are numbered by God and that all things are written before the eyes of God and gathered in a golden vessel, so to say (cf. Psalm 56:8).

From *Lectures on Genesis* (Luther's Works 6:123–24)

December 7

Life after Death

od does not inquire after sheep and cattle that have been slaughtered, but He does inquire after men that have been killed. Therefore men have the hope of resurrection and a God who leads them out of bodily death to eternal life, who inquires after their blood as after something precious, just as the psalm also says (116:15): "Precious is the death of His saints in His sight." This is the glory of the human race, which was won by the Seed when He crushed the serpent's head. This is the first example of that promise given to Adam and Eve, by which God shows that the serpent does not harm Abel even though it succeeds in having Abel killed. This is indeed why the serpent lies in wait for the heel of the woman's Seed. But while it bites, its head is crushed. Because of Abel's trust in the promised Seed, God inquired after Abel's blood when he was dead and showed that He is his God.

From *Lectures on Genesis* (Luther's Works 1:285)

Praise the LORD, all nations! Extol Him, all peoples!
For great is His steadfast love toward us,
and the faithfulness of the LORD endures forever.
Praise the LORD!

PSALM 117

They Must First Hear His Word

Now if all heathen are to praise God, this assumes that He has become their God. If He is to be their God, then they must know Him, believe in Him, and give up all idolatry. One cannot praise God with an idolatrous mouth or an unbelieving heart. And if they are to believe, they must first hear His Word and thereby receive the Holy Spirit, who through faith purifies and enlightens their hearts. One cannot come to faith or lay hold on the Holy Spirit without hearing the Word first, as St. Paul has said (Romans 10:14): "How are they to believe in Him of whom they have never heard?" and (Galatians 3:2): "You have received the Spirit through the proclamation of faith." If they are to hear His Word, then preachers must be sent to proclaim God's Word to them; for not all the heathen can come to Jerusalem or make a living among the small company of the Jews. Therefore the psalmist does not say: "Come to Jerusalem, all heathen!" He lets them stay where they are and calls upon them, wherever they may be, to praise God.

From *Commentary on Psalm 117* (Luther's Works 14:9)

December 9

*Praise the L*ORD*, all nations! Extol Him, all peoples!*
For great is His steadfast love toward us,
*and the faithfulness of the L*ORD *endures forever.*
*Praise the L*ORD*!*

PSALM 117

Real and Only Worship

he psalmist admonishes and instructs us how to serve the Lord. He urges us to give praise and thanks. Since of ourselves we are nothing but have everything from God, it is easy to see that we can give Him nothing; neither can we repay Him for His grace. He demands nothing from us. The only thing left, therefore, is for us to praise and thank Him. First we must recognize in our hearts and believe that we receive everything from Him and that He is our God. Then out with it, and freely and openly confess this before the world—preach, praise, glorify, and give thanks! This is the real and only worship of God, the true office of the priest, and the finest, most acceptable offering—as St. Peter says (1 Peter 2:9): "You are a royal priesthood, that you may declare the wonderful deeds of Him who called you out of darkness into His marvelous light." Yes, our mouths will be slapped for such praise; for the world does not want to hear it and cannot stand it. But that is the risk if one wants to bring this sacrifice to God; for it is written: "Praise the Lord, all heathen." It does not say that we should praise men or this world, but the Lord and His work or grace, not the works of men; for these are condemned.

From *Commentary on Psalm 117* (Luther's Works 14:32–33)

December 10

The Grace of God

There are unusually fine words in this verse, words which we should not skim over coldly or without feeling. In the first place, the psalmist speaks of "His steadfast love." This is not our doing, holiness, or wisdom; it is His grace and mercy. What, then, is the grace of God? It is this, that from sheer mercy, for the sake of Christ, who is our beloved Bishop and Mediator, God forgives all our sins. He abates all His anger, leads us by faith from idolatry and error to truth. And the Holy Spirit purifies our hearts, enlightens, sanctifies, and justifies us, chooses us as children, and heirs, adorns us with His gifts, redeems and protects us from the power of the devil, and finally gives us eternal life and blessedness. And yet He also supplies this transitory life with everything needful, gives and preserves it, through the service and co-operation of all creatures of heaven and earth. The whole world could not deserve even the tiniest of these gifts, much less all of them, or even some of the greater ones. In fact, because of its idolatry, ingratitude, contempt, and continual manifold sinning it has deserved nothing but anger, death, and hell. If this is true—and it undeniably is—then it follows that our works, wisdom, and holiness are nothing before God. For if it is God's love, then it cannot be our merit. And if it is our merit, then it is not God's love (Romans 11:6).

From *Commentary on Psalm 117* (Luther's Works 14:25)

December 11

Oh give thanks to the Lord, for He is good;
for His steadfast love endures forever!

PSALM 118:1

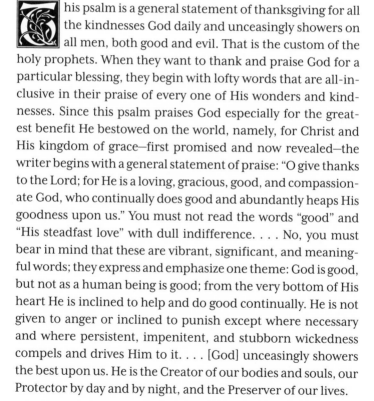

Showers of Kindness

his psalm is a general statement of thanksgiving for all the kindnesses God daily and unceasingly showers on all men, both good and evil. That is the custom of the holy prophets. When they want to thank and praise God for a particular blessing, they begin with lofty words that are all-inclusive in their praise of every one of His wonders and kindnesses. Since this psalm praises God especially for the greatest benefit He bestowed on the world, namely, for Christ and His kingdom of grace—first promised and now revealed—the writer begins with a general statement of praise: "O give thanks to the Lord; for He is a loving, gracious, good, and compassionate God, who continually does good and abundantly heaps His goodness upon us." You must not read the words "good" and "His steadfast love" with dull indifference. . . . No, you must bear in mind that these are vibrant, significant, and meaningful words; they express and emphasize one theme: God is good, but not as a human being is good; from the very bottom of His heart He is inclined to help and do good continually. He is not given to anger or inclined to punish except where necessary and where persistent, impenitent, and stubborn wickedness compels and drives Him to it. . . . [God] unceasingly showers the best upon us. He is the Creator of our bodies and souls, our Protector by day and by night, and the Preserver of our lives.

From *Commentary on Psalm 118* (Luther's Works 14:47–48)

December 12

Out of my distress I called on the LORD;
the LORD answered me and set me free.

PSALM 118:5

Skill above All Skills

Note the great art and wisdom of faith. It does not run to and fro in the face of trouble. It does not cry on everybody's shoulder, nor does it curse and scold its enemies. It does not murmur against God by asking: "Why does God do this to me? Why not to others, who are worse than I am?" Faith does not despair of the God who sends trouble. Faith does not consider Him angry or an enemy, as the flesh, the world, and the devil strongly suggest. Faith rises above all this and sees God's fatherly heart behind His unfriendly exterior. . . . Faith has the courage to call with confidence to Him who smites it and looks at it with such a sour face. That is skill above all skills. It is the work of the Holy Spirit alone and is known only by pious and true Christians. The self-righteous are ignorant of it. . . . Let everyone know most assuredly and not doubt that God does not send him this distress to destroy him, as we shall see in verse eighteen. He wants to drive him to pray, to implore, to fight, to exercise his faith, to learn another aspect of God's person than before, to accustom himself to do battle even with the devil and with sin, and by the grace of God to be victorious. Without this experience we could never learn the meaning of faith, the Word, Spirit, grace, sin, death, or the devil. Were there only peace and no trials, we would never learn to know God Himself. In short, we could never be or remain true Christians.

From *Commentary on Psalm 118* (Luther's Works 14:59–60)

December 13

Out of my distress I called on the LORD;
the LORD answered me and set me free.

PSALM 118:5

Becoming Real Christians

ou must learn to call. Do not sit by yourself or lie on a couch, hanging and shaking your head. Do not destroy yourself with your own thoughts by worrying. Do not strive and struggle to free yourself, and do not brood on your wretchedness, suffering, and misery. Say to yourself: "Come on, you lazy bum; down on your knees, and lift your eyes and hands toward heaven!" Read a psalm or the Our Father, call on God, and tearfully lay your troubles before Him. Mourn and pray, as this verse teaches, and also Psalm 142:2: "I pour out my complaint before Him, I tell my trouble before Him." Likewise Psalm 141:2: "Let my prayer be counted as incense before Thee, and the lifting up of my hands as an evening sacrifice!" Here you learn that praying, reciting your troubles, and lifting up your hands are sacrifices most pleasing to God. It is His desire and will that you lay your troubles before Him. He does not want you to multiply your troubles by burdening and torturing yourself. He wants you to be too weak to bear and overcome such troubles; He wants you to grow strong in Him. By His strength He is glorified in you. Out of such experiences men become real Christians.

From *Commentary on Psalm 118* (Luther's Works 14:60–61)

*It is better to take refuge in the L*ORD
than to trust in man.
*It is better to take refuge in the L*ORD
than to trust in princes.

PSALM 118:8–9

Worth Repeating

For this reason the psalmist declares twice: "It is better to take refuge in the Lord." He is telling us that men cannot comfort and advise us, and that princes cannot come to our rescue. For men do not have the right word or spirit to comfort and uphold a sorrowful heart. Nor do princes have a fist strong enough to help a wretched man and to suppress his enemies. God alone has the word of comfort and the fist for help, regardless of the size and the number of troubles and enemies. Experience substantiates this. When a person is really downcast, how, pray tell me, can all the emperors, kings, princes, and all the power, skill, possessions, and honor of the whole world comfort him? They are all less than nothing, even in the trouble caused by one little everyday sin, unless God's Word gives counsel and comfort.

From *Commentary on Psalm 118* (Luther's Works 14:66)

The LORD is my strength and my song;
He has become my salvation.
Glad songs of salvation
are in the tents of the righteous.
PSALM 118:14–15

Keeping the Rascal Away

hen the saints rejoice in the spirit and sing "The Lord is my Strength and my Song" (Psalm 118:14), then the devil is far away, and murmuring and impatience cease. But when the barrier has been trodden down, then the rascal comes. As long as those words of praise and thanksgiving resound: "I will bless the Lord at all times; His praise shall continually be in my mouth" (Psalm 34:1), and "I will exult in God, my Salvation, etc."—so long all trials of sadness and unbelief vanish, and heaven and Paradise are opened wide. Hell has disappeared.

From *Lectures on Genesis* (Luther's Works 7:127)

The LORD is my strength and my song;
He has become my salvation.
Glad songs of salvation are in the tents of the righteous.

PSALM 118:14–15

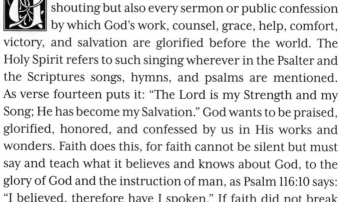

Everything Turns Out Just Fine

nder "singing" I include not only making melody or shouting but also every sermon or public confession by which God's work, counsel, grace, help, comfort, victory, and salvation are glorified before the world. The Holy Spirit refers to such singing wherever in the Psalter and the Scriptures songs, hymns, and psalms are mentioned. As verse fourteen puts it: "The Lord is my Strength and my Song; He has become my Salvation." God wants to be praised, glorified, honored, and confessed by us in His works and wonders. Faith does this, for faith cannot be silent but must say and teach what it believes and knows about God, to the glory of God and the instruction of man, as Psalm 116:10 says: "I believed, therefore have I spoken." If faith did not break forth, speak up, and confess, it would not be a true faith, even though it has to suffer and be cursed and persecuted, as the same psalm continues: "I was greatly afflicted." But faith has a Helper who is its Salvation. Verse fourteen teaches that such persecution does not harm our salvation but must promote it; for it defies and blasphemes God, so that He is driven to help, and the righteous are compelled to call on God and to pray to Him. Thus everything turns out just fine.

From *Commentary on Psalm 118* (Luther's Works 14:81)

I shall not die, but I shall live,
and recount the deeds of the LORD.

PSALM 118:17

Proof of Grace and God's Goodwill

hen we are afflicted and disciplined, our heart must be aroused against the feeling of evil, and we must say (cf. Psalm 118:17): "I shall not die, but I shall live, however different it may appear. Although I may, indeed, be compelled to despair of myself, I shall nevertheless hope in Him who made all things out of nothing and can restore me intact after being reduced to nothing, to my very great benefit and that of others." Therefore the fiercer our sufferings are, the greater and more wonderful are the things that are worked in the saints. It is a proof of grace and God's goodwill when they are disciplined by the cross and afflictions. For when they persevere by faith in the promise and endure, great and incredible blessings follow according to the statement in James 1:12: "Blessed is the man who endures trial, for when he has stood the test, he will receive the crown of life which God has promised to those who love Him," and in John 12:24 we read: "Unless a grain of wheat falls into the earth and dies, it remains alone; but if it dies, it bears much fruit."

From *Lectures on Genesis* (Luther's Works 6:355)

December 18

I shall not die, but I shall live,
and recount the deeds of the LORD.

PSALM 118:17

No More Than a Sleep

We should recognize this verse as a masterpiece. How mightily the psalmist banishes death out of sight! He will know nothing of dying and of sin. At the same time he visualizes life most vividly and will hear of nothing but life. But whoever will not see death, lives forever, as Christ says: "If anyone keeps My Word, he will never see death" (John 8:51). He so immerses himself in life that death is swallowed up by life (1 Corinthians 15:55) and disappears completely, because he clings with a firm faith to the right hand of God. Thus all the saints have sung this verse and will continue to sing it to the end. . . . At this point we should learn the rule that whenever in the Psalter and Holy Scripture the saints deal with God concerning comfort and help in their need, eternal life and the resurrection of the dead are involved. All such texts belong to the doctrine of the resurrection and eternal life, in fact, to the whole Third Article of the Creed with the doctrines of the Holy Spirit, the Holy Christian Church, the forgiveness of sins, the resurrection, and everlasting life. And it all flows out of the First Commandment, where God says: "I am your God" (Exodus 20:2). This the Third Article of the Creed emphasizes insistently. While Christians deplore the fact that they suffer and die in this life, they comfort themselves with another life than this, namely, that of God Himself, who is above and beyond this life. It is not possible that they should totally die and not live again in eternity. For one thing, the God on whom they rely and in whom they find their consolation cannot die, and thus they must live in Him. Besides, as Christ says, He is a God of the living, not of the dead and of those who are no more (Matthew 22:32). Therefore Christians must live forever; otherwise He would not be their God, nor could they depend on Him unless they live. For this little group, therefore, death remains no more than a sleep. But if it is true that they live in God, then it must first be true that they have forgiveness of sin. If they have no sin, they surely have the Holy Spirit, who makes them holy. If they are holy, they are the true Holy Christian Church, the little flock; and they rule over all the power of the devil. Then one day they will rise again and live forever. These are the great and lofty works of the right hand of the Lord.

From *Commentary on Psalm 118* (Luther's Works 14:87–88)

This is the day that the Lord has made;
let us rejoice and be glad in it.

PSALM 118:24

Oh Happy Day!

his is a happy day, as the psalmist here rejoices and says: "Let us be glad!" The light and teaching of grace gives the heart peace, rest, and joy in Christ. It realizes that its sins are without merit, that it is delivered from death, and that in God it forever has a gracious Father through Christ, as St. Paul says (Romans 5:1): "Therefore since we are justified by faith, we have peace with God through our Lord Jesus Christ." And then he further describes this peace and joy as something that endures in tribulation and gives courage. No unbeliever can know anything of this joy and peace, nor can those who by their works endeavor to be pious and wipe out their sins. . . . What could be more precious and nobler than an enlightened heart, a heart that knows God and all things, a heart that can judge rightly and speak truly in all things before God? Where could there be a higher or greater joy than in a happy, secure, and fearless conscience, a conscience that trusts in God and fears neither the world nor the devil?

From *Commentary on Psalm 118* (Luther's Works 14:100–101)

December 20

Remember Your word to Your servant,

in which You have made me hope.

This is my comfort in my affliction,

that Your promise gives me life.

PSALM 119:49–50

Suffering with Joy

he Church, placed in tribulation, reminds [Christ] of His promise, saying: "Remember Thy Word, in which Thou hast given me hope." For hope which is seen is not hope (Romans 8:24), therefore hope is in the Word, not immediately in demonstration. But He permits the Church to be afflicted and to hope for help. Otherwise, if she would be helped as quickly as she is afflicted, then also resistance to the adversaries would come about, so that they could not afflict. . . . Therefore help must be delayed and affliction grow and increase, so that she might learn to say: *This has comforted me in my humiliation*, that is, "in harassment, affliction, persecution, and tribulation for the sake of the Word of Your Gospel." Hope consoles them and causes them to suffer with joy, because they are made sure about the good things to come. Patience works hope (Romans 5:4), but hope does not make ashamed, indeed, it glorifies, calms, and consoles the conscience. *Because Thy Word has given me life*, as if to say: "For this reason I hope, because I am still alive, though I might die in sufferings. But I live by faith in Your Son, because Your Word has given me life. For the dead do not have hope, but the living."

From *First Lectures on the Psalms*, on Psalm 119
(Luther's Works 11:453)

December 21

Your Word is a lamp to my feet
and a light to my path.

PSALM 119:105

Led by the Word Alone

 wonderful statement! Why not a lamp to my eyes and a light for seeing? Can the feet be lighted or the paths see? But the nature of faith for this life is expressed. For eyes must be taken captive to the obedience of Christ and be led by the Word alone, which is perceived by the ears and is not seen with the eyes. For we believe the invisible but not the inaudible. Therefore the Word does not enlighten the eyes, but neither the ears. Yet it is a lamp, because it guides the feet and the heart, and faith does not require understanding. Not understanding, but willing, not knowing but doing, what is heard is the right thing. And you will not go astray if you believe and go, even though you do not see. Only walk securely in what you have heard, because His Word will be a lamp to your feet and a light for your paths. Nothing is required except that you do what you do not know, perform what you do not understand, go where you do not know [the way], following the leading of the Word, and become foolish, dismissing your own thought. . . . Faith leads it where it will be saved, and it does so through the hearing of the Word. The heart, hearing the Word, begins to walk after it, not knowing where. Therefore the Word of God, which gives light to the feet and the paths, is wonderful.

From *First Lectures on the Psalms*, on Psalm 119
(Luther's Works 11:485)

December 22

Your testimonies are my heritage forever,
for they are the joy of my heart.

PSALM 119:111

The Hope of Things to Come

 hose who purchase an inheritance on earth, the joy of their heart is not the testimonies of things to come, but the setting forth and possession of things present. . . . But the testimonies are signs and words, not the thing itself, and to esteem these as an inheritance for themselves and to rejoice in them is not a matter for the weak faith and hope of men. For through hope of future blessings in soul and body people rejoice more than all the rich with regard to their present possessions, yes, they rejoice even in torments because of this kind of hope. Thus for the greedy the testimonies of God are not joy and inheritance, because they do not know how to sing: "I was glad when they said to me: 'Let us go into the house of the Lord'" (Psalm 122:1). . . . This, however, is a happy inheritance because it is eternal, for he says, "I have purchased [it] for a heritage forever." The promises of God gladden the heart of those who believe and hope in them. Therefore in the meanwhile we rejoice in faith and hope of things to come which God has promised us. We rejoice, however, because we are certain that He does not lie but will do what He promised and will remove from us every evil of body and soul and will grant us every good thing, and this without end.

From *First Lectures on the Psalms*, on Psalm 119
(Luther's Works 11:490)

December 23

Princes persecute me without cause,
but my heart stands in awe of Your words.

PSALM 119:161

In Awe of the Words of God

f we could only ponder with due feeling what it means to say, "God speaks," "God promises," "God threatens!" Who, I beg you, would not quake from the foundation? It is a great word, a great and fearful sound to say, "Behold the Word of God!" Blessed are they who hear the Word of God, the Word of such great majesty, which holds, does, and ends all things by a nod. Here only a full faith is wanting. If it were there, it would cause full fear and trembling at the words of God, so that this happy boasting would belong to faith alone and to the most vigorous faith. "But the princes, who are nevertheless powerful, threatening, terrible, and more to be feared than others, not only resorted to threats to scare me, but they persecuted in deed and showed all their terror. And behold, I still did not fear them, but rather stood in awe of Your words, so that I might conquer fear of them." . . . The Church is not afraid of all the persecuting princes of the world, because she stands in awe of the words of God. This she would not do, unless, despising all things by faith, she savored eternal things alone.

From *First Lectures on the Psalms*, on Psalm 119
(Luther's Works 11:518)

To Savor the Invisible and Eternal

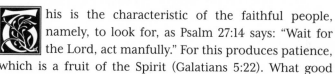his is the characteristic of the faithful people, namely, to look for, as Psalm 27:14 says: "Wait for the Lord, act manfully." For this produces patience, which is a fruit of the Spirit (Galatians 5:22). What good would it do to live in faith and hope only at the beginning and to be broken with weariness before the end and return to visible things, in which one lives without faith and hope, but in the reality and present? This is characteristic of the ungodly and unbelieving who do not know how to savor the invisible and the eternal. Therefore they go to earthly things and neither endure their adversity nor bear their prosperity but sin in both and are moved from one kind of sins to another. But those who wait are fixed and suspended in heaven. Therefore, whether adversity or prosperity comes, they are not moved, but abide, looking for other things. Therefore this expectation necessarily includes contempt of all earthly goods and evils. If it were not so, they would surely stop expecting, while despairing in adversity or enjoying themselves in prosperity, as others do. Hence he rightly says, "I will look for Thy salvation," not the salvation of the world or of the flesh, which can be taken away again or can also be looked for by the unworthy.

From *First Lectures on the Psalms*, on Psalm 119
(Luther's Works 11:529)

Behold, He who keeps Israel
will neither slumber nor sleep.

PSALM 121:4

Always Turn Back to the Promise

his is therefore the wisdom of the Christians, to endure the plans of God and to persevere by faith in the promise that has been given, for it is indeed sure and firm, and the Lord's covenant is faithful, according to the statement of Psalm 121:4: "Behold, He who keeps Israel will neither slumber nor sleep." But human reason replies: "These things are indeed excellently and beautifully spoken, but I am experiencing the contrary. He is not only sleeping but even snoring; to be sure, there is plainly no God at all to care for us and have regard for us." . . . All are silent and allow the devil to rage against the holy Church. Where is God now? We are often reminded and taught by examples of this kind that the promise must be apprehended by faith and that one must not doubt God when He makes promises. For as God cannot lie (Titus 1:2), so it is impossible for Him not to exercise care for us, especially if we adhere to the promise. For if this is firmly apprehended, it is impossible for us to be forsaken, because God is true. Accordingly, when He allows us to be tried, to be led down to hell, to be mortified . . . we must always turn back to the promise, and that horrible scandal by which we are being crucified must be removed from our eyes.

From *Lectures on Genesis* (Luther's Works 6:360)

But with You there is forgiveness,

that You may be feared.

PSALM 130:4

Insisting on Grace

ut there is forgiveness with Thee. Therefore there is no refuge in any other person where one could stand or abide. St. Paul says (Romans 8:31): "If God is for us, who is against us?" By the same token, who will be for us if God is against us? With Him alone is forgiveness. Therefore good works cannot help. If anyone wants to amount to something before God, he must insist on grace, not on merit. *That Thou mayest be feared.* As already stated, if anyone does not fear God, he does not implore, nor is he forgiven. In order, therefore, to gain God's grace, He and He alone is to be feared, just as He alone forgives. For if anyone fears something besides God, he seeks the favor and mercy of this other thing and does not care about God. But whoever fears God desires His grace and does not care about anything that is not God; for he knows that no one can harm him if God is gracious to him.

From *Seven Penitential Psalms*, on Psalm 130 (Luther's Works 14:191)

Enter not into judgment with Your servant,
for no one living is righteous before You.

PSALM 143:2

Gospel Promises

 am very frequently troubled by this trial, that I look about for works in which I may be able to put my trust, because I have taught much, have benefited many, and have borne many more indignities than I deserved. But I realize that in real conflicts all these are nothing, and I am driven to the well-known confession of David, who said: "Lord, I am nothing but a sinner" (cf. Psalm 32:5); and (Psalm 116:11): "I said in my consternation: 'All men are a vain hope'"; that is, every man who deceives and is deceived is useless. Likewise (Psalm 143:2): "Enter not into judgment with Thy servant." But I encourage myself with this hope alone, that in the Gospel I see that solace has been promised to the contrite, hope to the despairing, and heaven to those who have been put into hell; and the fact that the Son of God, without our knowledge, offered Himself for us to God the Father, His Father, on the altar of the cross, is sure proof of this hope. . . . Therefore when you feel that you are being humbled, cast yourself at the feet of your heavenly Father and say: "O Lord, if Thou dealest with me in this manner, I shall bear it patiently, and I confess that I have deserved something more terrible. Therefore be merciful to me. . . . Thou dost not owe me a thing by any right. Therefore I cling to Thy mercy." This is the true way by which we come to grace and salvation.

From *Lectures on Genesis* (Luther's Works 4:54–55)

December 28

For Your name's sake, O LORD, preserve my life!
In Your righteousness bring my soul out of trouble!
And in Your steadfast love You will cut off my enemies.

PSALM 143:11–12

By Grace Alone, Not by Merit

or Thy name's sake, O Lord, preserve my life! That is, that Thy name may be honored. God's name is honored when men declare that He gives life and righteousness by grace without merit. Then one can say: God is kind, gracious, merciful. These are His names that are to be praised. But the self-righteous honor their own names. They want to have life through their own righteousness. Therefore they despise the righteousness of God, which He grants the sinner by grace and by which He makes him alive in His freely given righteousness and in His truth. *In Thy righteousness bring me out of trouble!* He not only prays to be preserved in the face of his enemies, those who consider themselves great in their righteousness, but also to be led out from among them at last. For although the righteous are preserved among their enemies, yet they are like captives among them until they are brought out from them, or the enemies are converted. This God would do because of His righteousness, not that He seeks His own honor in this deliverance but that men may learn how God establishes the righteousness of faith in opposition to works. *And in Thy steadfast love cut off my enemies.* That is, on account of Thy mercy and grace, so that it may be praised and acknowledged.

From *Seven Penitential Psalms*, on Psalm 143 (Luther's Works 14:203)

December 29

He fulfills the desires of those who fear Him;
He also hears their cry and saves them.

PSALM 145:19

Perseverance in Prayer and Faith

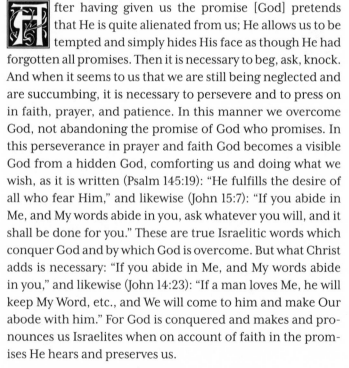

After having given us the promise [God] pretends that He is quite alienated from us; He allows us to be tempted and simply hides His face as though He had forgotten all promises. Then it is necessary to beg, ask, knock. And when it seems to us that we are still being neglected and are succumbing, it is necessary to persevere and to press on in faith, prayer, and patience. In this manner we overcome God, not abandoning the promise of God who promises. In this perseverance in prayer and faith God becomes a visible God from a hidden God, comforting us and doing what we wish, as it is written (Psalm 145:19): "He fulfills the desire of all who fear Him," and likewise (John 15:7): "If you abide in Me, and My words abide in you, ask whatever you will, and it shall be done for you." These are true Israelitic words which conquer God and by which God is overcome. But what Christ adds is necessary: "If you abide in Me, and My words abide in you," and likewise (John 14:23): "If a man loves Me, he will keep My Word, etc., and We will come to him and make Our abode with him." For God is conquered and makes and pronounces us Israelites when on account of faith in the promises He hears and preserves us.

From *Lectures on Genesis* (Luther's Works 6:259–60)

December 30

He declares His Word to Jacob, His statutes and rules to Israel.
He has not dealt thus with any other nation. . . .Praise the Lord!

Psalm 147:19–20

His Grace Is Sufficient

We can boast that God has given us His Word. Let it happen that others are rich and we poor, they powerful and we weak, they happy and we sad, they admired and we despised, they alive and we dead, they everything and we nothing—what of it? Still they have no God but must make a worthless, miserable god out of their own pittance. What poor material for a god! O pitiable godsmiths! But we have God, and we glory in the right God. This ruby they must leave with us; in comparison with it all their kingdoms are rotten dung and dirt. Even though we must suffer much, what difference does it make? It is written that if you want to be a Christian, "My grace is sufficient for you (2 Corinthians 12:9). Be grateful that you have My Word and Myself in My Word. How can distress, hunger, and pestilence hurt you? What damage can be done to you by the feuding of the bigwigs, the malice of the peasants, the rage of the Papists, the censure of the whole world, or the anger of all devils? You have God's Word; they don't! You are in My grace; they are not! You are My child; they are My enemies! Beloved, let My Word as Myself be a treasure, a kingdom, even a heavenly kingdom, to you in your poverty, misery, and woe. My Word is eternal, and in this Word you are eternal."

From *Commentary on Psalm 147* (Luther's Works 14:134–35)

December 31